D0467967

La Bella Cucina

La Place, Viana.
La bella cucina : how to
cook, eat, and live like
c2001.
33305015788320
MI   12/06/01

La Bella Cucina

HOW TO COOK, EAT, AND LIVE LIKE AN ITALIAN

VIANA LA PLACE

SANTA CLARA COUNTY LIBRARY

. 3 3305 01578 8320

CLARKSON POTTER/PUBLISHERS ✦ NEW YORK

Copyright © 2001 by Viana La Place

All rights reserved. No part of this book may be reproduced
or transmitted in any form or by any means, electronic or mechanical,
including photocopying, recording, or by any information storage
and retrieval system, without permission in writing from the publisher.

Published by Clarkson Potter/Publishers, New York, New York.
Member of the Crown Publishing Group.

Random House, Inc. New York, Toronto, London, Sydney, Auckland
www.randomhouse.com

CLARKSON N. POTTER is a trademark and POTTER and colophon
are registered trademarks of Random House, Inc.

Printed in the United States of America

Design by Louise Fili and Mary Jane Callister/Louise Fili Ltd
Illustrations by Melanie Parks

Library of Congress Cataloging-in-Publication Data
La Place, Viana.
La bella cucina: how to cook, eat, and live like an Italian / Viana La Place.
1. Cookery, Italian.   I. Title.
TX723.L22   2001
641.5945—dc21   2001016351

ISBN 0-609-60518-6

10   9   8   7   6   5   4   3   2   1

First Edition

TO THE SALENTO

Sapore di mare
Sapore di sale
Sapore di te

FROM A SONG BY GINO PAOLI

Acknowledgments

In Italy, to my friends in the Salento for
showing me the true meaning of the word generosity:

SIGNORA VIRGINIA

PINO

SIGNORINA MARIA

SIGNORA IDA AND SIGNOR FRANCO

ROSETTA, FRANCO, AND ZOÈ

LUIGI AND PASCAL

SARAH AND ALESSANDRO

BENEDETTO CAVALIERI

❧

In America, my thanks to:

ROY FINAMORE, for his insightful editing and for gently getting me back on track

LOUISE FILI, for her brilliant visual interpretation of the manuscript, *baci e abbracci*

WENDY DOWNING, who knocked on my door just when I needed her,
for her expert and passionate recipe testing

SUSAN LESCHER, who through astute agenting made it possible
for me to work with the people with whom I most desired to collaborate

❧

Books serving as resource and inspirational material:
Ricette Leccesi, Leda Maggiore
Cucina Populare ed Aristocratica di terra d'Otranto, Antonio Edoardo Foscarini
Cucini Pugliese, Antonietta Pepe
Flavors of Puglia, Nancy Harmon Jenkins
Honey from a Weed, Patience Gray
Bitter Almonds, Maria Grammatico and Mary Taylor Simeti

Contents

La Bella Cucina

La Bella
Vita

What is "la bella vita"? It is the good life. But what constitutes a life well lived? Our conceptions of what is needed to live well have changed. We now look to other cultures—with envy, with wistfulness, romanticizing perhaps—feeling deep within ourselves that the life we lead is lacking some of the most basic human needs. Most often, it is to Italian culture that people look to discover what it is to live well, to live *la bella vita.* ❧ I've always felt that one of the most damaging facets of American society is an aching loneliness that so many people feel at their core. The day rushes along, many hours spent at work or in the isolation of suburban homes or city apartments. Where is our sense of community, once so prominent in American life? Where is the family that, in the past, provided a sense of belonging, or made us feel we were a part of something bigger than ourselves? Children are occupied with after-school activities and spend precious little time at home. Men and women in the work force are gone all the live-long day. Arriving home tired, they assemble a quick meal and inevitably migrate toward electronic entertainments—television, videos, computers. ❧ This is where Italy enters into our imagination, with the imagery of *la bella vita.* We picture the extended family gathered at a long table, most often under a grape arbor, on a terrace surrounded by geraniums, with a view of the sea or a vista onto the countryside. This type of scene transforms Italy into a place that is unbearably desirable. ❧ But think carefully about this picture. What are the elements that compose it, that make it so enviable? Imagine what is placed on that table you've conjured up so vividly: large serving bowls of pasta with tomato sauce, platters of brightly colored vegetables, a bowl of tender salad greens from the garden, glistening olives, dark and crusty peasant bread, bottles of wine and mineral water, a bowl brimming with fresh fruit. This vision of joyous abundance reflects a generosity of spirit that many of us feel is lacking in our lives; it speaks of a desire to share with others what we have. Look now at who is seated at this table: generations of family and friends eat in each other's company. Eating is basic to human survival, and is generally repeated three times a day. To engage in something so necessary to survival in the company of others is a comfort and a joy. ❧ Look again at the picture and you'll notice that everyone at the table is seated in nature—not observing it, but actually in or very close to it. The olives come from the nearby silvery trees; in the garden, herbs flourish, fava beans take shape, and tomatoes hang on the vine. We see an intimate connection with nature, a sense of merging, of belonging to and being part of this earth. These are heady images that represent our deep longing to return to nature. ❧ We see wine on the table, for ages a symbol of happiness, a magic elixir that in Italy always accompanies meals, but is never drunk to excess. It is but one of the many components of the meal, but it adds a sense of well-being and enjoyment—*gioia di vivere,* the joy of living—to daily rituals. Another symbol of life, and for good reason called the staff of life, is the bread on the table. It is heavy and crusty—you could live on it. Bread like this truly provides sustenance. In the bread you are aware of the hand of the baker, another person connected to your life. We all want to be seated at this table that sustains body and soul. ❧ Another image of *la bella vita* that is deeply etched on our collective consciousness is that of an idle hour or two spent at an outdoor caffè. We can imagine ourselves sitting and watching the world go by, observing the others as they pass. By studying people, by observing them closely, we feel more connected to our own humanity.

Gradually we realize we are basically no different from anyone else, and we become at one with the flow of humanity. You thought you were short; well, just look at that fellow! You admire the beautiful cut of a man's suit. You see a group of children playing in the street and it makes your heart glad. Of course, men in Italy are still given to ogling the women in that passing parade. But the women are also front and center watching all the gorgeous men saunter by. You see rich and poor, children and old folks, some who move slowly and with difficulty, others who rush by—and it helps you find your place in the world.

Of course, food enters into this picture, too. In our minds, we see scoops of gelato in gleaming small metal goblets—dark brown, creamy brown, the pastel tints of fruit ice creams, pale strawberry pink, creamy lemon yellow. We see tiny cups of black espresso and frothy cappuccinos, accompanied by little pastries or *biscotti,* or an *aperitivo,* an aperitif, enjoyed on a sunny afternoon. These are all parts of the ritual of everyday Italian life! How fortunate Italians are to have made time for leisure, how civilized of them, or should I say how smart of them, to make time for such humanizing behavior.

And then there is August—the vacation month with full salary, the entitlement of everyone in Italy. Lazy days on the beach, eating almonds or bits of fresh coconut, taking *pranzo,* or lunch, at a seaside trattoria. Perhaps a month at one of the beautiful lakes, or up in the mountains, where the air is cool and fragrant with pine. In August everything shuts down except those businesses that cater to tourism; their vacation comes later, and lasts for the rest of the year!

Although this life still exists in Italy and is still at its core, certain modern realities have entered the scene, just as they have around the globe. Italy is changing; Italy will never change. These are the thoughts that, like a Ping-Pong ball, bounce back and forth in my mind.

But the culture of a place runs deep, like a plant's tap root, scrappy and persistent. You can try to pull the plant out of the ground, yank it hard, but the root grows deeper than you think. The plant springs up again.

Italy is like that. The superficial changes are obvious: *telefonini,* cell phones; a lonely panino lunch for one; families spreading hither and yon—unheard of until recently, except in situations of dire poverty that prompted migration to other regions in Italy and to other countries. There is more loneliness now among the elderly, more alienation among young people.

But the plant is tough and sturdy—its questing tap root suckling the earth for sustenance. The traditions of a culture run just as deep; they are embedded in one's DNA. The rituals do not fade away completely, even though they may change in certain ways.

The essence of Italian culture, which I feel is inextricably bound with Mediterranean cultures in general, continues to flourish in places far from the grasp of cities and towns where modern industrialized economies prevail and where, instead, an agrarian-based economy still exists. This essential Italianness is especially true in out-of-the-way places like Puglia, as far removed from moneyed Milano as you can get, and well off the tourist path. In fact, most people outside Italy would not be able to tell you where Puglia is located, or even if it is part of Italy. And the Salento, the southernmost part of Puglia, where I've spent a great deal of time, is that much more isolated than the rest of the region.

The Salento isn't an easy place to live. Conditions are severe: intense sun, craggy land, fierce winds, insufficient water. But the people of the Salento, like the people of so many challenging parts of Italy, have taken the flat, rock-strewn landscape and turned it into a habitable, productive land.

The Salento's natural gifts are many: a blue-green, pristine sea, an agrarian tradition that flourishes and feeds all of Italy and beyond with its extraordinary fruits and vegetables, its superb, super-abundant extra-virgin olive oil; and a verdant landscape in shades of muted green and olive gray.

Above all, what I've found in the Salento is a human-scale existence, where generosity and sharing are as natural as breathing. Perhaps it is the soulfulness of the people that has moved me the most and given me a sense of belonging.

Maybe it is because human survival demands interdependence that those cultural traditions run deeper in places like the Salento and in the small towns and villages that dot the Italian landscape. Nature, religion, agriculture, community, the local cooking—they all are alive and well here, nurtured by a tap root that must extend to the other side of the earth.

Communal participation and time to observe one's world, a basic respect and unbounded generosity toward fellow human beings, a strong connection with nature, feeling oneself to be an integral part of the natural world. These are some of the important aspects of living better, qualities found in Italy in general, but perhaps even more so in small towns in far-flung places like the Salento, less touched by the modern world, where the true meaning of *la bella vita* still exists in its purest form.

I've based this book largely on the time I've spent in Italy over the last five years, specifically in the Salento. During these years I've been able to stay for periods of greater length and frequency than at any other time of my life. I've cooked in my own kitchen by the sea or in the countryside. I've followed the daily patterns of Italian life, watched the seasons change.

I've made close and lasting friendships in the Salento. The people there, my friends, have shared so much with me, patiently answering all my questions as I searched to understand the real Italy. They have taken me into their homes and cooked for me, walked with me in their orchards and fields, picked fresh fruits and vegetables and given them to me by the basketful, shared precious reserves of homemade olive oil and wine.

With my friends in the Salento as my guides, I've worked in an olive grove, burning wood trimmings heaped in piles to prepare the fields for harvest; picked mulberries from a tree in the countryside during the dead of summer; gone diving along a rocky coast for sea urchins to eat raw with a crust of bread; foraged for wild arugula; and gathered tiny snails clinging to the dried stalks of summer fennel to cook up into a little stew.

The more I see, experience, and taste, the more I grow convinced that Italy represents an ideal paradigm for living *la bella vita* here at home.

We know the whole world loves Italian food. I strongly believe that this is because Italian cooking, more than any other ethnic cuisine I'm familiar with, allows the food to speak in a pure, simple way, with a direct expression of flavor and texture and with a lack of pretense or formality—and here I'm specifically talking about home cooking. Think of the foods on that imaginary table. In a sense, it is food that, because of its simplicity and lack of guile, almost transcends ethnic boundaries.

In *La Bella Cucina* I present the best and simplest versions of dishes that express authentic eating patterns, not just authentic dishes. The food and menus are based on what I have eaten during my sojourns in the Salento. I offer recipes for what an average Italian eats for breakfast, and later that day for lunch and dinner, as well as what one might snack on when a craving hits.

It is knowing how to cook simply, and the subtleties behind these seemingly simple dishes, that I hope to illuminate. A series of menus guide you through the day, and dishes appear and reappear as they would in a real Italian home.

In *La Bella Cucina,* I want to share the lessons I've learned through tasting and experiencing what has been given to me from the heart: the sweetest zucchini from my neighbor Signora Pantella; the garden peas cooked with wild fennel from another neighbor, Signora

Ida; Signorina Maria's homemade marzipan; and the bowl of freshly picked plums Signor Franco left on my doorstep.

I've attempted to get back to the origins of foods that have gone astray, sharing the true nature of Italian biscotti, that barely sweet and friable cookie that Italian families use in place of bread to dunk into their morning caffè latte. And I demonstrate the various ways in which Italians add nourishment to simple dishes—for example, the paper-thin slices of seared beef that top a bowl of pasta with tomato sauce.

In an Italian kitchen, familiarity means love, and simplicity is a way of life. An authentic Italian kitchen offers the reassuring cooking that is at the core of the Italian experience. In *La Bella Cucina*, more than anything, I hope to convey the passion with which Italians eat, the keen sense of pleasure they bring to gathering at the table. In essence, I want to show you the many ways in which Italians are frugal, joyous, generous, and respectful in their approach to food, cooking, and eating.

These are the important lessons at the heart of *La Bella Cucina*, so that we can eat better, more wisely, and more joyfully here at home.

{ Inside
an Italian
Kitchen }

*T*he kitchen is the soul of the Italian home. It scents the house with tomato sauce bubbling away, with onions cooking gently in fruity olive oil, a simple cake baking in the oven. From it emanates all the warmth and love associated with cooking and nourishing those we love. The Italian kitchen is where the heart of Italian life resides. *&* The kitchen in my summer rental flat in the two-story villa owned by Signorina Maria, who spends her summers in the ground-floor flat, is fully equipped. Signorina Maria has thought of everything. Actually, every kitchen I've ever seen in Italy possesses the same basic equipment: everything required to produce *la cucina Italiana*. *&* The Italian kitchen is utilitarian, in the sense that it is a workroom dedicated to the task of cooking. It is my opinion that the simpler a kitchen looks, the better the food. And Italian kitchens shine. Appliances look as if they have never been used, since no residue from cooking ever remains. Starting with the floor and working one's way up to the ceiling, the Italian kitchen must be spotless. *&* In my kitchen in the Salento, I am blessed with what I consider to be one of the most beautiful floors I've ever seen. The large terrazzo floor tiles are flecked with tiny chips of marble in pale pistachio green and white. When the temperatures climb, the floor stays cool, and the colors are refreshing to the eyes. In fact, most Italian kitchens have tile or terrazzo floors. Cleaned regularly with a particular mop contraption—basically a floor rag you purchase at any market that you push around with a type of broomstick—these floors help maintain an overall feeling of freshness and cleanliness. *&* In the center of the kitchen is a simple wooden table with a white marble top worn to a lovely dull luster and a set of wooden chairs painted blue. Windows that open to the breezes wrap around the kitchen—and outside I can almost touch the old-fashioned pink roses and little yellow plums that grow in the garden below. French doors lead out to a terrace in back that faces other gardens and other villas. ❧ A relatively new stove is shiny and white, with the *bombola*— a gas canister that fuels the stove—tucked away in its own compartment beneath the stovetop. A small refrigerator on the opposite wall hums with electricity. ❧ It is in the pantry that one really sees the inner workings of the Italian kitchen. The basic and essential tools are lined up on shelf after shelf and offer everything one needs to cook Italian. The tools include colanders in many sizes for draining pasta; a hand-cranked food mill with three disks having holes in various sizes for creating different textures—for making tomato sauces, smooth but textured soups, and other Italian-style "purees." There are several cheese graters (handheld, four-sided, big box contraptions with a grater that fits on top, and larger hand-cranked graters that attach to a counter). Of course there is an assortment of *formaggiere*—little glass serving pieces with hinged lids for holding the freshly grated cheese placed on the table at almost every meal. ❧ Moving on to coffee making, the pantry contains espresso pots, called Mokas, to make espresso on top of the stove: single-cup Mokas, Mokas for three cups, six cups, nine cups, and twelve cups—a whole family of Mokas all in a row. There is even an old, hand-cranked coffee grinder that looks like it hasn't been used for years. To serve the various coffee drinks, one finds numerous cups in a variety of sizes: tiny cups for espresso, large cups for caffè latte, and an assortment of other sizes for the occasional cup of tea or broth. ❧ Moving from cups to glasses, my pantry contains the everyday wineglasses, stemless, sturdy, and reliable, and diminutive glasses for liqueurs, *digestivi*, and *aperativi*—drinks that form a part of the ritual of eating in Italy. A few fancier wineglasses have made their way into the pantry, but most of the finer pieces are in the dining room credenza. Taller, but not too tall, glasses for homemade lemonade or cold tea are also lined up on pantry shelves.

Of bowls, there are many sizes: very large, shallow bowls for tossing together pasta and sauce, and a succession of bowls in ever decreasing sizes for salad making, for cooked vegetables, for olives, and individual shallow bowls for serving pasta.

You will always find at least one enormous pot for boiling pasta for a crowd, as well as a variety of pots in various sizes for other uses. And frying pans for frittatas, for frying zucchini in batches, for frying in general, a cooking method Italians have perfected and employ often, for when done properly the results are exceptional. Earthenware casserole dishes of various sizes look beautiful and produce the best-tasting food, and there is always a very large rectangular baking dish for making *pasta al forno* or lasagne.

Baskets for bread, carafes and pitchers for wine and water, and cruets for olive oil and vinegar are on another shelf. A big box of sea salt is always present. Salt shakers aren't used much since unadulterated salt tends to cake in a humid climate. Instead, salt is placed on the table in very small salt dishes, accompanied by equally small spoons. A pepper mill is also a kitchen basic.

Speaking of spoons, no Italian kitchen is complete without tiny spoons for espresso, medium-sized spoons for general use, and gigantic soup spoons, much larger than the ones we use in America for soup. And many wooden spoons to use for cooking. Forks are larger, too.

Knives are usually a motley assortment. Especially popular and useful are the plastic-handled serrated knives one buys at the outdoor markets where all manner of goods are sold. The knives are inexpensive and work incredibly well. The knives provided by Signorina Maria have bright rust-red plastic handles. The ones I have at home in San Francisco, with lime green plastic handles, I purchased at the outdoor market in Lecce.

In terms of small utensils, you'll find a meat pounder; a straight-sided pastry wheel for cutting pasta; a deep, slotted spoon for scooping stuffed pastas out of boiling water; and a thin, long rolling pin without ball bearings for rolling out pasta. And often, you'll find a cast-iron stovetop grill, and a cast-iron heat diffuser, to use under glazed terra-cotta pots on the stovetop.

The pantry also contains bottles of local olive oil, red wine vinegar, a variety of dried pasta shapes, and assorted piquant foods—jars of capers, pickled vegetables, spicy olive oil, and so forth. Of course, you'll find lots of granulated sugar for stirring into espresso. Big bottles of mineral water, six-packs, are ever present on pantry shelves, since Italians consume enormous amounts of bottled mineral water—usually a local brand. Also, a local brand of ground coffee, vacuum-packed, or one of the popular coffees made by larger industrial concerns such as Lavazza, is always tucked away in the cabinet.

It sounds like a lot of equipment, but it all fits very neatly in the medium-size pantry in the kitchen. The tools are basic, the ingredients simple, yet the results are profoundly good.

A Blueprint for Eating Like an Italian

As in most cultures, the rituals surrounding what to eat and when to eat are usually fixed: a set of rules and regulations to be followed by everyone. Italians still follow the basic patterns of eating that were established hundreds of years ago. ❧ *Sometimes the rules are connected to* religious doctrine; they can be dictated by climate; or they are determined by what is considered healthful and safe to eat. It is interesting to ponder why one culture eats in one way while another culture eats in an opposite style. And the differences run the gamut. ❧ Italy is no exception. The rules and regulations are a reflection of Italy's climate, its almost total immersion in Catholicism, and the foods that were historically provided by the terrain. Not much has changed over the years, although a certain "Americanization" has made its way into Italian popular culture, influencing eating habits. But this is more a worldwide phenomenon, not one specific to Italy. During my trips to Italy, I've noticed very few signs of people diverting from eating habits one would consider "Italian." ❧ Throughout *La Bella Cucina*, you will find brief essays on the ins-and-outs of Italian eating habits and the role mealtimes play in Italian life. Also, look to the chapter introductions for breakfast, and for morning and afternoon snacks for further insights into Italian eating habits. Before you know it, you'll be cooking, eating, and living like an Italian.

PRIMA COLAZIONE
breakfast

IN ITALY, BREAKFAST IS THE SIMPLEST MEAL OF THE DAY. ESPRESSO IS ALWAYS PRESENT IN ONE FORM OR ANOTHER. AND BREAD IS USUALLY ON THE TABLE AS AN accompaniment. American notions of a hearty breakfast have not caught on in this part of the world, where the main meal is eaten at midday.

The majority of Italians make espresso and caffè latte at home using a Moka, a stovetop espresso maker that costs very little and lasts for a very long time. A cappuccino, with its frothy topping of steamed milk, is more the province of the corner bar/caffè. Italians refer to this establishment simply as a bar, but it differs radically from what we call a bar here in America. Think "coffee bar" and you'll have the right idea.

At home in Italy, if you are not eating bread with your coffee drink, you are likely to have barely sweet biscotti, usually store-bought, to dunk into your espresso or caffè latte. The more elaborate breakfast sweets appear on counters or in the glass cases of bar/caffès, an enticement difficult to resist.

A granita, a granular flavored ice, is a breakfast favorite, notably in southern Italy, where the air turns incendiary as early as seven o'clock in the morning, and sometimes even earlier! Lemon or espresso granita are the most popular flavors and can constitute breakfast when it is just too hot to eat anything at all substantial. By the way, granita is never, to my knowledge, served as an after-dinner dessert. It is a mid-morning or mid-afternoon refresher.

One new wrinkle in this otherwise unchanging and time-honored morning ritual is a growing fascination with American-style cold cereals for breakfast, another symbol of the powerful pull of America. Although I've seen boxed cereals on supermarket shelves in Italy, I doubt that many Italians actually eat cold cereal for breakfast. But they do enjoy talking about it. I had a long conversation about cold cereal with the husband of a good friend of mine who lives in the city of Lecce in the Salento; he was fascinated by the number of cereals we have available here and the fact that they even put *caramelle,* candy, in some of them!

Remember, everyone in Italy is basically biding his or her time and priming the appetite for *pranzo*—what we call lunch, but what is, in Italy, the big meal of the day, served at about one o'clock in the afternoon after the first part of the workday has ended.

Caffè
COFFEE

ANY BOOK ATTEMPTING TO TRULY EXPRESS ITALIAN EATING HABITS MUST BEGIN WITH coffee. I remember my first impression of Italy when I traveled there with my family at the still tender age of twelve: it was the smell of coffee. It seemed to exude from everyone's pores. It was in the air, it permeated the furniture.

Recent studies have shown that simply breathing the scent of coffee causes a chemical reaction that increases one's sense of well-being—a form of aromatherapy. You don't even need to *drink* coffee to get a "high." Naturally, I was unaware at the time of this tidbit of coffee chemistry, but I did experience a tremendous sense of physical pleasure just from breathing in the warm, enveloping fragrance.

Breakfast Italian style is based on a variety of coffee drinks. It can be a straight espresso, referred to simply as *un caffè* in Italy, made at home or taken at a bar/caffè. *Espresso* for breakfast seems to be more a man's "macho" breakfast. It is often accompanied by at least one or two cigarettes. But straight espresso for breakfast is not exclusive to men; many women partake of espresso first thing in the morning.

A cappuccino usually has a ratio of one-third espresso, one-third steamed milk, and a topping of dense frothy milk that fills the rest of the cup. The amount of froth is rather minimal compared to what one sees here in America, and is creamy rather than fluffy. A cappuccino cup is equivalent in size to our standard coffee cup—never larger.

Cappuccino is most often ordered at the corner coffee bar on the way to work, along with a *brioscia,* brioche, or *cornetto,* croissant, sometimes filled with pastry cream—a particularly delicious variation. A cappuccino is also permissable at the mid-morning coffee break, but it is never ordered after 10 A.M. or, at the very latest, never after 11—a strict rule! And never order more than one—according to a friend in the Salento, a self-proclaimed expert on coffee-bar etiquette!

Another expert-friend explained the reason for this cut-off point. Milk on the taste buds muddies the flavors of food at the midday meal. Since in most parts of Italy that meal is still sacrosanct, nothing must interfere with its pleasures and the sense of satisfaction and well-being derived from it.

Caffè latte, a blend of espresso and plenty of hot milk, is a homemade drink; it is rarely ordered at a coffee bar. The ratio, depending on one's mood, is one or two tiny cups of espresso mixed with enough hot milk to fill a large cup the size of a bowl! This is drunk only first thing in the morning, and never later.

In Italy, ordering a cappuccino after a meal is considered barbaric. When I've mentioned to friends that it is done frequently in America, Italians react with complete and utter disgust: "All that milk on a full stomach!"

To an Italian, consuming coffee with meals is unheard of. When told it is an American tradition to have a cup of coffee, say, with lunch, the information is greeted with the same look of revulsion.

Espresso, on the other hand, can be consumed wherever, whenever, however, and as often as one is seized with the desire for a quick pick-me-up—an inch or two of that deep, dark brew. For Italians, the urge strikes frequently and with lightning speed. The only exception—and this is unwavering—is that espresso is never taken with meals, and very rarely with anything at all savory.

You would think that consumption of so much espresso would create a nation of hyped-up people. In fact, a cup of espresso contains less than one-half to one-third the caffeine in a cup of regular American coffee, owing to the type of beans used and roasting methods.

Coffee rituals in Italy are taken seriously. After all, coffee isn't just a beverage: it is part of the fabric of society. The variations on coffee drinks are too numerous to list in a land of bar/caffès that are found not just on every corner but two or three to a block. To single out a few of the most popular, though, one finds *espresso macchiato*, with just a "spot" of milk foam on top; *caffè corretto*, with a dash of brandy, grappa, or one's favorite liqueur; and *caffè ristretto*, literally meaning condensed or concentrated, an extra-strong espresso.

Italians are famous for the quality of coffee they drink, as well as the amount they consume. But in a country where there is intense rivalry between regions, provinces, towns, even hamlets regarding every aspect of life, each taking credit for the best of whatever it might be, probably even toothpicks, it is impossible to find a consensus on where to find the best coffee in Italy.

Leonardo Sciascia, the great contemporary Sicilian writer, described the south of Italy as beginning at "the palm tree line, the strong black coffee line." All the *Mezzogiorno*—literally meaning midday, but the term used to delineate the southern and hottest part of Italy—historically has excelled in coffee making. In the *Mezzogiorno*, espresso is darkest and strongest, and always served *ristretto*. *Due dita*—two fingers' worth, an Italian would say as a measurement—is a few sips of espresso beneath a thin layer of *crema*, the dense, creamy, light-brown foam that forms naturally on the surface of a properly made espresso.

It has been explained to me that in the south the beans are roasted longer but never to the point of scorching, producing a stronger, less acidic brew, since roasting removes acidity from the beans. But it intensifies the flavor, too, so the espresso might be perceived as slightly bitter to the uninitiated. A bit of sugar mellows out the bitterness to produce a perfect balance.

In the north, roasting time is shortened, therefore the espresso is less rich but also more acidic. Also, I'm told, a bit more espressso is served, about two and a half fingers' worth. In the Salento—most definitely a part of the *Mezzogiorno* where I've spent many summers and had many espressos—the coffee is of high quality, both inside and outside the home. But it is Naples that has had the reputation throughout Italy for producing the best coffee. And the coffee there is still superb, with master roasters and blenders at small artisanal companies. In fact, many small companies now exist all over Italy.

The north is responsible for some of the best and most widely distributed packaged coffees; Illy and Lavazza are two major players that come to mind. This is due, in part, to various geographical and economic considera-tions, but we will leave Italian socioeconomic issues for others to expound upon. Here, you are the final arbiter of the strength and length of your coffee, the person responsible for its quality. Find a source in your neighborhood for good, freshly roasted coffee beans and familiarize yourself with the various offerings. Just remember—well-roasted beans for espresso are dark brown, not black!

Finally, the amount of sugar added to these drinks is purely up to the individual. I've seen Italians piling spoonfuls of sugar into their espresso that would seem to render it more syrup than beverage. Others use it more sparingly. I like the equivalent of a small sugar cube or two in my espresso and cappuccino, and use none at all in my morning caffè latte.

{ How Italians Make Coffee at Home }

PROBABLY THE SINGLE MOST IMPORTANT PIECE OF KITCHEN EQUIPMENT IN THE ITALIAN *cucina* is the stovetop espresso maker, called *la Moka*. There's no need to buy a fancy electric espresso machine, since the results won't be as good anyway.

Some may argue that a colander for draining pasta is number one in ranking, or that a big pot for boiling spaghetti is the foundation of Italian cooking. But without a Moka on the stove first thing in the morning, it just wouldn't be Italy.

A Moka is a modestly priced piece of kitchenware. A stainless steel Moka costs more than one made of aluminum, but it is more durable and keeps its shiny finish longer. I prefer the heavier stainless steel model, not so much for its appearance but because I believe the heavier material acts as a shield against acids found in the coffee that can corrode the lighter material and introduce a slight metallic taste.

The Moka is shaped something like an hourglass, cinched at the waist, with cylindrical chambers that screw together at the center. Most Italian families have several sizes to suit various needs: small one-cup models, medium-size ones that make three to six cups of espresso, and larger Mokas that produce nine to twelve tiny cups of the dark brew. A small rubber washer is the only component that needs to be replaced occasionally.

A Neapolitan expert on the subject described to me in intense, passionate detail the proper way to make espresso. First, it starts with the beans. He said they must be freshly roasted to just the right degree. In America, most beans labeled "espresso" are roasted to the point of being burned; therefore, the espresso is exceedingly bitter and unpleasant. Espresso should be strong and rich, pleasingly bitter but not harshly so. Taste the offerings of various coffee bean establishments to find an espresso that pleases your palate. Or purchase Italian high-quality brands such as Illy.

Second, the beans should be ground just before using, or as close to that as possible. Here, we are speaking of the ideal. A handcranked coffee grinder yields the best results, since no heat is introduced. Electric grinders heat the beans as they are ground, which causes the beans to exude oil, dissipating the aroma and flavor. They also have a drying effect on the beans. But since the majority of us do not possess hand-cranked coffee grinders, or can't devote the extra time it takes to use one, an electric coffee grinder is next best. When using an electric grinder, pulse the beans until ground—that is, stop the machine every few seconds to keep the beans as cool as possible.

If you grind the beans in advance, keep the ground coffee in an airtight jar, either in the refrigerator or in a cool, dark place. I prefer the pantry, to eliminate the risk of moisture entering the jar.

A final alternative, and much inferior according to my expert friend, is to purchase the beans already ground. If you must, buy from a reputable purveyor with a large following to ensure the beans are freshly ground. Store in the same way as above.

To prepare the Moka, fill the bottom chamber with spring or filtered water to just below the steam vent. Tap water often has a strong chemical taste that can subvert the flavor of the coffee. My Neapolitan friend insists that his local water makes the best coffee, but lacking that, purified or spring water should be used—natural, not *frizzante,* or carbonated.

Insert the metal coffee filter into the bottom chamber. Add the ground coffee in spoonfuls, tamping down each spoonful firmly until the filter is full to the rim. The ground coffee should not be tamped down excessively hard, just pressed down to make it compact. Use the back of a spoon to smooth the top surface. Screw on the top chamber.

The slower the espresso emerges from the Moka, the better the coffee. Place the Moka on the stove and turn the heat on to the lowest setting. (My friend said that if it were possible, espresso should be made over a lighted candle since it would supply the least amount of heat possible and create the richest, least bitter brew!) The espresso will seep out slowly, producing the most full-flavored coffee that can be made at home.

Further, the cups must be hot. Dip the espresso cups in hot water. As soon as the upper chamber of the Moka is full of coffee, turn off the heat and pour the espresso into the hot cups. Add sugar to taste and stir quickly. Drink in one, at the most two, quick sips without pausing for breath until only a film of *crema* remains on the bottom of the cup.

Never wash out the Moka with dishwashing lotion or cleanser. Use only hot water and a soft cleaning pad. When the Moka is completely dry, place a small spoonful of fresh ground coffee in the bottom chamber, slip in the filter, and screw the compartments together. Store until the next use. (I never got to ask him why the ground coffee should be added to the Moka after washing, but my guess is that it aromatizes the pot for the next time and also absorbs any remaining moisture. The ground espresso in the bottom chamber should be discarded before making the next pot of espresso.)

Naturally, this is espresso making at its most fanatical. My friends in Italy usually buy already ground coffee, although it is always of excellent quality, fresh, and for the most part, locally roasted. They store it in a dark cupboard in the vacuum-packed bags in which coffee is sold, always rolled tightly on top, where wires running along the top edges of the bag help ensure a tight seal.

My friends start the Moka on a higher heat, with the lid open to keep an eye on the coffee's progress. As soon as the coffee starts to come out of the funnel into the top chamber, they close the lid and lower the heat. When the pot makes fast and furious sputtering sounds, the espresso is ready. I've never seen a friend at home heat the cup first, although it is an excellent way to keep a small amount of liquid hot. They pour the espresso immediately into cups, quickly stir in the sugar, and drink it fast. Or they pour the espresso and hot milk into a caffè latte cup, pouring both liquids simultaneously to control the strength of the drink.

Once you've bought your Moka, you are on your way to eating and drinking like an Italian. At home, you can be as fanatical or as casual in your espresso making as you wish. In short, it's a very long description for a very easy task. Making espresso in a Moka or making caffè latte is the work of a moment.

CHILDREN'S CAFFÈ LATTE

[serves 1]

CAFFÈ LATTE IS THE PROVINCE OF THE HOME KITCHEN, NOT THE CORNER BAR/CAFFÈ. STARTING AT A VERY YOUNG AGE, A CHILD WILL FIND A FEW DROPS OF ESPRESSO added to his or her morning hot milk. As my Neapolitan expert explained to me, children shouldn't be deprived of the pleasures of coffee. There should be just enough coffee to turn the milk a very light buff color. The amount of milk is generous—a bowlful, or enough to fill the oversize cups used for caffè latte.

Although the general concept may sound scandalous, in Italy it is common practice. I myself started drinking hot milk with a little coffee stirred into it when I was about five years old.

Obviously, amounts are variable. The following is a suggested amount of espresso, to increase incrementally as the child gets older. The caffè latte is always accompanied by fresh bread of some sort, dried bread for dipping, plain dipping biscotti, or a simple not-too-sweet breakfast cake or pastry. Nutella, a brand of chocolate-hazelnut spread, is a favorite with children, spread on a piece of plain bread. Dipping is not only permissible, it is part of the ritual!

Whole milk
Freshly made espresso
Sugar

Place enough milk to fill a large caffè latte cup in a small saucepan. Turn the heat to low. Meanwhile, set up the Moka as instructed on page 22. The milk is ready when it is hot but before it forms a skin or boils. Test with your fingertip. The Moka is usually ready at about the same time.

Pour the milk into a big cup and add a few drops of espresso—just enough to turn the white milk to pale tan. A teaspoon or so is sufficient. Add sugar to taste.

GROWN-UP CAFFÈ LATTE

[*serves 1*]

GROWN-UP CAFFÈ LATTE FOLLOWS THE SAME GENERAL PROCEDURE AS THAT FOR CHIL-DREN, THE DIFFERENCE BEING THE AMOUNT OF ESPRESSO ADDED TO THE HOT MILK. Again, it is a matter of preference, but basically, there is a great deal more espresso, at least a demitasse cup, added to the hot milk.

In Lecce, my good friend Rosetta's husband, Franco, told me he drinks practically a half-liter of hot milk with espresso every morning!

> *Whole or low-fat milk (nonfat milk is extremely*
> *watery, but it can be used if absolutely necessary)*
> *Freshly made espresso*
> *Sugar to taste*

The procedure is the same as for Children's Caffè Latte (page 23).

You may add 1 or 2 cups of espresso according to preference. Espresso for adult caffè latte can be made *ristretto*, or extra-strong.

For adults, the accompaniments are the same—barely sweet biscotti; bread, butter, and jam; or some form of breakfast cake or breakfast pastry.

{ *Pane, Burro, e Marmellata* }

BREAD, BUTTER, AND JAM

NO RECIPE IS REQUIRED, BUT A BRIEF EX-PLANATION IS IN ORDER TO REPRODUCE THE taste of this combination as served in kitchens every morning all over Italy. It is the standard accompaniment to the morning coffee drink.

When bread is fresh, Italians do not toast it. Fresh bread for breakfast is eaten straight from the bakery or pantry. It is often in the form of a roll, but the roll can be round, oval, hollow at the center, made from white flour or semolina flour—it just depends on the region. Bread that has dried out for a day or two is dipped in caffè latte until it absorbs some of the hot liquid and softens a bit, an absolutely delicious way to consume dried bread.

The butter, without exception, is unsalted. This makes an enormous difference. The sweet butter's creamy, fresh taste blends beautifully with the other components. Unsalted butter is fresher than salted, since salt is added as a preservative and can often serve to mask traces of rancidity.

This is the only meal at which Italians use butter on their bread. At lunch and dinner, butter disappears from the table. Again, Italians would find it unthinkable to butter their bread with lunch or dinner.

Jams and citrus marmalades—both referred to as *marmellata* in Italy—come in the usual range of fruit flavors, along with some unusual ones you may want to add to your collection, such as quince or pear jam, lemon or blood orange marmalade. Search them out for they are extraordinarily good.

The best preserves are those made with the sweetest, ripest fruits. They require less sugar, so the true fruit flavor can be better appreciated. Making jams at home is the best way to ensure quality. But if you are not inclined to make your own, farmers' markets are a good source of high-quality jams. Check the labels to make sure they contain only fruit and sugar, and no other additives.

BREAKFAST BISCOTTI

[makes 24 biscotti]

DON'T CONFUSE THESE BREAKFAST BISCOTTI WITH THE BISCOTTI POPULAR IN AMERICA, WHICH I CONSIDER TO BE MORE A DESSERT COOKIE.

As you can see by a quick scan of the ingredients, this recipe contains no nuts, chocolate, citrus zest, extracts, or liqueur. They are dry, crisp biscotti—plain and innocent, and not too sweet, made specifically for dipping into morning caffè latte. These biscotti have a less heavy crumb and are more friable than our biscotti.

Down in the Salento, each small town makes its own biscotti, and sells them in gigantic family-size bags with the name of the bakery, address, and phone number printed on a simple label affixed to the plastic bag.

Whenever I'm staying in the Salento, I always buy the largest bag available, figuring since they keep forever I'll never run out. But they are so good dipped in my caffè latte that each morning as I sit on my terrace staring out at the sea, I've dipped five or six, or even eight, biscotti into my coffee without even realizing it.

Before long I am back at the *salumeria,* the local little grocery store, buying another bag and swearing to cut back on my consumption!

6 eggs, separated
1 cup sugar
1½ cups unbleached all-purpose flour
1½ teaspoons baking powder
Pinch of sea salt

Heat the oven to 350 degrees and butter two 5 x 10-inch loaf pans.

Beat the egg yolks with all but 2 tablespoons of the sugar until thick and pale yellow in color.

Sift the flour with the baking powder and salt into the eggs a little at a time, mixing well after each addition.

Beat the egg whites with the remaining 2 tablespoons of sugar until stiff, then gently fold them into the batter.

Divide the dough in half and place each half in a loaf pan. Bake for 45 minutes or until a cake tester comes out dry.

Cool slightly before removing loaves from the pans. Slice each loaf into ½-inch slices. Lay the slices flat on a cookie sheet and return them to the hot oven. After 15 minutes, flip each slice over and bake for an additional 5 minutes, or until evenly brown. Briefly cool the biscotti on a rack.

Reduce the oven heat to 300 degrees. Put the biscotti back on the cookie sheets for a third baking. Bake them for 10 minutes on one side, then turn them over and bake an additional 10 minutes. Let cool.

The biscotti should be hard and crisp, perfect for dipping. Store in a sealed container. They last practically indefinitely, as long as you don't eat them all!

YOU WON'T TRULY BE LIVING LIKE AN ITALIAN UNLESS YOU SPEND AT LEAST 25 PERCENT of your free time in a local *piazza* or in its smaller cousin, the *piazzetta*.

In Italy, the *piazza* is the center of the town, its magnetic pull creating a hub of activity. *Piazzas* are the great communal living rooms of Italy where one can drop by anytime and everyone is welcome. A large *piazza* stimulates the senses with a wonderful confusion of images, smells, colors, and motion, while enclosing everyone in its big, safe embrace. The *piazzetta* is more like the communal den of the house that is the city, the center of a *quartière*, a neighborhood. Small and intimate, it is a quieter, more personal center, with its own less charged magnetic field.

Piazzas big and small are important focal points in the life of Italians. Men and women may crisscross the *piazza* many times a day— to go marketing, clothes shopping, banking, to visit a friend, pick up a child at school, go home for lunch, return to work, go to Mass at the local parish. A *piazza* is also a destination for hanging out, talking to your *amici* or watching your children run around in dizzying circles or wheel round and round on their tricycles and bicycles. If one were to make a diagram and each line represented a *piazza* crossing, it would probably end up being an impenetrably dense crosshatching.

If anything important happens, it takes place or is talked about in the *piazza*. The larger the *piazza* of a city or town, for each has many, the more important role it plays in the life of the inhabitants. The largest *piazza* of a city or town hosts political rallies, food fairs, religious events, social gatherings: the larger the *piazza*, the more important the politician or performer who takes his or her place on its stage.

A *piazza* usually offers a variety of dining options. In a *piazzetta* there may possibly be just a bar where you can gulp down an espresso, possibly an *espresso corretto*, or coffee with a discreet lacing of brandy. Of course, the bars that are located most prominently in the most important *piazzas* in a city attract *la crema* of local high society. Well dressed and immaculately groomed, and impossibly beautiful, they go daily to see and be seen. In small towns, a similar hierarchy occurs, but on a less grand scale.

Summertime finds *piazzas* teeming with locals. Each keeps a keen eye on all who pass by, since Italians by nature are highly curious about each other. The men in small towns in the deepest part of the south cluster in groups as though nothing had changed in the last several hundred years. The women often stay at home sitting on the threshold of their houses, knitting or making odd-shaped pastas with nimble fingers.

For the *pensionati*—retired people on pensions—the *piazza* is a full-time job. Clusters of men, especially, can be seen standing for hours, talking, gesticulating in the typical high-octane style of Italians. (Advancing age does not seem to diminish their capacity for the wild flailing of arms, ear-high shrugs, and intense, energy-driven conversation that takes place.) On the other hand, some of the men prefer playing the role of intent listener, rocking back and forth on their heels, hands held behind their backs, all the better to sharpen their concentration.

Since backyards are usually not a part of the way in which Italian cities and towns are structured, the *piazza* (or *piazzetta*) often serves as park and playground for children—from the time their mothers rock them back and forth in those huge, bulbous European perambulators in an attempt to quiet their crying, to the older boys who use the *piazza* to hone their soccer skills.

The *piazza* is where people meet and fall in love. They gather in large groups to check each other out even though they may have known each other since birth. The *piazza* is the place for making an *appuntamento,* a not very romantic word for a date. It is where young people kiss in the shadows of a restored fragment of an ancient amphitheater or passionately entwine their bodies in airtight embraces that seem suspended in time—the shadows of the softly illuminated *piazza* at night often being the only privacy they have in a world crowded with family—and every *piazza* has its shadows and secret places.

America had its town squares in the past. These were, I'm sure, modeled after the *piazza*. Perhaps ours were grassy parks rather than cobblestone or concrete, but a bandstand was at their center, a sign that communal life

existed. These town squares have gradually disappeared, giving way to strip malls and monolithic, sealed-in shopping centers where consumerism rather than conversation reigns supreme. The migration toward the suburbs directly correlates with the decline of the old town square and the subsequent increase in loneliness so prevalent in our society.

It is a thorny problem in America. Where does one go to simply be rather than do or buy? Where can one go sure of finding a friend and getting not one but two kisses, one on each cheek, the custom in Italy? Where can one feel free to spend several hours simply watching the motions of life being enacted in an open-air theater? There are no simple answers.

In recent years, there's been a proliferation of coffeehouses in America. These coffee emporiums have become neighborhood gathering spots that help fill a huge, gaping void in our society. But what is missing is that liberating expanse of space, the feeling of being at the center of life, at the center of one's universe.

If I were a politician, after making sure there was a chicken in every pot I would propose a *piazza* in every town and city in America. I would commission a glorious sculpture or fountain or obelisk to be placed at its center. The *piazza* would be ringed with caffès and offer outdoor seating, two or three chairs deep in summer. There would be plenty of free seating—benches and fountains with wide rims around their circumference where one could sit, and people would feel free to bring a portable chair if they preferred.

We would all gather in this open-air living room, from the littlest ones just learning to walk to the oldest men and women who are so often tragically marginalized out of existence. During the day, we would all be bathed in golden sunlight; at night we would bask in moonlight under a sky full of stars. And the *piazza* would be food for our souls because, even with a chicken in every pot, one can still go hungry.

TENDER CAKE WITH DRIED FRUITS AND NUTS

[*serves 6 to 8*]

A NOD TO A SLIGHTLY MORE SUBSTANTIAL BEGINNING TO THE DAY. THIS MIGHT BE SERVED TO A CHILD ALONG WITH HIS OR HER MORNING CAFFÈ LATTE.

Look in your local natural food store for dried fruits and nuts in bulk. Contrary to any posted signs, taste first before buying. Select unsulphured golden raisins and moist unsulphured apricots. Leathery dried apricots won't yield good results. If necessary, steam dried fruits over boiling water briefly to plump them up.

Buy walnut halves rather than pieces; they are more reliably fresh. Taste one or two to make sure they are impeccably fresh. The oil in walnuts is highly unstable and can turn rancid rapidly, become unhealthful as well as unappealing in terms of flavor, spoiling any dish in which they appear.

Butter and flour for cake pan
1 cup diced unsulphured dried apricots
(cut the fruit with flour-dusted scissors)
½ cup unsulphured sultana raisins
½ cup coarsely chopped walnuts
1⅓ cups unbleached all-purpose flour
2 teaspoons baking powder
½ cup (1 stick) unsalted butter, at room temperature
¾ to 1 cup sugar
2 eggs, lightly beaten
⅔ cup milk
1 teaspoon pure vanilla extract

Heat the oven to 350 degrees. Butter and flour a 10-inch round cake pan.

Toss together the apricots, raisins, and chopped walnuts.

Combine the flour and baking powder in a bowl. In another bowl, cream together the butter and sugar. Gradually stir beaten eggs into the butter and sugar mixture.

Alternately beat in the flour and milk, beginning and ending with flour. Stir in the vanilla, dried fruits, and nuts. The batter should be thick. Transfer the batter to the pan.

Bake for 35 minutes or until a wooden skewer inserted in the center comes out clean. Let cool in the pan, then unmold.

The cake lasts for 4 or 5 days. Place in a tin with a lid, wrap in waxed paper or plastic wrap, and store in a cupboard.

❧

PASTICCIONI
PLUMP PASTRIES
[makes 18 pasticcioni]

PASTICCIONI ARE THE CLASSIC BREAKFAST PASTRY OF THE SALENTO. FOR BREAKFAST, NOTHING IN THE WORLD COULD POSSIBLY TASTE BETTER THAN A SMALL PASTICCIONE with a strong espresso or caffè latte at home, or with a cappuccino at the local bar/caffè.

I find them irresistible—the tender, cakelike pastry, the filling of fresh, lemon-scented pastry cream. Ideally, they should be eaten warm or not long after they've been baked. But I also love them hours later, when the cake is less tender but a nice sugary crust has formed.

Naturally, each town claims to make the best *pasticcioni*. My friend the Baron insists that a certain bar/caffè in Lecce makes the finest ones—he meets his aging father there every morning for *prima colazione*. But, he cautions, you must go early in the morning, when they first emerge from the oven, warm and tender.

In the Salento, the *pasticcioni* would be made in small oval molds. Here in America, miniature muffin tins come closest to duplicating the experience. Select a nonstick miniature muffin tin that can produce 18 muffins.

Pastry flour is specifically called for in the recipe. It has a lower gluten content than all-purpose flour and creates a more tender crumb. It is widely available.

By the way, *pasticcioni* is a generic word for big, or plump, pastries, but in the Salento it means only one thing!

2 egg yolks

⅔ cup sugar

¼ cup cornstarch

2 cups whole milk

*Grated zest of ½ lemon (1¼ teaspoons),
preferably organic*

FOR THE PASTRY BATTER

Butter and flour for muffin tin

1 cup less 2 tablespoons sugar

*14 tablespoons (2 sticks less 2 tablespoons)
unsalted butter, at room temperature*

1 whole egg

3 egg yolks

½ teaspoon pure vanilla extract

Grated zest of ½ lemon, preferably organic

3 cups pastry flour

4 teaspoons baking powder

Pinch of salt

Whisk the egg yolks and sugar together in a small, heavy saucepan. Dissolve the cornstarch in ½ cup of the milk, then gradually add the rest of the milk and mix well. Slowly pour the milk mixture into the egg mixture, whisking until well blended.

Place over low heat and cook for 10 to 12 minutes, stirring constantly, until mixture is as shiny and thick as pudding. Stir in the lemon zest.

Transfer to a bowl. Cover with plastic wrap directly on the surface of the pastry cream to prevent forming a skin. Cool.

The pastry cream can be refrigerated for several days. If separation occurs, whisk until smooth. The recipe makes 2 cups pastry cream.

Heat the oven to 400 degrees and lightly butter and flour the nonstick muffin tin.

Beat together the sugar and butter until creamy. Then, one at a time, beat in the whole egg and egg yolks, beating well after each addition. Blend in the vanilla and lemon zest.

Put the flour, baking powder, and salt in a sifter and stir with a fork to blend. Sift about one third of the flour mixture over the egg mixture and fold it in. Add in the rest, in thirds, until well blended. It will be very thick.

Using about one quarter of the batter, with floured fingers, distribute batter into molds and form a well in the center of each one. Using approximately half of the pastry cream, fill each well with 1 generous tablespoon of the pastry cream. (You can use the remaining pastry cream to fill a cooked tart shell and garnish it with fresh fruit.) With the rest of the dough, form a lid over the filling, enclosing it as best you can. Don't make too thick a layer of cake batter over the top or the pastries will be less delicate.

Bake for about 20 minutes or until the pastries are golden.

Remove from the oven and let cool a little. Serve warm or at room temperature.

GRANITA DI LIMONE CON BRIOSCIA

[*serves 6*]

ALTHOUGH IT MAY COME AS A SURPRISE THAT ITALIANS EAT GRANITA FOR BREAK-FAST, ITALIANS WOULD BE JUST AS SURPRISED TO LEARN THAT AMERICANS SERVE granita for dessert!

In Italy, granitas, like gelato, are consumed as summer refreshers, in the morning in place of breakfast, as an afternoon snack, or late on a hot summer night when taking a *passeggiata*, a walk, with friends.

A lemon granita and a brioche from the bakery make a great morning meal in Italy when it is too hot to eat, too hot to move. It is considered very *rinfrescante*.

During the most torrid months of summer, Italians have been known to keep home-made lemon granita in the freezer, and dip into it as the need arises!

If you can't locate Meyer lemons, a sweet lemon similar to those found in Italy, and you must use Eurekas, increase the sugar to make up for the greater level of acidity.

3 cups spring or filtered water
⅓ cup sugar or to taste
1 cup fresh Meyer lemon juice
Individual brioches from a best-quality bakery (optional)

Stir together 1 cup of the water and all the sugar until the sugar granules dissolve. Add the remaining water and lemon juice. Stir well. Transfer the mixture to a metal pie dish (it chills the mixture more quickly) and place in the freezer.

Stir every 30 minutes to break up the ice crystals that form. The granita is done when it has the texture of a rough sorbet.

The granita can be served immediately. Simply spoon some granita into a glass and accompany with a brioche, if desired. (If you remember, chill the glass in advance.) Or it can be stored in the freezer for future use. If storing, transfer the granita to a glass or plastic container with a tight-fitting lid. Lemon granita stays sparkling fresh for about a week in the freezer.

GRANITA DI CAFFÈ

[serves 4]

ON A HOT, SULTRY MORNING WHEN A PERFECT LITTLE CUP OF STEAMING ESPRESSO SOUNDS OPPRESSIVE, ITALIANS TURN TO GRANITA DI CAFFÈ, OR COFFEE ICE. IT CAN BE served with or without *panna,* unsweetened whipped cream.

As with lemon granita, in addition to breakfast, coffee granita is consumed between meals, as a mid-morning or afternoon energizer, or perhaps late in the evening, as one lingers at a caffè in the dead of summer—but not as an after-dinner dessert.

I'll never forget the shock of pleasure I experienced the first time I tasted a *granita di caffè con panna.* I was twelve and had never traveled outside my sleepy suburban California town. I was sitting at an outdoor caffè in a *piazza* in the center of Palermo, on one of those infamously hot days. There was the icy dark espresso and the cool, naturally sweet cream whipped to soft mounds. I clearly recall using a long silver spoon to bring the first taste of cold espresso and cream to my mouth. Naturally, my head was spinning for hours afterwards!

2 cups hot, strong espresso (use your Moka)
¼ cup sugar
Unsweetened cream,
preferably not ultra-pasteurized, whipped (optional)

Stir together the hot espresso and sugar until the sugar granules dissolve.

Pour the mixture into a metal pie plate and place in the freezer. Stir after 20 minutes, breaking up ice crystals that form on sides of pan. Return to the freezer and repeat process every 15 minutes. It is ready when it is the texture of a rough sorbet.

Serve immediately, plain or topped with softly whipped fresh cream. Or transfer to a glass or plastic container with an airtight lid and return to the freezer. The granita is at its peak for two to three days.

SPUNTINI

morning and afternoon snacks

HOW DO ITALIANS QUELL THEIR APPETITES BETWEEN BREAKFAST AND LUNCH? THEY HAVE A SNACK, BUT NOT THE TYPE YOU MIGHT IMAGINE. WHEN ITALIANS stop for the ritualized mid-morning or mid-afternoon *spuntino*, or *merenda*, as the afternoon snack is sometimes called, what they reach for varies tremendously. The candy bar as we know it here has yet to make inroads in Italy. What that snack might be depends on several factors: whether you are a child or an adult, whether you are at home or at work, and, of course, personal preferences.

Children in Italy get a mid-morning break from school. In Palermo, street vendors might supply a schoolchild with *pane e panelle*, thin chick-pea fritters stacked in a semolina roll, or an *arancino*, a deep-fried, saffron-tinted rice ball with a tasty center of tomato veal sauce. In Rome, a school-break snack might consist of *pizza al trancio*—long trays of pizza cut into generous squares. In the Salento, kids in small towns stop at the local bar/caffè for a piece of stuffed focaccia filled with greens or tomato and anchovy. A schoolboy might pull out of his pocket a *panino*, a roll filled with a slice of dark chocolate, placed there by *la mamma* to tide him over until the main event.

Adults might do the same, or they might content themselves with one last cappuccino at the corner bar/caffè—that is, if it is before ten or eleven o'clock in the morning, the technical cut-off time for any coffee and milk drinks such as cappuccino and caffè latte. They might smoke a cigarette or two, and possibly have a breakfast pastry, almost as an extension of *prima colazione.*

In the afternoon, big-city dwellers such as Romans love their *tramezzini*—little sandwiches like our tea sandwiches, only with typically Italian ingredients such as prosciutto, or tomato and mozzarella, possibly accompanied by an *aperitivo*. These little sandwiches usually never constitute a meal, the opposite of our sandwich tradition. Alas, in many large, industrialized cities in Italy, where many workers do not have the luxury of time, or can't travel the distance home for lunch, as well as for the new high-powered technology moguls who eat at their desks, a panino often becomes the meal. But this is considered a very sad way to eat, a definite reduction in quality of life.

At home, a piece of bread and some fresh ricotta might hit the spot. Or bread with a drizzle of olive oil and a dash of salt. Or bread with a bit of jam. Dieters (yes, there are dieters in Italy) might eat a small container, half the size of one of ours, of lean plain yogurt, or one flavored with gooseberries and kiwis, with sweetened rice, or any other fruit flavors you can imagine.

Of course, there is no wrong time to eat a gelato. A hot mid-morning, mid-afternoon, or midnight in summer is ice cream or granita time. Gelato is appropriate any time of the day or night. Italians are simply addicted to their *gelati.*

Times are changing, though. Television and films have influenced children not just in Italy but all over the world. A bag of *patatine* (potato chips) might end up as a child's snack. With fast-food outlets in major cities in Italy, it might be a serving of French fries. Teenagers enjoy the cachet of hanging out in front of the local version of McDonald's, or an actual McDonald's—I'm thinking of the one at the foot of the magnificent Spanish Steps of Rome. *Che sacrilegio!*

Just as in America, television ads bombard Italians with images of packaged cookies and other snacks, trying to impart a feeling of wholesomeness and old-fashioned goodness to their industrialized, rather than artisanal, products. One company particularly adept at this is Il Mulino Bianco. The prefabricated breakfast biscotti or pastries appear on many kitchen tables in Italy, only to resurface as a child's mid-morning snack.

While America may have introduced a modern reality into the Italian dream, that practice of snacking—nibbling all day on one thing or another—is simply not part of the Italian tradition. Many people don't snack at all between meals. The ritual of mealtimes and the importance placed on those meals is deeply ingrained in Italian society and is respected by everyone.

FRISELLA (OR FRISA) AL POMODORO

[serves 1]

FRISELLE OR FRISE ARE ONE OF THE MOST TYPICAL FOODS OF THE SALENTO. BASICALLY, THESE ARE ROUNDS OF BREAD SOMETHING LIKE A BAGEL, SPLIT HORIZONTALLY, AND cooked twice, until hard as a bone. Made from either durum wheat or barley, this last a nod to the original grain used, the friselle last forever—a pantry basic in every Salento kitchen.

By immersing the friselle very briefly in water, they magically swell up and become nearly as tender as fresh bread. The process reminds me of hydrating pop-up sponges, but the results are much tastier!

Once the friselle are softened, ripe tomatoes are dragged over the surface, and seasonings—wild arugula, capers, Mediterranean oregano—add tangy notes. Naturally, abundant extra-virgin olive oil enters into the equation.

Friselle are beginning to appear in Italian specialty food stores. Gallette, hard-baked bread rounds from Liguria, can be substituted and may be easier to locate. Lacking both, a crust of dried rustic bread makes a fine replacement.

1 whole frisella
Spring or filtered water
Extra-virgin olive oil
A ripe tomato or several small cherry tomatoes
Sea salt
Dried Mediterranean oregano, either Italian or Greek
Wild or cultivated arugula, just a few leaves
A few capers, wild or cultivated

Very briefly dip the frisella halves into cold spring or filtered water and shake off the excess, or squeeze out the water between your palms.

Drizzle the olive oil onto the softened bread. Cut the tomato in half and rub the cut side into each frisella half. Season with salt. Top with either a sprinkling of dried oregano, arugula torn into small pieces, or capers—or all three.

BREAD AND WINE-WASHED ARUGULA

[*serves 1*]

PICTURE A DRIVE THROUGH THE NARROW ROADS THAT WIND THROUGH THE SALENTO COUNTRYSIDE ON THE WAY TO THE BEACH, WITH NOTHING TO EAT OR DRINK IN THE CAR but a loaf of bread and some wine—not even the customary bottle of mineral water that is a fixture in cars in summer. You spot a big clump of arugula growing wild, "wash" a few leaves with a spritzing of homemade wine, and have an impromptu picnic by the roadside under the shade of an ancient fig tree.

At home, you might add some olive oil to the bread and a scattering of sea salt—but at that moment, nothing could have tasted better than the flavor of pungent, fresh-picked arugula growing in the hot sun and the taste of wine and bread.

Arugula, wild or cultivated
Light red wine
Bread, preferably made from durum wheat flour
Extra-virgin olive oil
Sea salt

Rinse a few leaves of arugula and dry well. With a thumb on the opening of the wine bottle, shake wine over the leaves.

Tear the bread into chunks (or if you have a knife handy, slice the bread thickly). Drizzle the bread with olive oil and salt. Top with arugula leaves.

TOMATO PANINO WITH
WILD OREGANO AND GARLIC

[serves 1]

THIS SANDWICH IS AS BASIC AS THE BEST FOOD OF THE MEDITERRANEAN OFTEN IS— REDUCED TO A FEW SIMPLE ELEMENTS, EACH OF WHICH ARE AT THEIR PEAK OF FLAVOR.

I make this *panino* often during the summer when I'm staying in the Salento. No cooking is necessary—a great boon during the hottest days. I usually have a stash of wild oregano in the kitchen and some wild garlic, recently uprooted, still fresh and moist—the wild garlic that grows right above the *scoglio*, the rocky bluffs above the sea, especially delicious in June.

Assemble the ingredients and the panino basically makes itself.

A panino (bread roll), split in half,
or 2 slices rustic bread

Extra-virgin olive oil

A tomato or two, vine-ripened and
streaked with green, crisp and a little tart

Wild or cultivated garlic

A bunch of wild or cultivated
Mediterranean oregano, dried

Sea salt

Lay out the bread and drizzle with a little olive oil. Slice the tomato and arrange on one slice of bread.

Finely dice a small bit of garlic and scatter over the tomato slices.

Hold the bunch of oregano at the stem ends and shake over the tomatoes. Let some of the dried oregano leaves fall on the sandwich.

Sprinkle with a little more olive oil and season with sea salt. Cover with the other slice of bread.

PANINO DI PROSCIUTTO E PROVOLONE

[makes 1 panino]

I'M CONVINCED THE BEST-TASTING FOOD IS SPONTANEOUSLY ASSEMBLED AND EATEN ON THE SPOT. ON A DRIVE ON THE IONION COAST ON THE WESTERN SIDE OF THE Salentine Peninsula, we had arrived as far as Punta Prosciutto, the northernmost point of the province of Lecce, when hunger struck. We pulled up to a small market, bought some rolls—not the freshest—excellent slices of prosciutto (perhaps Point Prosciutto influenced our decision), and the incredible aged provolone of the south. We assembled the sandwiches in the shade of an ancient stone watchtower and devoured them in the bracing sea air.

Aged provolone is an extremely tangy cheese that defies being neatly sliced since its texture is crumbly rather than creamy. Sliced domestic provolone routinely put in deli sandwiches in America is bland and flabby. *Provolone stagionato,* aged provolone, knocks your socks off with flavor. A little goes a long way. In Italy, provolone is highly regarded and considered one of the country's greatest cheeses.

3 or 4 thin slices best-quality imported prosciutto
1 panino (roll), split in half
A few thin shards of aged provolone cheese

Layer the prosciutto in the roll and scatter the cheese over the cured meat. Cover with the other half of the roll.

GRILLED PANINO WITH
RICOTTA AND WINTER SAVORY

[makes 1 sandwich]

HERE'S ANOTHER SPONTANEOUS SANDWICH, THIS ONE INSPIRED BY THE SALENTO BUT PREPARED IN MY SAN FRANCISCO KITCHEN. SINCE SPENDING SO MUCH TIME IN THE Salentine countryside, I've become a big fan of winter savory, which grows wild all over the Salento. It has become a permanent addition to my herb garden here at home.

Naturally, the cultivated herb lacks the heady intensity of the wild plant, but the resemblence is sufficient to bring back memories of that wonderful, untamed landscape.

1 panino or pita bread (unorthodox but delicious)
A few big spoonfuls of artisanal ricotta
Extra-virgin olive oil
Sea salt and generous grindings of black pepper
A few leaves of fresh winter savory, coarsely chopped
A hot grill (I use a cast-iron stovetop grill
for impromptu snacks such as this one)

If using a bread roll, split it in half without cutting all the way through. Pull out some of the interior of the roll. Reserve and let dry for another use.

Spread the ricotta on one side of the roll or pita without coming too close to the edges. Drizzle with a little olive oil. Season with salt and abundant pepper. Sprinkle with winter savory. Close the sandwich and press down gently to "seal" the edges.

Grill briefly on a hot stovetop grill, until a few grill marks show and the ricotta has warmed up. Eat the panino right away, being careful not to burn your tongue if the ricotta has gotten too hot.

❧

PANE E PANELLE

[serves 4 to 6]

ANOTHER SNACK FOOD, THIS, ONE OF THE QUINTESSENTIAL STREET FOODS OF PALERMO. SCHOOLCHILDREN DURING THE MORNING BREAK WILL BUY THIS PANINO STACKED WITH chick-pea fritters to tide them over until *pranzo*.

I first tasted this panino on that epochal trip to Italy when I was twelve years old. I remember tasting it up at the top of Monte Pellegrino by the shrine of Santa Rosalia, patron saint of Palermo. I think I confused my epiphanies—rather than feeling closer to God upon entering the sacred grotto, I experienced a form of ecstasy when I bit into that panino I got from a concession stand just outside the shrine!

½ pound fresh chick-pea flour, unseasoned
3¼ cups spring or filtered water
2 teaspoons sea salt
Extra-virgin olive oil for frying
Rolls, preferably semolina encrusted with sesame seeds
Wedges of lemon, if you like

Place the chick-pea flour in a medium, heavy-bottomed saucepan. Add the water and salt, and whisk until there are no lumps.

Turn the heat to medium and stir with a wooden spatula. As the mixture begins to thicken, switch to a whisk and whisk continuously to prevent lumps from forming. Cook for about 15 minutes, or until the mixture is thick but still soft and easy to pour.

Immediately pour the mixture onto a clean flat surface such as a very large cutting board or slab of marble. Working quickly, use a long, flexible metal spatula to spread the mixture to a ⅛- to ½-inch thickness. When cool, cut into squares or rectangles the size of the rolls. An alternate method is to pour the mixture into a dampened loaf pan. When cool, unmold and slice with a string. In Palermo, special molds are sometimes used to form the patties.

Pour enough olive oil in a frying pan so that the panelle will float in the oil (about 1 to 2 inches up the side of the pan is sufficient). Heat the oil, but do not allow it to smoke. Fry the panelle in the hot oil, a few at a time, turning them once to cook evenly on both sides until golden brown and slightly puffed up. Drain well on paper towels, sprinkling the patties with salt while hot.

Stack several of the hot patties in a split roll and eat immediately. If desired, squeeze lemon over the panelle after stacking them in the roll.

PIZZA DOUGH

[makes enough dough for four 8-inch pizzas]

I PREFER MY PIZZA CRUST JUST A LITTLE THICKER THAN THE CRACKER-THIN ONES CUR-
RENTLY IN VOGUE. IN THE SOUTH (CALLED THE MEZZOGIORNO, MEANING MIDDAY BECAUSE
the sun is so hot and strong), the mark of a great pizza is a resilience when you bite into it,
tender and chewy at the same time, but not crackly crisp.

To me, this kind of dough provides a better base for toppings, as well as giving pleasure
in the texture of the pizza crust itself. A slightly charred pizza crust, blistered a bit and golden
brown along the perimeter, is a beautiful sight to behold!

Pizza dough is so easy to make and so sensually satisfying that taking out the food processor seems a colossal waste of time and energy, and a lost opportunity for some sensual
gratification.

¼ cup lukewarm spring or filtered water
1 package active dry yeast (not the quick-rising type)
About 3½ cups organic unbleached
all-purpose flour, more or less as needed
3 tablespoons extra-virgin olive oil
1½ teaspoons sea salt
1 cup cold spring or filtered water

Place the lukewarm water in a small bowl and sprinkle the yeast over the top. Let rest for
about 5 minutes or until it becomes a little frothy on top. Don't worry if no yeast action
occurs as long as the expiration date is still valid.

Place the yeast mixture in a large mixing bowl. Add about 2 heaping cups of the flour,
the olive oil, salt, and cold water. Stir with a wooden spoon until a thick batter forms.
You may have to add more flour, enough for the dough to start to pull away from the
sides of the bowl.

Sprinkle a work surface lightly with flour. Transfer the dough to the work surface. Begin
kneading in the remaining flour, a little at a time, until the dough is soft and elastic. It is
better to err on the side of too moist rather than too dry. Shape the dough into a ball.

Lightly coat the inside of a large bowl with a very thin film of olive oil and wipe away
any excess. Place the ball of dough in the bowl and turn it over once, in order to moisten
the outside of the dough with oil. This prevents the dough from drying out as it rises. Cover

tightly with plastic wrap and keep in a warm, draft-free place for about an hour. It should double in bulk.

Sprinkle a work surface with flour. Divide the dough in quarters. Roll each piece into a smooth ball, making sure to knead out any air pockets. Place the balls on a lightly floured surface, cover with a clean cloth, and let rest for an hour.

To form the pizza, take one ball of dough and place on a lightly floured surface. Sprinkle a little flour on top. Use your fingertips to begin to spread the dough out evenly into a flat circle about ½ inch thick.

Place the dough on the back of your fist and gently stretch and rotate it using both fists side by side. Continue this process until the pizza is a little thicker than ¼ inch in the center portion, and a bit thicker still around the rim. The pizza should measure about 9 inches across.

The pizza is ready for the topping, which should be applied without delay, and then immediately slipped into the hot oven. Meanwhile, cover the remaining balls of dough with a kitchen towel. Repeat the procedure for the remaining dough balls.

PIZZA ALL'INSALATA

[makes enough for four 8-inch pizzas]

DURING A HEAT WAVE, THE WORST IN A HUNDRED YEARS, THE PAVED STREETS OF LECCE BEGAN TO MELT. WALKING IN THE CITY DURING THE DAY WAS ONLY FOR THE STURDIEST— and even they could be seen wiping foreheads and complaining bitterly. Not even the setting sun brought relief. The nights were in the high nineties and humid as a wet towel.

One evening, late, about ten or eleven o'clock, a friend and I went out for a pizza. The city, normally lively at this hour, was deserted and I suddenly understood why. Everyone was at this particular trattoria eating *al fresco*. The brilliant white umbrellas bathed in the dark night were a cooling sight. *Pizza all'insalata,* which appeared on just about every table, was the perfect food for withered appetites—basically a caprese salad on top of a beautifully charred and blistered crust.

4 large meaty tomatoes,
vine-ripened and streaked with green
2 large balls fresh firm mozzarella, well drained
1 recipe Pizza Dough (page 44)
Extra-virgin olive oil
Sea salt
Fresh green basil leaves

Place a baking stone on the top rack of the oven. Turn the oven to 500 degrees and let the stone heat at least 30 minutes or up to an hour before cooking.

Meanwhile, slice the tomatoes and let drain in a colander to remove any excess water and seeds. Slice the mozzarella and drain on a clean kitchen towel.

One at a time, stretch a dough ball into a 9-inch circle according to directions on page 45. Keep the remaining dough covered with a clean kitchen towel. Place the stretched pizza dough on a floured peel and drizzle pizza with a little oil, especially around the rim. Slip into the preheated oven. Cook for about 7 minutes or until the pizza is light brown and slightly charred.

Quickly assemble pizza by overlapping tomato and mozzarella slices over the top, salting the slices as you go. Scatter basil leaves torn into large segments over the top and drizzle with olive oil.

Continue with remaining dough.

PIZZA ALLA TORRE DEL MAR

[makes four 8-inch pizzas]

A FAVORITE PIZZA TOPPING OF A FRIEND, PARTICULARLY GOOD WHEN PREPARED IN THE OLIVE WOOD–BURNING PIZZA OVEN OF THE BEST PIZZERIA IN THE SMALL COASTAL town in the Salento where I spend summers. The pizza tastes great with a cold Italian beer.

The wild arugula the family-run pizzeria scatters on top of the pizza is pungent and aromatic—a few leaves are more than enough to pack a wallop. Here, we can just increase the amount of arugula to achieve a similar result.

1 28-ounce can imported San Marzano plum tomatoes, drained
2 tablespoons extra-virgin olive oil
Sea salt and grindings of black pepper
Pinch of dried Mediterranean oregano
1 recipe Pizza Dough (page 44)
Chunks of tuna preserved in olive oil, 2 or 3 ounces
4 small balls fresh mozzarella, drained, thickly sliced into rounds
24 unseasoned, brine-cured green olives,
pitted and cut into large segments
Handful of arugula leaves, trimmed of tough stems

Place a baking stone on the top shelf of the oven. Turn the oven to 500 degrees and heat the stone for at least a half hour or up to an hour in advance.

Put the tomatoes, olive oil, and salt and pepper to taste through the medium disk of a food mill. Stir in the oregano. The sauce is ready for the pizza—it cooks on the pizza and keeps the tomato flavor fresh and lively by not cooking it twice.

Meanwhile, place one ball of rolled-out pizza dough on a floured peel. Keep the remaining balls covered with a clean kitchen towel. Spoon one quarter of the sauce over the top using the back of the spoon to spread it evenly over the crust. Flake one quarter of the tuna and scatter over the top. Arrange slices from one ball of mozzarella on the pizza—there should be just a few slices dotting the surface. Sprinkle the pizza with one quarter of the green olives.

Drizzle the pizza lightly with olive oil. Slip the pizza into the preheated oven. Bake for about 7 minutes or until the pizza crust is golden and a little charred and blistered. Remove the pizza from the oven and scatter arugula leaves over the top.

Repeat with the remaining dough.

SCEBLASTI

[serves 6]

ONE OF THE STRANGEST FOOD FESTIVALS I'VE EVER ATTENDED WAS THE SAGRA DELLA SCEBLASTI. I WAS CURIOUS TO KNOW WHAT A SCEBLASTI WAS SINCE NO ONE AMONG MY friends seemed to know!

When we first arrived in the small town of Zollino where the festival was advertised as taking place, we assumed we'd made a mistake; perhaps the festival was on another night since the town was completely dark and deserted with not a soul in sight. As we wandered down the empty streets in search of signs of life, we began to detect the sounds of a band in the distance.

As it turned out, absolutely everyone in town was at the festival, which was taking place just outside the village under a lightly trafficked elevated highway! The concrete reinforcement beams of the overhead freeway didn't create much atmosphere, but the crowd, the food, the music, and the dancing more than made up for the odd setting.

And what is the mysterious *sceblasti?* It is a type of focaccia with tomato and zucchini, slightly piquant like so much food I've encountered in the Salento—and quite delicious.

FOR THE DOUGH

1⅓ cups warm spring or filtered water

1 tablespoon active dry yeast (not the quick-rising type)

1 tablespoon sea salt

3 tablespoons extra-virgin olive oil

4 cups organic bread flour, more or less as needed

FOR THE FILLING

Olive oil for the baking sheet
(using two sheets, one inside the other, will protect
the bottom of the sceblasti from scorching)

1 small, firm zucchini

Sea salt

1 small onion

2 tablespoons extra-virgin olive oil

1 large ripe, meaty tomato, peeled, seeded, coarsely chopped,
and drained in a colander

¼ teaspoon hot red pepper flakes

½ cup pitted oil-cured black olives, coarsely chopped

Put the warm water in a large bowl and sprinkle the yeast over the top. Let it rest for 5 minutes and then gently stir to dissolve the granules.

Add the salt and olive oil, and, using a wooden spoon, gradually blend in the flour, cup by cup. When it begins to pull away from the sides of the bowl, transfer the dough to a clean floured surface. Knead for about 10 minutes, or until the dough is smooth and elastic. Form into a smooth, tight ball.

Oil a clean large bowl and wipe off any excess oil. Place the dough ball in the bowl and turn over, so both sides of dough are lightly oiled. Cover tightly with plastic wrap and let rise in a warm place until doubled in size, 1 to 2 hours.

Place a baking stone in the oven on the middle rack and turn the heat to 450 degrees. Oil a rectangular baking sheet that measures about 10x15 inches and place it in another sheet of the same size to protect focaccia from scorching.

Cut the zucchini into thin rounds. Place in a colander. Sprinkle with salt and let drain for 15 minutes.

Meanwhile, sliver the onion and gently sauté in the olive oil until the onion is tender and translucent. Wipe the zucchini dry. Add the zucchini to the pan and toss in the oil. Cook for a minute or two, so the zucchini absorbs some of the flavors in the sauté pan. Stir in the tomato, salt to taste, and hot pepper flakes and cook another minute or two to evaporate some of the excess water. Off the heat, stir in the olives. Let the mixture cool.

Remove the dough from the bowl. Punch down the dough to remove air pockets. Briefly knead in the tomato and zucchini mixture, just long enough to distribute the ingredients. Use your fingertips to spread the focaccia evenly in the baking sheet. Drizzle lightly with olive oil and sea salt. Place the focaccia in the oven, preferably on a baking stone, and bake for about 30 minutes, or until the surface is golden brown. Serve warm or at room temperature, cut into squares.

POTATO CROQUETTES

[makes 12 to 15 croquettes]

IN KEEPING WITH THE TRADITION OF STREET FOOD, THESE LITTLE FINGERS OF MASHED POTATOES TANGY WITH GRATED CHEESE AND PERFUMED WITH HERBS MAKE ONE OF THE best snacks ever invented. Or serve them with drinks as an appetizer.

1 pound medium russet potatoes
¼ cup grated pecorino sardo cheese
¼ cup grated Parmigiano-Reggiano cheese
2 eggs, lightly beaten
1½ tablespoons finely chopped fresh mint
1 tablespoon finely chopped fresh oregano
Sea salt
3 cups fine bread crumbs
Olive oil, preferably extra-virgin, for frying

Boil the potatoes until tender. Drain and peel. Put potatoes through a ricer to create a smooth puree. (A food processor turns potatoes into glue.)

Add the cheeses, eggs, herbs, and salt to taste to the potatoes and stir with a wooden spoon to combine ingredients.

With lightly dampened hands, form the seasoned potatoes into logs about 1 inch in diameter and 2½ inches long.

Roll the logs in the bread crumbs.

Pour enough olive oil into a skillet to measure ¼ inch deep and warm over medium heat. When the oil is hot but not smoking, fry the croquettes, a few at a time, turning them so that they are an even light brown.

Drain on butcher paper and season lightly with salt. Serve hot.

How Italians Stay Healthy

DOES THERE STILL EXIST THE STEREOTYPE OF THE BIG ITALIAN MAMMA, A CORPULENT figure clad in black? In actual fact, one sees very few men or women in Italy with severe weight problems. Italians have a healthy self-esteem that expresses itself in a desire to make a good impression, to look good—*fare una bella figura* they call it.

Most people look trim. I'm not referring to gym muscles hard as petrified wood and bodies thin to the point of emaciation—our current misguided definition of fitness in so many affluent nations. I'm speaking about bodies whose muscles are used to perform actual tasks by people of all ages whose active lives maintain their body tone.

Italians seem to radiate a healthy glow. This may verge on exaggeration on my part, but whenever I leave Italy, I come away with the strong impression that this is a population that knows how to take care of itself.

The structure of mealtimes and the importance placed on each meal, as well as what is brought to the table, is of primary importance in maintaining health, and I discuss this at length in the pages of this book.

But exercise integrated into daily life is an equally important component of staying healthy. Cities and towns are architecturally structured so that one walks daily to the mar-

ketplace for groceries and sundries. Carrying all those bundles of vegetables, packages of cheeses and meats, bottles of wine, and huge plastic bottles of mineral water (the bottles sometimes purchased six at a time in shrink-wrapped plastic) is a real workout. I've done it often enough that I can attest to its strenuousness. In Italian cities and towns, pedaling one's bicycle to work makes sense and is "do-able"—yet another example of exercise as an integral part of life.

In small towns, I often see men and women who are quite elderly bicycling around on bikes that look as old as they are—running errands, buying groceries, visiting friends. Sometimes I see these same old folks pedaling the same ancient bikes on the soft shoulder of the highway, slowly, tranquilly, making their way toward their destination while sleek Italian cars whiz by at death-defying speeds leaving the bicyclist in a cloud of dust.

This sense of staying in motion, of using one's body, is, no doubt, still encoded genetically in Italians from the days of an all-agrarian society, where "the fruits of one's labor" was an expression that could be used literally, not merely figuratively. Italians are incredibly active people, putting intense energy into everything they do—above and beyond the normal energy that goes into one's form of employment, be it at a bank or one that involves physical labor. It is a high-energy style of simply being in the world, a nonstop openness to what the moment offers—a conversation with a friend, or the daily challenge of shopping for the best and freshest food—each activity requires total concentration and complete involvement. Just think of the super-charged energy that goes into all that gesticulating! Italians don't just talk with their mouths, they talk with their entire bodies—from the tops of their heads down to the tips of their toes.

In Italy, ritualized snacking, rather than our ongoing snackathons, is another factor that influences health. See the introduction to the chapter on snacks to learn further about Italians' sensible approach to snacktime and how it reflects a respect for healthful, "real" food and mealtimes, as opposed to our compulsive need to snack to replenish our nutritional reserves, which were not adequately addressed in the first place. We are a society addicted to the taste of sugar, to sweet foods, for the boost of energy it gives us, but also (and here I offer a personal theory) because it returns us to the comfort and warmth of childhood and family.

A highly social society cuts down on loneliness, one of the main reasons I feel we in America are addicted to snacking—to fill the hole in our soul. Italian life is structured so that people are in constant contact with one another. They greet each other ten times a day, each time as though they'd found a long-lost friend. And if you, as a foreigner, stop at the same little bar on the corner for two days in a row, you'll become a part of this very large extended family.

Or, perhaps this desire to stay *in forma*, in good shape, is simply because Italians want to be able to fit into all those exquisitely designed clothes, or they are thinking ahead to the summer months spent at the seashore where the Italian pastime of people-watching goes into high gear!

All these elements—the rituals of mealtimes, a reverence and respect for food and nurturing, a sense of purposefulness in being physical and using one's body, and the tremendous value, perhaps above and beyond everything else in Italian life, placed on human interaction and connection—are interwoven and together contribute to a society that has basic healthy patterns of living that we would do well to emulate here at home.

STUFFED FOCACCIA WITH TWO FILLINGS

[*serves 6*]

A CROSS BETWEEN A CALZONE AND A FOCACCIA, THESE STUFFED FOCACCIAS ARE POPULAR SNACKS IN THE SOUTH—EVERY BAR / CAFFÈ FEATURES THEM IN THEIR GLASS display cases. They taste great any time of the day—mid-morning, mid-afternoon, or, in the heat of summer, at midnight with a cool glass of local wine.

Many variations exist, but I offer recipes for two fillings that are my favorites—one with bitter greens and black olives, the other with the freshest ricotta and slivers of high-quality salami.

1 recipe Pizza Dough (page 44)
for each stuffed focaccia
1 recipe filling (recipe follows)

Put a baking stone on the middle rack of the oven and turn the heat to 450 degrees. Let the stone heat for about 30 minutes.

If not using a peel, lightly oil a baking sheet large enough to accommodate a 12-inch round focaccia and place the sheet inside another sheet of the same size (this protects the bottom of the focaccia from scorching).

Punch down the dough and divide into two pieces, one measuring one third of the dough and the other measuring two thirds of the dough. Lightly flour a work surface. Roll out the dough into two disks 12 inches in diameter.

Place the thicker disk on a floured peel or on the lightly oiled baking sheet. Spread the filling in the middle of the disk, leaving a border of about an inch or so without filling. Cover with the other disk and seal the edges, pressing down with your fingertips or with the tines of a fork. Use a fork or thin bamboo skewer to prick holes over the top surface. Lightly oil the top with your fingers or a clean pastry brush.

If using a peel, slide the focaccia directly onto the baking stone. If using a baking sheet, place it directly on the baking stone.

Bake for approximately 30 minutes or until the top is golden brown. Serve warm or at room temperature.

(CONTINUED)

DANDELION AND BLACK OLIVE FILLING

2 pounds small, tender dandelion greens,
trimmed of tough stems, leaves coarsely chopped

Sea salt

2 tablespoons extra-virgin olive oil

2 garlic cloves, finely chopped

12 oil-cured black olives, pitted and coarsely chopped

2 tablespoons capers, rinsed of excess brine

2 anchovy fillets, finely chopped

Cook the dandelion greens over medium heat in just enough water to barely cover them and add salt to taste. Drain when tender. When cool, press out any excess water between the palms of your hands. Chop medium-fine.

Over low heat, warm the olive oil and garlic in a sauté pan for a few minutes. Add the greens and toss in the oil to coat the leaves. Add the olives, capers, and anchovies and stir to distribute the ingredients evenly. Let warm over low heat briefly to unite the flavors. Let filling cool.

RICOTTA FILLING

1 pound high-quality (preferably
artisanal) ricotta, drained

¼ cup slivered fine-textured salami

2 eggs, lightly beaten with a fork

½ cup grated pecorino cheese

Grindings of black pepper

Combine the ingredients in a bowl. Stir with a fork until well amalgamated. Refrigerate if making the filling in advance.

INSALATE
salads

SOME FORM OF SALAD, EITHER INSALATA VERDE (GREEN SALAD), INSALATA MISTA (MIXED GREEN SALAD), OR A COOKED VEGETABLE SALAD, IS EATEN BY EVERY Italian every day, usually twice a day.

The following salads include raw or cooked ingredients, and sometimes a combination of the two. Fairly small by our standards, Italian salads are also somewhat restrained in terms of the number of ingredients. I have noticed Italian food magazines including more American-style salads—that is, main-dish salads with combinations of fruits, nuts, vegetables, and so forth, in their pages. But I don't recall actually seeing an Italian prepare or eat one of these more elaborate creations.

Eating salads on a twice-daily basis is another way in which Italians maintain their health. These salads are as intrinsic to Italian eating patterns as the taste of espresso at the end of a meal.

TERESA'S BLOOD ORANGE SALAD
FROM NEAR BARI

[serves 4]

SOME PEOPLE MAY NOT BE FAMILIAR WITH THE IDEA OF ORANGES DRESSED WITH OLIVE OIL, BUT IT IS AN EXTRAORDINARILY GOOD AND REFRESHING COMBINATION. MY FRIEND Teresa told me about this salad, served in March for the Festa di San Giuseppe.

Most important is finding sweet, juicy blood oranges—some lack sweetness and are pulpy. The juices should run blood red and the flavor be a cross between ripe oranges and berries. The best varieties are Tarocco, the sweetest, and Moro, the "bloodiest," or most red, blood orange, but quality here in America is still spotty.

The purpose of adding the hot water? An informal discussion with Teresa yielded a few possibilities. The most plausible one is that the hot water helps create a bit of dressing, since it blends with the olive oil and citrus juice. Heat also brings out the perfumes of olive oil and citrus.

6 large, juicy blood oranges
Extra-virgin olive oil
Hot spring or purified water
Sea salt
Generous grindings of black pepper

Use a paring knife to cut away peel and pith of the oranges. Cut oranges horizontally into rounds.

Divide slices among four salad plates. Drizzle each plate with olive oil. Then top each serving with 2 or 3 tablespoons hot water. Season with salt and black pepper.

Serve immediately.

PINK BEET SALAD WITH CELERY LEAVES

[serves 2 to 4]

CELERY LEAVES ARE A DELICIOUS ADDITION TO SALADS. IN ITALY, NO ONE WOULD THINK OF THROWING AWAY THE LEAVES; THEY WOULD BE USED AS PART OF A FLAVOR BASE FOR soups and pasta sauces. In the beet salad, they add a strong, unexpected herbal flavor to sweet, earthy beets.

To make a complete meal of the salad, serve with a few slices of ricotta salata or fresh pecorino cheese.

1½ pounds small pink chioggia,
or golden beets, or other varieties
¼ cup extra-virgin olive oil
1 tablespoon fresh lemon juice
Zest of ½ lemon, preferably organic
Sea salt and freshly ground black pepper
½ cup celery leaves, both dark green and yellow

Trim the leaves off the beet tops, leaving a tuft of stems. If the leaves are very fresh, reserve them and cook as you would any greens (see Verdura all'Insalata, page 57).

Boil the beets in salted water until tender but firm. Drain. When cool enough to handle, peel and cut into chunks. While still warm, season the beets with olive oil, lemon juice, and the lemon zest. Season with salt and black pepper to taste. Toss and adjust seasonings. You can make this up to a day in advance. Bring to room temperature before proceeding.

Just before serving, sprinkle the beets with celery leaves and toss gently once or twice.

❧

VERDURA ALL'INSALATA

COOKED GREENS SALAD

[serves 4]

IN ITALY, GREENS COOKED IN THIS MANNER ARE AS BASIC AS BREAD ON THE TABLE OR A DISH OF SPAGHETTI IN TOMATO SAUCE. THE TYPE OF GREEN MAY VARY—FROM MILD to peppery—but the cooking method remains pretty much the same.

If possible, try to incorporate cooked greens into mealtimes once or twice a day. I'm convinced it is one of the main components of a healthy Italian style of eating. Vary the varieties: remember, spinach isn't the only leafy green.

3 pounds tender broccoli rabe, dandelion greens,
Swiss chard, or other seasonal greens
Extra-virgin olive oil
Sea salt
Lemon wedges (optional)

Clean and trim the greens according to the type you are cooking. Cook in salted boiling water; the amount depends on the variety of greens. Cooking times will vary for different greens, so taste frequently. Drain when tender, reserving the cooking water; it makes a deliciously herbal hot "tea." Let cool to room temperature. Do not refrigerate; cold temperatures affect the flavor of greens adversely.

Just before serving, toss in a little olive oil and season with salt to taste. Serve with lemon wedges, if desired.

SAGRA DELLA PATATA

SALAD FROM THE POTATO FESTIVAL

[serves 4]

ONE OF MY FAVORITE MEMORIES OF THE SALENTO: A POTATO FESTIVAL IN THE SMALL TOWN OF PARABITA, ON A WARM JULY NIGHT WHEN AIR TEMPERATURE AND BODY TEM-perature became one—it was a feeling of merging into the night. Everyone in town was there. A band played and a singer with a wild mane of pitch-black hair sang. The moon was so large and red it was absolutely frightening.

Every potato dish I tasted was extraordinarily good. This region, close to the sea and salt-air breezes, produces famous potatoes with fine golden flesh and paper-thin skin. You can keep your truffle festival—I'll take my potato festival any day!

1 pound very small Yukon Gold potatoes
5 tablespoons extra-virgin olive oil
4 tablespoons mellow white wine vinegar
Sea salt and black pepper
2 crisp vine-ripened medium tomatoes, cut into small cubes
1 firm cucumber, peeled, seeded, and cut into small cubes
¼ cup roughly chopped arugula leaves
¼ cup finely diced sweet red onion
1 tablespoon pickled fennel blossoms (see Note)
or 1 tablespoon capers, preferably salt-cured, well rinsed
1 teaspoon dried oregano, preferably Mediterranean

Cook potatoes in salted boiling water until tender but firm. Drain well. When cool enough to handle, peel and cut into small dice. While still warm, dress the potatoes with olive oil and vinegar, and add salt and pepper to taste.

When potatoes are at room temperature, add remaining ingredients and toss gently. Correct seasoning, adding more oil, vinegar, salt and pepper as needed.

NOTE: When wild fennel is in season, pluck the blossoms just before they bloom. Rinse well and let dry thoroughly overnight. Place blossoms in a jar with a tight-fitting lid. If desired, add hot red chili pepper. Generously cover with white wine vinegar. Refrigerate. Lasts for months.

THE FAMILY'S SUMMER SALAD

[*serves 6*]

THIS SALAD APPEARED ON OUR DINNER TABLE THREE OR FOUR TIMES A WEEK DURING THE SUMMER MONTHS. WE ALWAYS USED THE ITALIAN OREGANO MY GRANDMOTHER GREW in the backyard—dried, the way it is preferred for salads. My mother would cut up the garlic for the salad with a simple table knife. The pieces were so big they would make my mouth burn! But I always loved this salad and couldn't stop eating it until it had vanished from the bowl, juices and all.

This typical Italian salad needs vine-ripened tomatoes to really taste authentic. During tomato season, head straight to the farmers' market or grow the tomatoes yourself. Romano green beans—a wide, flat version popular in Italy—are delicious in this salad, another reason to head to the farmers' market or a market in an Italian neighborhood.

1 pound small Yukon Gold potatoes of about the same size
6 tablespoons extra-virgin olive oil
5 tablespoons imported red wine vinegar
Sea salt and grindings of black pepper
2 teaspoons dried Mediterranean oregano
2 garlic cloves, finely chopped
1 pound tender green beans, any variety, ends trimmed
4 medium crisp, vine-ripened tomatoes

Cook the potatoes in a generous amount of salted boiling water until tender but firm. When cool enough to handle, peel and cut into chunks. Place in a shallow salad bowl. Drizzle with half the olive oil and vinegar and season with salt and pepper. Sprinkle with oregano and garlic. Toss gently.

Meanwhile, cook the green beans in another pot of salted boiling water. Drain when tender but firm and add to the potatoes. Toss.

Cut the tomatoes into chunks and add to the bowl.

Drizzle in the remaining olive oil and vinegar and gently toss the salad. Taste and correct seasonings.

PALERMO MARKET SALAD

[serves 4]

CAN YOU IMAGINE A MARKET WHERE YOU COULD BUY, NOT PREPARED SALADS, WHICH ARE USUALLY DISAPPOINTING AND EXPENSIVE TO BOOT, BUT FRESHLY COOKED SALAD ingredients: freshly boiled green beans, roasted onions, roasted peppers, and other "prepared" vegetables, ready to take home and assemble into your own fresh salad?

When I was a child my mother would describe to me the Vucciria, the famous market in Palermo—its scent of ripe fruit, the colors, the cries of the vendors. On scorchingly hot summer days, all the ingredients for a salad made from the freshest market produce were available freshly cooked—without herbs or seasonings of any kind. All that was needed was your own olive oil and vinegar, and some fresh basil. And everyone had basil growing on their balconies, to pluck fresh and throw into a salad or a pasta sauce.

2 large onions
3 medium Yukon Gold potatoes
1 sweet red pepper
1 sweet yellow pepper
½ pound fresh Romano green beans,
or regular green beans
5 tablespoons extra-virgin olive oil
¼ cup imported red wine vinegar
Sea salt and grindings of black pepper
2 or 3 small crisp, vine-ripened tomatoes
Handful of basil leaves

Roast the onions in a preheated 350 degree oven until tender, about 1 hour. Let cool. Peel and cut into thick slices.

Meanwhile, prepare the remaining vegetables.

Boil the potatoes until tender but firm. Drain and when cool enough to handle, peel and cut into chunks.

Roast the peppers over coals, over a gas burner, or under the broiler until charred. Peel and remove core, seeds, and thick white membrane. Cut into thick strips.

Trim the beans. Cook in abundant salted boiling water until tender but firm. Drain well and place on a large platter.

Add the other vegetables. Drizzle with olive oil and vinegar. Season with salt and pepper to taste. Toss gently. Taste and correct seasonings. Garnish with chunks of tomato, salted, and basil leaves, torn into large fragments.

༄

BREAD SALAD WITH TOMATO, ARUGULA, MILD HOT GREEN PEPPER, AND WINTER SAVORY

[serves 4]

AN IMPROMPTU BREAD SALAD I MADE ON A HOT DAY IN THE SALENTO WITH INGREDIENTS ON HAND. THE VARIETY OF HOT GREEN PEPPER I WOULD USE IN THE SALENTO FOR this dish is not available here. Substitute Anaheim or poblano peppers.

Also, wild arugula grows everywhere in that rugged landscape, rising out of the brick-red earth. It has a much more intense flavor than our market arugula. The good news is that seeds are available through Renee's Garden Seeds for a wild arugula that they call Rustic Arugula. It is easy to grow and the results are fabulously good.

4 thick slices day-old country bread, cubed
4 crisp, juicy vine-ripened tomatoes, coarsely diced
Handful of arugula leaves, preferably wild, chopped
1 tablespoon finely julienned mild
hot green pepper, such as Anaheims or poblanos
2 tablespoons capers in salt, rinsed and dried (see Note)
1 tablespoon chopped fresh winter savory or
1 tablespoon chopped fresh thyme
¼ cup extra-virgin olive oil
A splash of red wine vinegar
Sea salt and freshly ground black pepper

Combine all the ingredients but the oil, vinegar, and salt and pepper and gently toss. Drizzle with olive oil and vinegar. Season with salt and pepper. Toss again to distribute dressing. Taste and correct seasonings.

Serve immediately or let rest for an hour at room temperature to let flavors develop.

NOTE: Capers cured in salt retain more of the caper flavor and texture. They require rinsing to remove excess salt. If unavailable, substitute capers in brine. Rinse thoroughly and dry well.

THE BARONESSA'S RICE SALAD

[serves 4]

THIS VERY REFRESHING RICE SALAD WAS PART OF A COOL-TEMPERATURE LUNCH AT THE SUMMER RETREAT OF MY FRIEND, THE BARONE. THIS ELEGANTLY APPOINTED VILLINO WAS a former pigsty, part of a vast tract of family-owned land deep in the Salento countryside.

Across acres of Italian garden is the massive *castello*, which the baron has recently transformed into a luxurious Italian-style bed and breakfast.

1 cup raw rice, preferably superfino arborio

¼ cup extra-virgin olive oil

Sea salt

Black pepper

3 ripe but firm garden tomatoes, diced small

1 cucumber, peeled, seeded, and cut into small dice

3 celery stalks, tender ones, finely diced

1 small carrot, peeled and finely diced

1 tablespoon capers, rinsed and carefully dried

¼ cup fresh lemon juice

Very fresh cut basil, preferably just picked

Cook the rice in abundant salted boiling water until al dente. Drain well.

Place in a medium bowl and toss with 2 tablespoons extra-virgin olive oil. Season with salt and freshly ground pepper to taste. Let cool.

Add prepared vegetables and capers. Season with remaining 2 tablespoons olive oil and the lemon juice, and adjust seasonings. Let rest for 30 minutes.

Before serving, sprinkle with basil and toss once or twice.

{ A Civilized Lunch During the Workday }

SINCE MOST AMERICANS EAT LUNCH OUTSIDE THE HOME, IN A RESTAURANT OR FAST-FOOD outlet, or carry their lunch with them in a paper bag, it is important to keep the principles of the Italian *pranzo*—the complete midday meal—in mind.

After all, this is the nutrition that will carry us through the rest of our workday. It will especially aid in that afternoon slump so many of us experience, when we grab a candy bar or something sugary to boost our flagging energy. It is precisely at this time, mid-afternoon, that Italians, after having eaten well and rested, are ready to return to work refreshed and renewed.

Even if you can't sit down to a relaxed meal among family members, you can seek out eating establishments that offer complete menus. Yes, but the price, you say! It is true that many restaurants that offer higher quality and more varied selections tend to be expensive, but one can still search for a small establishment that might offer a greater variety of foods at more reasonable prices. Ethnic restaurants are a tremendous resource. The prices are usually low and many of the menus feature a number of different items to choose from, including a selection of cooked seasonal vegetables, one of the keys to good health.

For example, San Francisco's North Beach neighborhood, where my writing studio is located, is adjacent to a bustling Chinese neighborhood. Many of the small and modest restaurants there offer four or five different varieties of cooked greens—mustard greens, Chinese broccoli, sautéed pea shoots, and so forth. The comparison to an Italian trattoria is obvious: one often sees platters of the day's seasonal cooked greens—Swiss chard, spinach, rapini—on display in the trattoria window. You can be sure that nearly everyone who enters the trattoria will order one of the greens, served simply with a cruet of extra-virgin olive oil for drizzling over the top. And the same is true at the Chinese restaurant (minus the olive oil!).

Of course, North Beach is a mecca for Italian restaurants. Yet, eating lunch out nearly every day, I'm faced with attempting to construct a civilized meal without depleting my financial resources. Getting to know the proprietor of a small family-run place can be tremendously helpful. Once you are a regular, they are more inclined to respond to your personal requests. For example, if I order roast chicken at one of my favorite restaurants, I may just want a simple tomato salad served on the side, and a cruet of olive oil. Since I eat there often, they accommodate a certain flexibility in the menu. This particular family-run trattoria reminds me so much of Italy—the father behind the grill, the son and daughter waiting tables. If I am in the mood for just half a glass of wine, they don't mind pouring me a generous half, which I pay for the next time I order a half-glass.

Another option might be a restaurant, say,

that serves hamburgers. Instead of eating one like a sandwich, ask that it be served on the plate with the bun on the side, and use the tomato, lettuce, and onion to make a simple mixed green salad. Always ask for cruets of olive oil and vinegar or lemon wedges, and dress the salad yourself. Most restaurant salad dressings are gloppy affairs that weigh down the ingredients and completely obscure the delicate flavors of salads—most are industrially produced and loaded with additives and preservatives. If you live where cruets of extra-virgin olive oil and red wine vinegar are not so readily available, you may consider carrying small, leak-proof containers with you at mealtimes to add that authentic Italian note to your food. May I also suggest carrying a small shaker of sea salt? It sounds extreme, it may even sound crazy, but minor adjustments like these make all the difference in the world.

And, if it *is* financially feasible, spend a bit more money on lunch, since, if you follow the Italian custom and go the whole route, you will be dining on a smaller amount of food in the evening. It may seem extravagant, but ultimately, your body will thank you and the financial expenditure may even out in the end.

Eating at your desk presents its own set of challenges. The infamous sack lunch containing a sandwich, chips, and piece of fruit still prevails. A diet-conscious eater may replace the sandwich with a yogurt and have two pieces of fruit instead. Inevitably, the afternoon slump will descend upon you, as well as a general feeling of deprivation for a lonely meal out of a brown paper bag.

Again, imagination plays a role in turning the quickie lunch into a meal. As with the hamburger, instead of assembling a sandwich, why not pack a roll of rustic bread, a few slices of mozzarella or prosciutto, a small container of sliced tomatoes seasoned with olive oil, and a bottle of mineral water. Add the salt later so the tomatoes do not become watery (you have that little shaker handy).

Pack a plate, knife, fork, and spoon, and even a glass. It is amazing how much more satisfaction comes from eating on a real plate and using actual cutlery. You may even want to pack a cloth napkin. Arrange the ingredients on the plate, and season to taste. Pour yourself a glass of mineral water, set the napkin on your lap, and feel the satisfaction of eating in a manner that lends a feeling of contentment and of having eaten well.

If these ideas seem absurd to you, or impossible to achieve owing to time considerations, the fact is, a soggy sandwich you took the time to put together in the morning or the night before would be infinitely more desirable if you had kept the ingredients separate and had given each one the integrity it deserves.

And back to that sandwich in a sack. A well-prepared panino with appropriately chosen ingredients of exceptional quality on slices of good rustic bread or tucked into a roll, a vegetable accompaniment of some kind—for example, a few slices of grilled eggplant or red peppers made in big batches at home to last for several days—and a nice piece of fruit can be a civilized style of eating if you slow down just a little and savor the "courses."

A take-out salad-bar salad can be elevated to a higher degree of flavor and satisfaction by sticking with what is seasonal and then using your stash of olive oil, vinegar or lemons, and sea salt to fashion your own personalized dressing when you return to your desk or the eating area of your office. Again, if possible, transfer the salad to a plate and eat it with real cutlery.

Delicatessens may offer simple chicken cutlets. A squeeze of lemon (a wedge cut from a lemon in the basket on your desk!) will enliven the cutlet. Cook a green vegetable the night before or, if time permits, that morning, and take it to work with you. Place the chicken cutlet on the plate and accompany with the cooked vegetable. Follow with a sliver of cheese and a piece of fruit.

Or pack some sliced turkey breast (the real thing), a ball of fresh mozzarella cut into generous dice, and lots of tender sliced celery stalks and chopped celery leaves for a simple salad that you won't find at any of the local spots. Arrange it on your plate. Use your secret arsenal of seasonings—they have never failed me and they will never fail you when assembling a delicious and appetizing salad. Add a crusty roll, a piece of excellent seasonal fruit, and a small piece of dark chocolate to finish.

These are just a few suggestions. A little imagination goes a long way when it comes to attempting to duplicate an Italian *pranzo* during an American lunch hour or, horrors!, half-hour.

After lunch, if there is the opportunity, try to rest, even briefly, before returning to work. You'll have to figure out if this is feasible given where you work and the nature of your job. But if actually lying down somewhere is an impossibility, even sitting quietly at your desk or wherever it is you've eaten will help you digest your food with less strain on your body, as well as offering a bit of repose and restoration.

MOZZARELLA AND SUMMER VEGETABLE SALAD

[*serves 4*]

THE COMBINATION OF MOZZARELLA AND TOMATO IS THE CLASSIC ITALIAN SUMMER SALAD CAPRESE. BUT OTHER VEGETABLES ARE AT THEIR PEAK DURING THE HOT MONTHS AND are delicious combined with *mozzarella fresca*, the type purchased immersed in water.

*1 pound (4 medium balls) fresh
mozzarella, well drained, cut into medium-large dice*

*2 to 3 medium ripe but firm tomatoes,
cut into medium-large dice*

*1 large sweet yellow pepper,
seeded and cut into medium dice*

2 medium carrots, peeled and sliced

*2 to 3 tender celery stalks
with leaves, stalks sliced, leaves left whole*

Handful of radishes, thinly sliced

¼ medium red onion, finely diced

1 garlic clove, finely chopped

6 tablespoons extra-virgin olive oil

¼ cup fresh lemon juice

Sea salt and freshly ground black pepper

1 small bunch basil, leaves torn into small fragments

Combine the cheese, prepared vegetables, and garlic in a large but shallow bowl.

Drizzle with olive oil, add lemon juice, season with salt and pepper, and toss carefully. Taste and correct seasonings.

Scatter basil over the top and serve.

TUNA SOTT'OLIO WITH PURSLANE AND TOMATO

[serves 2]

TUNA CONSERVED IN OLIVE OIL IS A TIME-HONORED TRADITION FROM THE DAYS WHEN TUNA WAS A SEASONAL FISH. IN MAY, THE FISHERMEN WOULD GO OUT TO SEA FOR THE *mattanza,* as it is called in Sicily, a bloody ritual, and bring in the tuna.

The fish would be cooked, cut into large chunks, and covered completely with olive oil. Storing it in large barrels preserved the tuna long past the season by not exposing it to the air.

In Italy, one can still find tuna *sott'olio*—literally, "under oil," in large containers—to be bought by the piece. Here, we can buy canned tuna in olive oil, a good substitute.

This is one of those impromptu salads I make during my summers on the Salento coast. I gather wild purslane, then with a few tomatoes and tuna, create a salad that satisfies my diminished summertime appetite.

Purslane is considered a weed. But I learned from my Sicilian grandmother that it is delicious in salads—crisp, succulent, with a slight lemony tang. Here, it can be purchased at farmers' markets that cater to ethnic populations—Italian, Greek, and Middle Eastern. Or, in certain dry, hot parts of the country, it can be found growing in the wild. The usual precautions apply: do not pick any wild food growing near roadsides or where there is any danger of pesticides or other toxins in the soil.

1 3-ounce can imported tuna in olive oil
Handful of fresh purslane
2 or 3 small garden tomatoes
A few thin slivers of red onion
Extra-virgin olive oil
Red wine vinegar
Sea salt
Fresh grinding of black pepper

Drain the oil from the tuna. Place the tuna on a dinner plate without breaking up the chunks. Coarsely chop the purslane, stems and all, and sprinkle it over the tuna. Slice the tomatoes and arrange them around the tuna. Sprinkle red onion slivers over the top.

Drizzle with extra-virgin olive oil and red wine vinegar. Season with salt and pepper. Toss gently. Taste and correct seasonings.

INSALATA DI MARE

[makes 4 small first-course servings]

EVERY SEASIDE SHACK OR TRATTORIA IN THE SALENTO SERVES THIS SIMPLE VERSION OF A SEAFOOD SALAD. SEAFOOD INSALATA MAKES FOR THE BEST KIND OF AL FRESCO hot-weather eating.

I remember staying at the summer house of friends. The little nineteenth-century villa was perched on a hill nestled in a pine grove through which you could see slivers of blue sea. One day, after my daily morning swim, I went to one of the two very simple trattorias in the little town, more just a cluster of small villas by the sea than a real town. The trattoria was just a few steps above the rocky swimming beach.

As I sat under the large rush awning eating my seafood salad and looking out at the sea, I saw a young boy hoist himself out of the water and fling an octopus in the direction of the trattoria—no doubt destined for the next batch of *insalata di mare!*

For ease of preparation, buy already cleaned squid. Cooked octopus, thinly sliced and tender, can be found at Japanese fish markets.

¾ pound cleaned squid
1 pound mussels, debearded and well scrubbed
½ pound small shrimp in the shell
½ pound sliced cooked octopus
½ cup extra-virgin olive oil
3 tablespoons fresh lemon juice
1 garlic clove, finely chopped
2 tablespoons chopped Italian parsley
1 tablespoon capers, drained and rinsed
Sea salt and grindings of black pepper

Cook the squid in boiling salted water for 3 minutes, or just until it is opaque and tender.

Place a small amount of water in the bottom of a large sauté pan. Add the mussels. Turn the heat to high. Cover the pan. Shake the pan once or twice to expose all the mussels to the heat. Uncover and remove mussels as each one opens. Reserve liquid in pan. Set mussels aside to cool. Working over a bowl to catch the juices, remove mussels from the shells and discard shells. Combine juices from the pan and bowl. Strain and set aside.

Boil shrimp in abundant salted water until just cooked, a matter of 2 or 3 minutes. Drain and let cool. Peel the shrimp.

Combine the olive oil, lemon juice, garlic, parsley, capers, and reserved mussel juice in a serving bowl. Season lightly with salt and pepper. Beat gently with a fork. Add the cooked seafood. Toss and taste. Adjust seasonings.

You can serve the salad immediately, but the flavor improves if it marinates for several hours in a cool spot. Or refrigerate, and bring back to cool room temperature before serving.

❧

SIGNORA PANTELLA'S CHICKEN SALAD

[serves 2 for a light dinner]

SIGNORA PANTELLA HAS A WAY WITH FOOD. THE SIMPLEST DISH ALWAYS HAS A FINESSE ABOUT IT. THIS SALAD ARRIVED PRETTILY ARRANGED ON A WELL-WORN DINNER PLATE carefully wrapped in plastic wrap.

The lettuce was from Signora Pantellas' garden and it was velvety to the touch, light green, sweet and tender. In fact, everything about the salad seemed so fresh that all the vegetables must have been just harvested. I didn't ask, but I'm convinced the chicken had been, until recently, residing in a neighbor's backyard.

1 head butter or Bibb lettuce
1 lightly sautéed skinless, boneless, and split chicken breast
2 or 3 small Yukon Gold potatoes, cooked, peeled, and sliced
2 or 3 small white beets, cooked, peeled, and sliced
2 garden tomatoes streaked with green, cored and cut into wedges
Extra-virgin olive oil
Red wine vinegar
Sea salt and grindings of black pepper

Wash the lettuce well. Home-grown lettuce usually requires extra rinsing to remove the soil trapped between the leaves. Check for bugs. Finding one is a good sign: it means no pesticides were used. Dry the lettuce thoroughly. Tear into large bite-size pieces.

Mound the lettuce on a plate. Slice the chicken into several strips and arrange on lettuce. Arrange the remaining vegetables on the lettuce leaves.

Serve with a cruet of olive oil and wine vinegar, sea salt, and a pepper mill.

GRILLED FRESH SHRIMP ON TENDER LETTUCE

[serves 2]

WITH A SEEMINGLY SIMPLE SALAD SUCH AS THIS ONE, THE CORRECT INGREDIENTS ARE ESSENTIAL. I HAD THIS "SALAD" AT A SMALL SEASIDE TRATTORIA IN THE WHITEWASHED town of Otranto on the dazzling Adriatic coast. It was an order of grilled shrimp, but I turned it into a warm salad by incorporating the few lettuce leaves that formed a bed for the shrimp.

This recipe begins with fresh, not frozen shrimp. Look for it in Asian markets and specialty fish markets. Fresh shrimp has a sweetness and tenderness of flesh pretty much impossible to achieve with frozen shrimp no matter how careful the cooking. If fresh shrimp are simply not available, frozen will have to do, but take extra care not to overcook them. The shrimp must be cooked over natural coals or embers, which imparts a certain smoky richness otherwise unattainable.

Finally, just a few tender green leaves with a touch of crispness to the flesh are needed to form the base. Find a small, very green butter lettuce, as fresh as possible.

¼ pound fresh medium shrimp in the shell, head and all
Extra-virgin olive oil
Sea salt
Grindings of black pepper
8 medium-small leaves green butter lettuce
Lemon wedges

Prepare a grill using natural wood and no lighter fluid. Start the grill about 30 minutes ahead of time to create a hot bed of coals.

Meanwhile, toss the shrimp in enough olive oil to lightly coat the shells. Season generously with salt and pepper. Wash the lettuce leaves and dry well.

When the coals are ready, grill the shrimp a few minutes on each side, until the shells turn pink and are very slightly charred.

Arrange the leaves on two dinner plates. When the shrimp are just cooked through, place the whole shrimp on the lettuce. The lettuce will wilt slightly and the shrimp shells will flavor the leaves. Peel the hot shrimp and move the peels to one side of the dish (the shells are very flavorful and delicious to suck on). Cut the shrimp into sections. Cut the lettuce into medium pieces. Toss together shrimp and lettuce, drizzling with a few drops of lemon juice.

Signora Pantella

I CAN SEE HER FROM THE KITCHEN WINDOWS OF MY VILLA APARTMENT EARLY IN THE MORN-ing. Dressed in her flowered housecoat, some-times with a scarf tied around her head, she looks at the vegetables in the garden, carefully and lovingly scrutinizing each plant.

She examines the figs dangling from the big shady tree to see if they've ripened to the right point: has the skin begun to split at the stem end, the sign they are bursting with honeyed juices? She scans the rows of toma-toes and I can tell she is calculating how many more days before the big tomato-can-ning event will take place. Kilos and kilos of tomatoes to cook and can! She brushes past the basil plants and I can almost see the haze of perfume surround her; even though it is morning, it is already quite warm and min-gled fragrances rise from the vegetation, the red clay earth absorbing the sun's hot rays.

I watch as she bends to pick zucchini flow-ers. She walks toward the house with the bril-liant bouquet in her hand. No doubt she will be preparing her stuffed zucchini blossoms or her zucchini blossom fritters for lunch. And no doubt she has already decided what other vegetables and fruits will soon be making an appearance at the kitchen table.

No summer shower, not even a summer downpour, stops her from her morning perusal of the garden. Only her clothing changes: instead of her light cotton housecoat, she dons galoshes and an old raincoat, and carries an umbrella.

Signora Pantella is in her early eighties, but she has a youthful air about her. Her skin is smooth and soft, and her eyes are those of a young girl. It must be the result of all those years of looking at plants that her eyes remain so soft and sweet in their aspect. Her hair is gray and she wears it in a braided bun pinned at the nape of her neck, just as my country grandmother did. Her basic daily attire is black. Remember, we are in a small town in the Salento where the old customs still are honored. She has worn black since the day her husband died, and she will continue to wear black until she passes on to the next world.

Since I've begun spending my summers in this small town on the Salentine coast, she has been like a mother to me. Her dishes appear at my door, carried over by one of her adult children who live nearby and visit her often, while she keeps a watchful eye on me from the windows of her modest villa. Her dishes contain everything anyone could possibly desire—fragrance, flavor, heat, and, yes, love —extended to a stranger in a strange land. And she always reserves a portion of a special dish for me to taste.

What did I do to deserve such beneficence? How can I thank her? What can I give her to repay her for her kindness? A beautiful embroi-dered linen tablecloth? A crystal decanter? Both pale in comparison in the face of such pure generosity. She accepts nothing in return, since she tells me she does it *dal cuore,* from the heart. For Signora Pantella, the joy is in the giving.

Signora Pantella owed me nothing, yet she cared. I was a woman alone in a sometimes harsh land. Through her dishes I became a part of her family and in this way she protected me. She protected me with her ruffled lasagnette with its delicate tomato veal sauce strewn with basil, with her simple baked lasagne, her bowls of boiled greens.

It was with great pleasure that I entered the kitchen of this kind woman, her inner sanctum. Signora Pantella's kitchen is a large square room almost completely devoid of decoration. An old wooden table is at the center surrounded by old wooden chairs. A well-worn but spotless and freshly pressed tablecloth covers the table. A gas stove of immaculate cleanliness sits in one corner. Nearby, an old wood-burning stove, rarely used, looks a bit forlorn. The room is simple and orderly, everything put away in cupboards and cabinets, the counters amazingly clear of clutter.

Signora Pantella's kitchen floor is lined with large terrazzo tiles, common in this part of Italy, composed of tiny flecks of beige and white marble, the flecks so small they resemble grains of pepper.

The walls are lined with light ocher enamel tiles with a floral design in pastel golden green that creates a continuous, sinuous line of slender garlands around the room. These tiles travel approximately one-third up the walls, above which the plaster walls and high vaulted ceiling are painted a blindingly clean, pure white, the fresh-looking whitewash one sees everywhere. A simple opaque glass hanging lamp with its own small floral garland casts a pool of light over the table at night.

All the colors in this special room are muted and quiet, and the garlands are subtle in design. It is a peaceful room, this kitchen, where I could happily spend many hours. And it is from this plain workroom, as simple as a country church, that Signora Pantella cooks her wonderful dishes.

WARM-WEATHER BEEF SALAD

[serves 4]

THIS IS A GOOD MAIN DISH INSALATA TO PREPARE IF YOU HAVE MADE BROTH AND THE LEFTOVER MEAT IS TENDER AND FLAVORFUL (SEE PAGE 184 FOR HOW TO KEEP LEFT-over boiled beef tender). The simple dressing of olive oil and vinegar is used often with boiled beef and other meats.

Look for spring onions at farmers' markets. You will recognize them by the green tops still attached to the juicy white onion bulbs—a sign they've just been pulled from the earth.

*1 pound boiled beef, trimmed of all fat
and sinew, thinly sliced*

2 very small fresh spring onions, finely diced

1 small tender lettuce, torn into bite-size pieces

*Handful of basil leaves, coarsely chopped with just a
few strokes of the knife blade (otherwise the basil turns black)*

5 tablespoons extra-virgin olive oil, more or less

5 tablespoons red wine vinegar, more or less

Sea salt

Grindings of black pepper

3 hard-cooked eggs, quartered

2 tomatoes, cut into wedges

Basil leaves, not too large, for garnish

Combine the beef, onions, lettuce, and basil. Drizzle with the olive oil and vinegar as needed. Season with salt and black pepper to taste. Toss gently.

Garnish with eggs and tomato wedges, both seasoned with additional salt and pepper. Sprinkle with basil leaves.

MINESTRE

soups

THE SOUPS IN THIS CHAPTER MAKE NO PRETENSE OF BEING ANYTHING OTHER THAN WHAT THEY ARE: SATISFYING MAIN-DISH SOUPS IN THE RUSTIC TRADITION. Contrary to what one might expect, the majority of these soups require very little time spent on preparation. Only when beans are involved does the cooking time lengthen, but the stove is doing all the work!

I particularly like the fact that the soups are hearty but not *pesanti*, or heavy. They have a certain delicacy while providing abundant protein.

The three exceptions to this rusticity are the broths—fish, chicken, and beef—which are served with pasta as a *primo piatto*. The fish or chicken or beef can then sometimes be served as a second course depending on directions in the individual recipes. These can be special-occasion broths that cook for hours to extract every drop of flavor, like the chicken and beef, or a rapidly made fish broth that is light and delicate.

SUMMER BARLEY, TOMATO, AND BASIL SOUP

[*serves 4 to 6*]

SOUPS FEATURING GRAINS OFTEN SEEM MORE A PART OF WINTER EATING. THIS SUM-MERY SOUP—WHICH DOES CONTAIN CHEWY GRAINS OF EARTHY BARLEY—HAS A BRIGHT, fresh flavor from the cherry tomatoes and basil that makes it appealing for summer meals.

3 to 4 young leeks, cut into thin rounds
2 tablespoons extra-virgin olive oil
1 basket plump cherry tomatoes
1 bunch tender Swiss chard, leaves only, chopped
2 cups cooked barley
8 cups light chicken broth or spring or filtered water
Sea salt
A handful of fresh basil leaves

Sauté the leeks in the olive oil in a soup pot until tender. Add the whole cherry tomatoes, Swiss chard, barley, and enough of the broth or water to generously cover. Season with salt to taste.

Cook at a lively simmer for 10 minutes or until Swiss chard is tender.

Before serving, adjust salt and sprinkle with a generous amount of chopped basil.

MINESTRA DI TINNIRUMI

[*serves 6*]

TINNIRUMI IS SICILIAN DIALECT FOR THE TENDER LEAVES AND STEMS OF A LONG, CON-
VOLUTED, PALE GREEN SQUASH MUCH APPRECIATED BY SOUTHERN ITALIANS (SEE NOTE).

The squash itself is commonly called *zucchina da pergola* since it is grown dangling from a trellised pergola. It reminds me of those circus balloons twisted into shapes resembling animals or fantasy figures. The seeds I've bought here in America refer to the squash as *tromboncini*, little trombones, again, a nod to its strange shape.

In this summertime soup, the leaves and stems of the *zucchina da pergola* are cooked with cubes of the squash, ripe tomatoes, and a generous amount of fresh basil. The finishing touch: small pieces of pecorino cheese that cook briefly in the soup, just until they soften and add their flavor to the broth.

If desired, add a handful of pasta to the soup during the final minutes of cooking. Spaghettini broken into short lengths is the pasta of choice.

1 medium onion, finely diced
3 garlic cloves, coarsely chopped
6 tablespoons extra-virgin olive oil
3 red, ripe plum tomatoes, peeled and cut into small dice
1 medium zucchina da pergola, *cut into small dice*
2 cups chopped tinnirumi *(see above)*
Sea salt and freshly ground pepper
Spring or filtered water
¼ cup pecorino sardo cut into very small pieces
1 bunch basil, leaves coarsely chopped or torn
Extra-virgin olive oil for drizzling

Sauté the onion and garlic with the oil in a soup pot until tender.

Add the tomatoes. Cook briefly until juices thicken.

Add the squash and the greens and toss briefly in the sauce, adding salt and pepper to taste.

Cover with water and bring to a boil. Simmer until zucchini and greens are tender, about

20 minutes. A few minutes before the soup is ready, toss in the small cheese cubes and cook briefly until the cheese softens.

Off heat, stir in basil and drizzle with olive oil.

NOTE: Short of growing the squash in your own backyard (seeds are available through mail-order catalogs), a farmers' market or Italian produce market may be the best resource.

ᣟᣟ

HOT RED PEPPER OLIVE OIL

[makes 1 liter spicy olive oil]

POSSIBLY NOWHERE IN ITALY IS SPICY FOOD MORE APPRECIATED THAN IN PUGLIA. RED AND GREEN HOT PEPPERS MAKE AN APPEARANCE IN SOUPS, PASTA SAUCES, VEGETABLE dishes, fish and meat stews, and just about everything else except dessert.

Many types of spicy condiments are routinely found on dining tables. One, a conserve of very hot green peppers in tomato sauce, is strong enough to set the house on fire!

Hot red pepper olive oil is a common tabletop condiment, to be added at the diner's discretion. It is particularly good as a final flavor boost for rustic soups, especially bean soups, bread soups, soups featuring grains, actually just about any of the soups in the chapter except broths or a delicate vegetable soup.

1-liter bottle extra-virgin olive oil
¼ cup hot red pepper flakes
4 fresh bay leaves, 2 leaves threaded on each
of 2 bamboo skewers the length of the jar
(if fresh bay leaves are unavailable, omit them)

Open the bottle of olive oil, carefully removing the screwtop and stopper. Use a funnel to add the hot red pepper flakes to the olive oil in the jar.

Insert the skewered bay leaves into the jar. Make sure they are completely submerged in oil to prevent mold from forming.

Replace the stopper and screwtop. Place the bottle in a dark, cool pantry for about a month, or longer, if you prefer a hotter version of the spicy oil.

GREEN CAULIFLOWER AND SEMOLINA SOUP

[serves 4]

MY MOTHER REMEMBERS THIS SOUP FROM HER CHILDHOOD IN PALERMO. THE UNIQUE-SOUNDING COMBINATION OF INGREDIENTS PROMPTED AN ATTEMPT TO REPRODUCE IT IN my own kitchen.

Romanesco broccoli, jade green with an unusual structure composed of a swirl of small conical peaks, is actually a cauliflower. (In certain parts of Italy cauliflower is called broccoli.)

Romanesco broccoli is very tender and cooks quickly. Look for it at farmers' markets and specialty produce stores. As alternatives, try the more readily available broccoflower or a very fresh white cauliflower.

Semolina thickens and enrichs the broth, giving the soup an appealingly creamy texture.

½ small onion, finely diced
3 tablespoons extra-virgin olive oil plus extra for drizzling on soup
1 garlic clove, finely chopped
2 fresh bay leaves
Pinch of hot red pepper flakes (optional)
8 cups spring or filtered water
½ cup semolina
Sea salt and black pepper
1 romanesco broccoli, trimmed of leaves and stalk
Freshly grated pecorino sardo or pecorino pepato cheese (optional)

Sauté the chopped onion in 2 tablespoons olive oil in a soup pot until soft. A few minutes before the onion is lightly golden, add the chopped garlic, bay leaf, and optional hot red pepper.

Add the water and bring to a boil.

Whisk in the semolina gradually. Stir until fully incorporated. Simmer for 15 minutes, adding salt and pepper to taste.

Meanwhile, cut the broccoli into very small pieces. Sauté for a minute or two in the remaining 1 tablespoon olive oil, seasoning with salt to taste.

Add the broccoli to the soup pot and stir. Cook for 10 minutes or until meltingly tender. Correct the seasonings.

Serve hot drizzled with extra-virgin olive oil and optional grated pecorino cheese.

FARRO SOUP WITH BASIL AND RICOTTA SALATA

[serves 4]

ALSO CALLED SPELT, FARRO IS AN ANCIENT GRAIN THAT HAS MADE A COMEBACK. AS HAS HAPPENED WITH OTHER FOODS CONSIDERED PART OF THE TRADITION OF CUCINA *povera*, such as polenta, farro is suddenly *di moda*, fashionable. The finely diced vegetables and topping of grated ricotta salata and fresh basil add a sophisticated note to this soulful grain.

I was served this soup at a refined country hotel in Puglia situated deep in the heart of miles of olive groves.

2 cups raw farro (to yield about 3 cups cooked)
1 celery stalk, cut in half
1 carrot, peeled and cut into 4 pieces
1 medium onion, quartered
1 fresh bay leaf
Spring or filtered water
¼ cup finely diced onion
2 tablespoons extra-virgin olive oil
with more to drizzle on soup
Sea salt
¼ cup finely diced celery
¼ cup finely diced carrot
¼ cup chopped Italian parsley
Ricotta salata for grating
Finely slivered basil leaves

Place the farro in a soup pot with the large pieces of celery, carrot, and onion, and the bay leaf. Add enough water to cover by about an inch. Bring to a boil. Cook over medium heat for about 30 minutes, or until the farro is tender but not soft. Remove from heat. Discard vegetables.

Meanwhile, in another soup pot, sauté the diced onion in olive oil and a pinch of salt over medium heat for about 5 minutes.

Add the celery, carrot, and parsley, and cook for an additional 5 minutes. Add the farro and enough of the cooking liquid to make a soup of medium density. Let it simmer briefly to blend flavors.

Serve each portion with a drizzle of extra-virgin olive oil, grated ricotta salata, and a sprinkling of fresh basil.

CREAMY CHICK-PEA SOUP WITH
FRESH BAY LEAVES

[*serves 6*]

HERE, A CREAMY PUREE OF CHICK-PEAS IS INFUSED WITH THE SCENT OF FRESH BAY LEAVES AND ROSEMARY, AND FINISHED WITH SHORT RIBBONS OF GOLDEN FETTUCCINE.

Italian tomato paste (a small amount is called for in the recipe) is quite different from what we buy in small cans in our markets. The Italian *doppio concentrato* is a loose paste sold in tubes resembling toothpaste tubes.

But even truer to the taste of the *mezzogiorno* is the tomato paste called *estratto,* which is made from tomato sauce dried under a torrid sun until it is dark and dense (see Note). This would be my first choice, but I've never seen it sold in America, although perhaps someone, somewhere is producing it or importing it for sale. It is a rather arduous and labor-intensive artisanal product, so even in Italy it is becoming more difficult to find.

The first time I sampled the real thing I was at the outdoor market in Siracusa, Sicily. I didn't even know what I was being offered to taste—it was so dark red it almost looked black, and it was piled up, almost sculpted, like some form of strange mortar or clay! But the flavor was extraordinary, entirely different from even the best purchased tomato paste from Italy.

Our cooked-down canned tomato paste tastes overly sweet and metallic. The *doppio concentrato* in tubes has a better flavor, and it keeps much better since all you have to do is screw the cap back on.

2 cups dried chick-peas

1 medium onion, cut in half

3 celery stalks with leaves, cut into short lengths

1 sprig of fresh rosemary

6 fresh bay leaves (omit if only dried are available)

2½ quarts spring or filtered water, brought to a boil

⅓ cup extra-virgin olive oil, with more to drizzle over soup

3 garlic cloves, crushed

1 to 2 tablespoons imported tomato paste
(doppio concentrato; see above)

Sea salt

¼ pound dried egg fettuccine, broken into short pieces

Grindings of black pepper

Soak the chick-peas overnight in abundant water to cover. Drain.

Place drained chick-peas, vegetables, and herbs in a soup pot. Cover with boiling water. Cook at a steady simmer, covered. Cooking times will vary depending on the freshness of the dried beans. Cook the beans until they are completely tender. This may take an hour or two, possibly longer.

Remove the vegetables and herbs from the pot. Put the beans and liquid through a food mill, which will catch any tough skins in the sieve. The beans should emerge with a smooth, creamy consistency. Return them to the pan.

Put the oil and garlic into a small sauté pan. Cook over medium heat, stirring often with a wooden spoon, until the garlic is golden. Remove the garlic.

Dilute 1 tablespoon tomato paste with a few tablespoons of water. If you would prefer a stronger tomato presence, add the second tablespoon of tomato paste and a little additional water. Add the diluted tomato paste to the oil and simmer for several minutes. Stir into the chick-pea soup.

Bring the soup to a boil, adding additional water if it is too thick. Add salt to taste. Add the fettuccine pieces, stir well, and cook until tender/firm, a matter of a few minutes.

Serve drizzled with a few drops of fresh olive oil and grindings of black pepper.

NOTE: Sun-dried tomato paste would seem to be an appropriate substitute for *estratto*. Unfortunately, I can't recommend it, since the ones I've tried here in America include various seasonings that distract from the essential pure flavor of *estratto*.

PANCOTTO

BREAD SOUP WITH GREENS

[serves 4]

A HEARTY SOUP OWING TO THE PRESENCE OF COUNTRY BREAD. AS THE VEGETABLES COOK, THE BREAD BREAKS DOWN TO ADD A CREAMY CONSISTENCY.

If the greens called for below are unavailable to you, substitute other bitter greens such as escarole, endive, broccoli rabe, or whatever you can find locally. If sweet-tasting wild fennel is not available, omit it or add thinly sliced bulb fennel in its place.

2 tablespoons extra-virgin olive oil, with more for drizzling

1 thick slice pancetta, cut into small pieces

1 medium onion, diced

Sea salt

Pinch of hot red pepper flakes

1 pound dandelion greens, tough stems removed, leaves chopped

1 pound arugula, tough stems removed, leaves chopped

1½ cups sliced and chopped tender wild fennel stalks and tops

1 pound Yukon Gold potatoes (about 3 medium
potatoes), peeled and cut into ½-inch dice

Spring or filtered water

½ pound day-old rustic Italian bread, torn into bite-size pieces

Freshly grated pecorino sardo

Heat 2 tablespoons of olive oil in a soup pot over medium heat. Add the pancetta and cook for about 3 minutes.

Add the onion, a little salt, and red pepper flakes. Sauté the onion for about 10 minutes, or until lightly golden.

Add the greens, wild fennel or sliced fennel bulb, and diced potatoes and enough water to cover. Bring to a boil, lower the heat, and add the bread.

Simmer gently for 30 minutes or until the greens and potatoes are very tender and the bread has absorbed enough liquid to break down into meltingly soft pieces. The ingredients should form a kind of coarse puree. Stir occasionally to make sure everything cooks evenly.

Garnish with a drizzle of olive oil and a sprinkling of grated pecorino sardo or other tangy grating cheese.

WHITE BEAN AND DITALINI SOUP
WITH WILD FENNEL

[serves 4 to 6]

THE COMBINATION OF PASTA AND BEANS IS BASIC TO ITALIAN COOKING. I FIND THAT WHEN THE MAJORITY OF THE BEANS ARE TO BE SERVED WHOLE IN THE SOUP, WHITE BEANS are a good choice since their flavor is light and delicate.

Added flavor lift comes from the irresistably sweet and aromatic licorice taste of wild fennel.

*2 cups dried cannellini beans, soaked overnight
in a generous amount of spring or filtered water
1 medium onion, quartered from end to end so pieces remain intact
1 carrot, peeled and cut in half
2 celery stalks with green leaves, cut in half
1 small bouquet of wild fennel
10 plump, ripe cherry tomatoes, cut in half, seeds removed
1 fresh bay leaf
2 garlic cloves, cut in half
Spring or filtered water
¼ pound ditalini pasta
Extra-virgin olive oil or Hot Red Pepper
Olive Oil (page 77) to drizzle over soup
A sprinkling of coarsely chopped Italian parsley leaves
Freshly grated Parmigiano-Reggiano cheese (optional)*

Drain the white beans and place in a soup pot. Add the vegetables, bay leaf, and garlic. Cover with a generous amount of water.

Cook over medium-low heat until the beans are tender, about 2 hours. When tender, turn off the heat and let the beans cool in the broth.

Bring a medium pot of water to a boil and cook the pasta until half-done.

Meanwhile, remove the large vegetable pieces from the beans and broth and discard (or eat, seasoned with a little extra-virgin olive oil drizzled over and a bit of sea salt). Puree or mash 1 cup of the beans until smooth and return them to the soup. Add the pasta to the soup pot and bring to a simmer.

When the pasta is al dente, ladle soup into bowls. Garnish with extra-virgin olive oil or Hot Red Pepper Olive Oil, chopped parsley, and grated cheese.

FISH BROTH WITH CAPELLINI

[*serves 4 to 6*]

THIS IS A CLEAR, PURE, AND FRESH-TASTING FISH BROTH. SELECT ANY SMALL PASTA SHAPE APPROPRIATE FOR SOUPS THAT COOKS QUICKLY—BROKEN PIECES OF CAPELLINI work especially well. The pasta must cook quickly in the broth, absorbing the broth's flavor, but not all the broth.

The cooked fish can be served separately as a second course or as a light lunch, or included as part of an *insalata di mare*.

2½ pounds assorted nonoily "white" fish fillets
1 small onion, quartered
2 celery stalks, quartered
Handful of Italian parsley
1 fresh bay leaf
1 small lemon, preferably organic, thinly sliced
Sea salt
1 cup dry white wine
Spring or filtered water
Freshly ground black pepper
Handful of capellini broken into short lengths
(crush the pasta with your hands as you add it to the soup)
Extra-virgin olive oil, lemon juice, and
chopped Italian parsley to season cooked fish

Wrap the fish in cheesecloth. Place fish in a deep braising pan. Top with vegetables, herbs, and lemon slices. Season with salt. Add wine. Cover with water and bring to a boil. Cook at a low simmer for 20 to 30 minutes, or until fish is fully cooked.

With a large spatula, carefully lift fish out of broth. When the fish is cool enough to handle, remove cheesecloth. Serve fish warm or at room temperature drizzled to taste with olive oil and lemon juice, a sprinkling of coarsely chopped Italian parsley, and salt and pepper.

Meanwhile, strain the fish broth and discard the vegetables.

Bring the liquid to a lively simmer in a soup pot. Adjust the seasonings. Add the broken capellini to the broth and stir to prevent the pasta from sticking.

When the capellini are tender, a matter of a few minutes, the soup is ready. Grated cheese is never used with fish broth.

HEN BROTH WITH TINY SHELLS

[serves 6]

IN THE PAST, A FLAVORFUL HEN WOULD BE USED TO MAKE THIS CHICKEN BROTH RESERVED FOR SPECIAL OCCASIONS. TINY SHELL-SHAPED PASTA IS THE APPROPRIATE choice to add to the boiling broth a few minutes before serving.

Use a free-range organic chicken to duplicate the rich taste of a broth made from the backyard hen.

Always save the hard rinds of Parmigiano—the part that remains after all the cheese has been grated. It is an Italian cook's secret ingredient for adding flavor to soups and pasta sauces. Stored wrapped in waxed paper in the refrigerator, the bits and pieces of rind last indefinitely.

FOR THE BROTH

1 large chicken, about 4 pounds, preferably organic

Spring or filtered water, enough to generously cover chicken

1 large onion, quartered

3 celery stalks with leaves, cut in half

3 thick slices fennel bulb

1 peeled Yukon Gold potato

2 carrots

3 to 4 canned tomatoes

*1 small piece dried Parmigiano-Reggiano cheese rind
(which contains cheese too dry to grate)*

Sea salt

1 or 2 handfuls of miniature shell-shaped pasta for soups

TO SEASON THE COOKED CHICKEN

Extra-virgin olive oil

Red wine vinegar

Sea salt and freshly ground black pepper

Place the chicken in a large stockpot and cover generously with spring water. Slowly bring to a boil and let boil for a few minutes, skimming surface of all impurities. Add the vegetables and Parmesan cheese rind. Simmer at a low heat for from 1½ hours to 3 hours for a very rich broth. Taste broth and add salt as needed.

(CONTINUED)

Strain the broth through a colander lined with several layers of dampened cheesecloth. Refrigerate and when cold, remove congealed fat on the surface of the broth.

Bring broth back to a boil. Add a handful or two of tiny shell-shaped soup pasta and cook until al dente. No grating cheese is required since the broth has been flavored with the cheese rind.

If the broth is cooked the shorter length of time and the chicken itself is still flavorful, the chicken meat can be served separately. Pull the meat from the bones and remove all skin, fat, and other undesirable matter. Cut chicken into large bite-size pieces. Season with olive oil, vinegar, salt, and black pepper. If desired, serve with a salad of tart lettuces or sliced garden tomatoes.

If you have made a very rich broth, simmered the full 3 hours, discard all solids; the chicken will be flavorless and not good to eat.

᪐

BEEF BROTH WITH ANELLINI

[*serves 4 to 6*]

NOT SIMPLY A FLAVORING BASE FOR OTHER DISHES, DELICATELY FLAVORED ITALIAN-STYLE BEEF BROTH IS AN EXQUISITE SOUP UNTO ITSELF. IT IS AT ITS FINEST AND MOST elegant when served crystal-clear with a flotilla of delicate pasta circles and freshly grated Parmigiano-Reggiano cheese.

Bring the grated cheese to the table in a *formaggiera*, a special small serving piece with a hinged lid to prevent the cheese from drying out. Each person sprinkles the cheese on the broth as desired.

This is the soup Italians turn to when not feeling well, their version of our chicken soup. See the chapter "Foods for When You Are Not Feeling Well" for a complete description of Italian "prescriptions" for foods that heal.

1 pound flank steak
1 pound beef shanks, cut into 2-inch pieces
Spring or filtered water to cover meat
1 unpeeled onion, trimmed of root fibers
1 carrot, peeled and cut in half
1 celery stalk with leaves, cut in half

2 small whole tomatoes
1 unpeeled garlic clove
2 sprigs of Italian parsley
Sea salt
4 black peppercorns
2 egg whites, lightly beaten
1 or 2 handfuls anellini or other small pasta shape for soup
Freshly grated Parmigiano-Reggiano cheese

Place the meat and bones in a soup pot. Cover with water and bring to a boil. Scrupulously skim off all impurities that rise to the surface.

Add the vegetables, garlic, parsley, salt, and peppercorns. Turn down heat to a bare simmer. Cook over low heat, with the lid ajar, for about 3 hours.

Strain the broth and discard solids.

Bring the strained broth to a simmer. Add the lightly beaten egg whites. Simmer until the egg whites have formed a solid mass that contains all the remaining impurities. Strain again through dampened cheesecloth.

Bring the soup to a boil. Add salt to taste. Add anellini or other soup pasta shapes and stir. Cook until pasta is al dente.

Ladle into soup bowls and serve with grated cheese.

VERDURA
vegetables

NOTHING IS MORE IMPORTANT TO THE PUGLIESE DIET THAN VEGETABLES. VEGETABLES ARE EATEN IN ABUNDANCE FOR LUNCH AND DINNER. MEALS ARE COMPOSED of vegetables with a little bread or pasta added to form a whole.

The vegetables of the Salento are some of the best I've tasted. Is it the ferrous red soil, rich in iron? Is it the salt air that travels across the narrow peninsula within a peninsula? Is it the time-honored methods of cultivation? Whatever the reason, the result is produce of extraordinary quality and flavor: the wonderful small, golden potatoes grown near the coast, with fine-textured flesh and full flavor; tomatoes grown with the least amount of water possible, literally drops of water per plant—the leaves look practically dead but the tomatoes are pungently spicy, sweet and tart.

Cooked cultivated greens play an important role at mealtime, as do wild greens. Pleasingly bitter, some taste slightly of artichoke, others of mineral essences. Greens go into pastas, soups, meat dishes—but are at their best served alone, with the liquid in which they've cooked, a few drops of extra-virgin olive oil, and a scattering of sea salt. Puglia also boasts extraordinary artichokes, fava beans, peas, fennel.

This region is still basically agrarian. Olives grow everywhere—Puglia's huge production of extra-virgin olive oil is a major component of many oils labeled from other parts of Italy, notably the more fashionable north. Puglia's olive oil is superb, made mostly from Coratina, Ogliarola, and Cellina di Nardò olives. Many families, or should I say most, own several hectares of olive groves and produce enough oil for their own family's consumption.

This is the oil I was lucky enough to have on hand in my pantry for pouring over my cooked wild greens or for drizzling over a salad of home-grown tomatoes, thanks to the generosity of my friends and neighbors.

Local vegetables and local oil—this is the ideal. But we are lucky here in America to have access to excellent produce from farmers' markets. Olive oil is trickier since so much that enters the country labeled extra-virgin simply isn't. Buy olive oil from a highly reputable source. Find someone who has access to some inside information on which oils are really, truly what they claim to be. This is a problem with oils that come from all over the world, and is not exclusively an Italian problem.

A final word on vegetables, one you have heard before, but that bears constant repeating. When vegetables are peak, at the height of flavor, the less you do to them the better. Simplicity is the word. A cookbook allows for only so much simplicity, since its very nature requires manipulation of the raw ingredients to formulate a recipe. I've tried to present the simplest vegetable recipes I know, and the ones I invariably enjoy over and over again.

FRIED BABY ARTICHOKE FANS

[serves 4]

IF YOU ARE AN ARTICHOKE LOVER AND HAVEN'T DISCOVERED BABY ARTICHOKES, PRE-PARE YOURSELF FOR A REAL TREAT. THESE OFFSHOOT ARTICHOKES ARE NOT TRUE BABIES since they do not develop in size, never maturing into the large artichokes most of us are familiar with.

The delightful fact about the diminutive ones is that they never develop chokes, that spiny, fuzzy mass at the center of larger artichokes. Therefore, with a little basic trimming, the baby artichokes become entirely edible.

Fried in a light "breading" of egg and flour, they become golden and a little crisp, impossible to stop eating.

½ lemon
6 to 8 "baby" artichokes
2 eggs, preferably organic from cage-free chickens
Sea salt
Unbleached all-purpose flour
Extra-virgin olive oil for frying
Grindings of black pepper (optional)

Prepare a big bowl of cold water and add the juice of the lemon half and the rind. Push a clean dishtowel into the bowl, soaking it and covering the surface.

Trim the artichokes one at a time.

Snap off the tough outer leaves until arriving at the pale green ones. Cut off the top third of each artichoke. With a paring knife, strip off the tough outside layer of fibers from the stems but leave the stem attached. Cut each artichoke into thin lengthwise slices that resemble fans. Slip the artichoke slices under the wet towel and into the lemon water to prevent discoloration.

Place the eggs in a shallow pasta bowl. Season with a little salt and beat them lightly with a fork. Place a mound of flour on a dinner plate.

Heat enough olive oil to come up about 1 inch on the side of a sauté pan. Heat until hot but not smoking.

Meanwhile, working with just a few slices at a time, drain the artichokes well in a colan-der, then dry well on clean kitchen towels. Dip an artichoke slice on both sides in flour and shake off the excess. Then dip in the egg mixture and let excess drip back into the bowl.

Slip the artichoke slices into the hot oil, making sure not to crowd the pan. Fry on both sides until the coating is golden, a matter of a few minutes total. Drain on paper towels and sprinkle with salt while the fried artichokes are hot. If desired, add a grinding of black pepper. Continue until all the slices are fried.

Serve immediately.

❧

BRAISED WHOLE ARTICHOKES WITH FRESH MINT

[serves 4]

MATURE ARTICHOKES ARE DELICIOUS, BUT IN A DIFFERENT WAY FROM THE BABIES. THE PROCESS OF EATING THEM, LEAF BY LEAF, FORCES YOU TO SLOW DOWN AND REALLY savor the flavors. Then there is the excitement of working your way toward the prize, the meaty artichoke heart.

I enjoy cooking artichokes, medium-size, not the overly large ones that are tough and practically flavorless, in a simple manner that does not involve a lot of tedious trimming. It's easier; besides, all that would usually be trimmed actually adds tremendous flavor to the finished dish.

This way I can enjoy one of my favorite vegetables as often as I like. The slow braising creates delectable juices to be sopped up with good bread or just brought to your lips in a big soup spoon.

1 lemon, cut in half
4 artichokes, medium-size, with leaves
tightly closed like a clenched fist
Spring or filtered water
6 garlic cloves, coarsely chopped
Handful of mint leaves, stems removed, coarsely chopped
Extra-virgin olive oil
Sea salt
Grindings of black pepper

Prepare a big bowl of cold water. Squeeze in the juice of both lemon halves and throw in the rinds.

Working one artichoke at a time, start by snapping back a few of the tough outer leaves.

(CONTINUED)

With a paring knife, strip off the tough outer layer of fibers from the stems, leaving stems attached. Use kitchen shears to cut off the spiny tips of the artichoke leaves. Submerge each trimmed artichoke immediately in the lemon water. Top with a clean dish towel, the weight of which, when soggy with water, keeps the artichokes covered with lemon water and prevents discoloration. Continue until all artichokes are trimmed.

Select a braising pan that is large enough to snugly contain all the artichokes in one layer.

Evenly cut off all but ½ inch of the artichoke stems. Reserve the stems. Arrange the artichokes in the braising pan, placing the stems in all the nooks and crannies, the interstices, to keep the artichokes upright and in place.

Add enough water to the artichokes to come up about a third of the way. Scatter with the garlic and mint, drizzle with a little olive oil, and season with salt.

Cover and cook over medium heat until the artichokes are tender. Time varies according to the freshness of the artichokes, but check after 15 or 20 minutes. If a leaf pulls out easily and a thin wooden skewer inserted in the heart slides through with the barest bit of resistance, the artichokes are ready. Taste the broth and add salt as needed.

To serve, place an artichoke in a shallow pasta dish. Add some of the artichoke broth, a piece of stem, a tiny sprinkling of sea salt, and a grinding of pepper over each artichoke. Drizzle with a little raw olive oil. Repeat with each artichoke.

Have an empty bowl or two on the table for the leftover debris of scraped artichoke leaves and inedible chokes.

These artichokes are great served hot, warm, or at room temperature.

ASPARAGUS WITH GARLIC
AND PECORINO CHEESE

[serves 4]

A SPRINKLING OF TANGY GRATED PECORINO CHEESE GIVES NORMALLY DEMURE ASPAR-
AGUS AN EARTHY PERSONALITY.

1 bunch tender, erect, bright green asparagus spears
4 tablespoons extra-virgin olive oil
Sea salt
3 garlic cloves, finely diced
3 heaping tablespoons grated pecorino cheese

Line up the stem ends of the asparagus spears. Snap off the bottom end of one spear to see the breakoff point; this is generally where the tough fibers end. Use this as a guide and cut off the bottom of the spears, an inch or so, depending on where the asparagus snapped off. No need to peel each spear when the asparagus is fresh and cooked to the right point.

Place the olive oil in a sauté pan or two sauté pans large enough to contain the asparagus in one layer. Add the asparagus, coating them with the oil. Cook uncovered over medium heat, seasoning with salt to taste, and adding the garlic after the first few minutes of cooking. The spears are ready when they just begin to droop slightly when raised up with a pancake flipper. The garlic should be lightly golden. Taste one spear to make sure it is cooked through, tender but firm.

Use the flipper to carefully transfer the asparagus to a serving platter. Cooked asparagus is delicate and the skin frays easily with overhandling. Sprinkle evenly with pecorino cheese.

Serve immediately, with each portion getting its share of grated cheese.

FRESH FAVA BEANS WITH MINT

[serves 3 or 4]

THE SKIN OF THE FAVA BEAN MUST BE GREEN; IF IT IS YELLOW OR YELLOWING, THE SKIN IS TOO TOUGH FOR THIS PREPARATION.

A spring onion is one that is freshly pulled, white and juicy, with its leaves still green. They are available during springtime at farmers' markets and specialty produce stores.

Along with a touch of fresh mint, this elemental dish with its lovingly chosen and handled ingredients is an exquisite experience.

4 pounds fresh unshelled young fava beans
1 small spring onion, finely chopped
3 tablespoons extra-virgin olive oil
Handful of small tender spearmint leaves, torn in half
½ cup spring or filtered water
Sea salt

Shell the beans. The skin of the beans should be green and tender so that there is no need to peel them. You should end up with about 2 cups of fava beans. Set aside.

Sauté the onion in the olive oil. When the onion is tender, add the fava beans and torn mint leaves. Stir to coat beans in oil. Add the water and add salt to taste.

Cook at a simmer until the favas are completely tender, about 15 minutes or so depending on size. If necessary, add more water, a little at a time, as needed.

ROMANO BEANS BRAISED
WITH GARLIC IN SPRING WATER

[*serves 4*]

A ROMANO BEAN RESEMBLES A REGULAR GREEN BEAN, EXCEPT IT IS FLAT AND WIDE. THE FLESH COOKS TO THE SWEETEST BEAN FLAVOR YOU CAN IMAGINE. SINCE THEY ARE meatier than typical green beans, they take well to braising. Romano beans should be cooked until they are completely tender.

Here, keeping with the theme of simplicity, I braise them in spring water to cover and a generous amount of raw chopped garlic. The garlic is not first sautéed in olive oil; it goes straight into the water in its natural state—which brings out its mild side. And so does the olive oil—just a bit goes in, to enrich the broth. Cooking the beans and garlic in water creates a broth full of vegetable sweetness that I drink straight out of the bowl when I'm done with the beans.

Look for Romano beans in markets featuring Italian produce or at farmers' markets.

2 pounds Romano beans
6 medium garlic cloves, finely chopped
Spring or filtered water
1 tablespoon extra-virgin olive oil plus extra for drizzling
Sea salt and grindings of black pepper

Cut or snap off the ends of the beans. Place the beans and garlic in a medium braising pan. Add enough water to cover, a tablespoon of olive oil, and salt and pepper to taste.

Bring to a boil and then simmer, uncovered, until the beans are tender but not overcooked. Depending on the freshness of the beans, this will take 10 to 20 minutes, possibly longer if the beans are very mature. The best guide is to taste one every so often after the first 10 minutes to gauge doneness. Season with salt as needed during the cooking process.

To serve, ladle the Romano beans, garlic, and juices into shallow individual pasta bowls. Drizzle with a few fine threads of olive oil.

CHICK-PEAS BAKED IN A WOOD-FIRED OVEN

[serves 4 to 6]

A FRIEND OF MINE IN PUGLIA SAYS HE PREPARES THIS ONCE A YEAR, IN WINTER, IN THE OLD WOOD-BURNING STOVE IN THE KITCHEN OF THE FAMILY'S TWO-HUNDRED-YEAR-old stone house. Nowadays, the old stove isn't often used, having taken a backseat to the modern convenience of one fueled with gas. Still, imagine the wonderful aromas of chick-peas and olive wood that must fill the house during this once-a-year ritual.

Here, we can bake the chick-peas in the oven—less romantic, less aromatic, less nostalgic of days gone by, but quite delicious nonetheless. Baking is an excellent way to cook chick-peas. They keep their shape better and retain more of their unique nutlike flavor.

1 pound dried chick-peas, soaked overnight
in water to generously cover, drained and rinsed
Spring or filtered water
Sea salt
A few sprigs winter savory or rosemary
3 large garlic cloves, lightly crushed
Tiny pinch dried hot red pepper (optional)
Grindings of black pepper
Extra-virgin olive oil for drizzling

Heat the oven to 375 degrees.

Place the chick-peas in a large, deep, glazed terra-cotta braising pan, or, second best but still perfectly fine, a heavy metal ovenproof braising pan. Add water to cover generously and a pinch of salt. Add the remaining seasonings, including the optional hot red pepper and a few coarse grindings of pepper.

Cover and place the pan in the oven. Bake until the chick-peas are tender. Times will vary according to how old the dried chick-peas are, but count on at least an hour or maybe even two. Check the water level every so often, adding hot water as needed to cook the chick-peas completely. A couple of inches of flavorful broth should remain when the chick-peas are done. Also check for salt, adding it as needed while the chick-peas bake.

To serve, ladle the chick-peas and some of the broth into shallow pasta bowls. Dress simply with a drizzling of olive oil and grindings of pepper. Any leftovers can be used in numerous ways, such as in soups and pasta dishes.

DRIED FAVA BEAN PUREE WITH
LEEKS AND BITTER GREENS

[serves 4]

A PUREE MADE OF SLOWLY COOKED DRIED FAVA BEANS, WHEN SERVED ALONGSIDE A DISH OF GREENS GLISTENING WITH THE BEST SOUTHERN ITALIAN OLIVE OIL, IS A DISH made in heaven specifically for formerly poverty-stricken Italians. Favas, an ancient crop, grow easily and can be kept in their dried form. The wild greens originally used were foraged in the fields among the grasses and wildflowers.

In the ironic twists and turns concerning which foods are considered high or low, this supremely rustic dish has been elevated to high status, and has become rather chic. High or low, when the fava puree, greens, and olive oil come together, a kind of food magic takes place.

Since the type of wild green typically used in this dish is unavailable to us here, I think rapini is the best substitute—full of mineral flavor, tangy, and, when properly trimmed and cooked, extremely tender and succulent.

2 tablespoons extra-virgin olive oil
plus lots more for generous drizzling
1 cup finely diced young leeks
1 sprig spearmint
1 sprig fresh Italian oregano or 1 teaspoon
dried Mediterranean oregano
1 pound dried fava beans, soaked overnight and peeled
(about 4 cups peeled)
1 medium russet potato, peeled and thinly sliced
Spring or filtered water
Sea salt
1½ pounds fresh, green rapini, stem ends trimmed
(thick and fibrous stems need to be cut off completely)

Heat 2 tablespoons of the olive oil with the leeks and herb sprigs in a medium pot or braising pan over a low heat until the leeks are very tender.

Add the peeled fava beans, sliced potato, and enough water to cover the ingredients. Add a generous pinch of salt and a drizzle of olive oil. Cook over medium heat until the fava

(CONTINUED)

beans break down into a puree. To help the mixture become a puree, use a wooden spoon to mash the ingredients against the side of the pan. Stir often and add water as needed to prevent the puree from sticking to the pan. The puree will be ready in 30 to 45 minutes or longer depending on the "freshness" of the dried beans. Taste and add salt and a little olive oil as needed to flavor the puree.

Meanwhile, cook the rapini in abundant salted boiling water. When tender, drain in a colander until the greens are free of excess moisture. Chop the greens very coarsely—just a few strokes of the knife blade.

For each serving, spoon some of the fava puree onto one side of a shallow pasta bowl. Place some of the greens next to the fava puree. Generously drizzle olive oil over the top.

I always have a bottle of my favorite olive oil and a container of my favorite sea salt on the table when I make this dish. This lets guests put the finishing touches on the seasonings according to their preference. A splash more of olive oil, a dash more salt are crucial to making the dish just right.

҉

CARDOON TIELLA

[*serves 4*]

ONE OF MY BIG FOOD REGRETS THUS FAR IS THAT I DID NOT STOP TO BUY THE TENDEREST, THINNEST STALKS OF CARDOON I'VE EVER SEEN IN MY LIFE. I WAS IN OTRANTO ON the Salentine coast, visiting the town for a few weeks. It was October, cold and rainy. I had booked a small apartment equipped with a kitchen.

I remember how the woman looked, her black dress, head scarf, and gray hair pulled back in a braided bun. She had set up a card table in front of her house on a narrow but busy road that winds through the town, her garden cardoons on display. And I walked right past her.

Being the absolute only tourist in town that time of year, I was feeling very conspicuous. I felt as though all eyes in town were watching me—and they were! So my self-consciousness prevailed.

I know that in the Salento and other parts of Italy, young cardoons are highly regarded. But even the large stalks that we get in our markets—like gigantic, pale whitish green celery stalks—when properly cooked, are delectable, a cross between cooked celery and cooked artichoke hearts.

Here, they are prepared as a gratin. If cardoons are not available, I've prepared this very successfully with fleshy, pale green celery stalks, first removing all strings, then cooking in boiling water until tender.

*About 3 pounds cardoons, the smallest
and most tender ones you can find, or about 3 cups
short lengths of trimmed celery
1 lemon, cut in half
Sea salt
Spring or filtered water
4 eggs
Grindings of black pepper
¼ cup grated pecorino cheese
¼ cup chopped Italian parsley
½ cup bread crumbs
Extra-virgin olive oil*

Heat the oven to 425 degrees.

Clean the cardoons, eliminating all the side leaves on the stalks. Use a cut lemon to rub the cut parts of the cardoons as you work to prevent discoloration. Remove the strings as you would with celery. If it appears that you are stripping the cardoons into nothingness, eliminate this step. Cut the stalks into 2-inch pieces.

Cook in a generous amount of salted boiling water until tender. Drain.

Beat together the eggs, salt and pepper to taste, the pecorino, and parsley.

Lightly oil a *tiella*—a glazed terra-cotta gratin dish—or a baking dish. Arrange a single layer of cardoon pieces on the bottom, and drizzle with some of the egg mixture. Continue layering the remaining ingredients. Sprinkle the top with bread crumbs. Drizzle generously with olive oil.

Cook in a hot oven for 15 to 20 minutes or until the top is golden brown. Serve immediately.

SIGNORA PANTELLA'S
BASIC ROASTED EGGPLANT

ROASTING EGGPLANT WHOLE ON A STOVETOP IMBUES THE VEGETABLE WITH A SMOKY FLAVOR THAT YOU WOULD SWEAR CAME FROM COOKING OVER A WOOD FIRE. IT IS A SIMple technique, and the cooked eggplant fillets are great to have on hand, the way Signora Pantella does, to make into a simple eggplant salad, to add to pasta, or to mix with other roasted vegetables, such as those wonderful Pugliese green peppers—narrow, tapered, and just a little spicy.

The key to keeping the eggplant fillets fresh-tasting after cooking is to season the strips just before serving. Olive oil, especially, should be used only at the time of assembling and serving.

Here is the most important part of the recipe: you must seek out small, firm eggplants with glossy skin and no soft spots. Large eggplants usually have many developed, tough seed clusters, the flesh is watery, not dense, and it can tend toward bitterness. You end up with a much greater ratio of eggplant flesh when you've selected the smaller ones. It is a real delight when you slice into a small raw eggplant and see practically no seed clusters, or when you peel off the blackened skin of the roasted eggplant and see all that pure creamy white flesh.

Small, firm eggplants with green
"leaves" at stem end, a sign of freshness

Use your fingers to snap off the "leaves." Do not puncture the eggplant or the juices will drain out during the roasting.

Place the eggplant or eggplants over a gas flame or a grill, or under the broiler. Keep turning the eggplant with tongs until all sides are charred and the eggplant has collapsed. Check for doneness by inserting a thin wooden skewer through the flesh.

When cool enough to handle, peel away the charred skin. Place the peeled eggplant in a clean bowl. Carefully divide the eggplant into fillets; it should naturally come apart in thick, long strips. Remove the seed clusters and discard, attempting to reserve as much of the flesh as possible. If using the same day, it is best to leave the eggplant covered with a clean dishtowel and unrefrigerated. Otherwise, refrigerate and use within a couple of days.

MUSTARD GREENS WITH OLIVE OIL
AND RED WINE VINEGAR

[serves 3 or 4]

LACKING JUST PICKED WILD MUSTARD GREENS, SEARCH OUT THE TENDEREST MUS-
TARD GREENS YOU CAN FIND. FARMERS' MARKETS ARE ALWAYS A GOOD SOURCE.

A really fine red wine vinegar is crucial. Good red wine vinegar, not flavored or doctored with preservatives, is hard to find.

The finest one I ever came across was from a natural food store, an organic product with a slightly mellow quality that was so different from the sharp, thin, highly acidic ones on supermarket shelves.

Balsamic vinegar is totally inappropriate here. In fact, it is used inappropriately most of the time, splashed on everything, including the tenderest salad greens. This sweet, aged vinegar must be used sparingly, and only when it serves as a perfect accent. On tender green salads, it is too sweet and syrupy, and obliterates the taste of the leaves. But a few drops of balsamic vinegar on roasted peppers, for example, really enhances their natural sweetness.

1½ pounds mustard greens
Spring or filtered water
3 tablespoons extra-virgin olive oil plus extra for drizzling
2 tablespoons best-quality red wine vinegar
Sea salt
Black pepper

Since most mustard greens I've found in markets tend to be overly large and tough, I always completely strip the leaves off the ribs and discard the ribs and stems. Trying to cook the mustard greens until the ribs and stems are tender, if ever, reduces the leaves to mush.

Once you've stripped the leaves from the stems, cook the mustard greens in abundant salted boiling water until tender, as little as 5 minutes if the greens are very young, but usually longer. The leaves should be completely tender and not at all tough or stringy. Drain well and let cool.

Arrange the mass of barely warm or room temperature cooked leaves on a cutting board and cut into ½-inch strips. Fluff up the strips a bit to separate the mass. Divide the cooked greens onto separate plates.

(CONTINUED)

Just before serving and not a moment sooner, toss with the olive oil and red wine vinegar and season with salt and pepper to taste. Serve accompanied by additional olive oil, red wine vinegar, and sea salt so each person can perfect the seasonings at the table. Dressing greens just before serving them creates a very fresh, clean-tasting vegetable. Also, keep in mind that vinegar and other acidic ingredients cause greens to discolor.

❧

DANDELION GREENS WITH
FRESH BAY LEAF AND PECORINO CHEESE

[serves 2]

NOTICE HOW THE DANDELION GREENS ARE COOKED JUST IN WATER AND ONLY THEN IS OLIVE OIL ADDED—IN ITS PURE, UNCOOKED STATE. THIS GIVES TREMENDOUS FLAVOR TO the finished dish and keeps the vegetable and olive oil flavors pure and clean.

A fresh, just-picked bay leaf, at the height of its powers, "sweetens" the greens by adding its elusive lemony/vanilla taste and perfume.

1 bunch tender dandelion greens, preferably
no longer than 6 inches or so, about ½ pound, rinsed,
dried, and cut into thick strips (see Note)
1 small fresh bay leaf
Pinch of hot red pepper flakes
Sea salt
½ cup spring or filtered water
Extra-virgin olive oil
Grated pecorino cheese

Combine the dandelion greens, bay leaf, red pepper flakes, a pinch of salt, and the water in a medium sauté pan. Cook over medium-low heat until the dandelion greens are completely tender. Timing will vary based on the tenderness of the greens.

To serve, put the greens and their cooking liquid in a dish, drizzle with olive oil to taste, and stir in a sprinkling of freshly grated pecorino cheese. Add a bit more salt if needed.

NOTE: If you prefer a less bitter flavor, cook the dandelion greens in abundant salted boiling water for a few minutes and drain. Then proceed with the recipe. This will eliminate some of the bitter tang in the leaves.

RAPINI WITH GARLIC BREAD CRUMBS

[*serves 2 to 4*]

I ADORE RAPINI. ITS DEEP GREEN COLOR, THE SUCCULENT SLENDER STEMS, TENDER LEAVES, AND SMALL FLORETS—AN EARTHY BITTERNESS—MAKE YOU FEEL HEALTHIER just by looking at it.

Rapini needs very little in the way of embellishment. In this case, less is more. A sprinkling of freshly made garlic bread crumbs adds just a bit of crunch as a pleasing contrast of textures, but does not intrude on the singular flavor of *la verdura*.

1 bunch rapini, very green and fresh, with tightly closed
florets and no little yellow flowers in evidence
½ cup spring or filtered water
Sea salt
½ cup bread crumbs
3 tablespoons extra-virgin olive oil
1 teaspoon chopped garlic

Trim the stem ends of the rapini. If the stems are tough and fibrous, cut them off completely.

Select a pan large enough to hold the full length of the rapini and add the water. Bring to a boil, adding salt to taste. Add the rapini and cook until they are tender. Most of the liquid will be absorbed or evaporate, but add more water as needed. Drain rapini in a colander, if any excess water remains.

Meanwhile, over low heat, toast the bread crumbs in olive oil until lightly golden. Add the garlic and cook for a few minutes more, until the garlic is tender and a little golden and the color of the bread crumbs has deepened to a golden brown.

Arrange the rapini on a serving plate with tops and stems lined up. Drizzle with olive oil and season with salt, turning the rapini stems gently to flavor each stem. Scatter the bread crumbs over the top.

ASSORTED "WILD" GREENS
WITH A SLICE OF RICOTTA

[serves 4]

ALL SORTS OF WILD EDIBLE GREENS GROW IN ITALY. AS YOU DRIVE DOWN NARROW
COUNTRY LANES, YOU MIGHT SEE MEN AND WOMEN, BENT OVER, PATIENTLY GATHERING
the leaves. During my Salento sojourns, I've had the opportunity to eat many varieties of
wild greens—for me, a real thrill.

Although we've lost, for the most part, that agrarian tradition, a new generation of foragers is out in the countryside, combing the land for edible wild greens. Sometimes the wild
leaves pop up at farmers' markets. I grow my own wild arugula, and believe me, nothing
could be simpler to cultivate. Wild plants are hardy.

Leaving behind the world of wild greens, we can create a highly successful dish using
cultivated varieties—the deep, tangy, rich flavors of greens found at markets. I've listed a
mix of greens that should not be too difficult to track down.

Serve the tangy greens with slices of firm sweet-tasting ricotta for a complete meal,
earthy, rustic, and satisfying.

2 pounds ricotta, preferably artisan-made (sheep's milk, if available)
Spring or filtered water
½ pound rapini, trimmed of tough stems
½ pound arugula, trimmed of all stems
½ pound dandelion greens, trimmed of all stems
½ pound mustard greens, leaves stripped from ribs, and stems trimmed off
Extra-virgin olive oil
Sea salt
Grindings of black pepper

Dampen three layers of cheesecloth large enough to line a colander. Drain any excess water
from the ricotta by slightly tipping the container over the sink. Upend the ricotta container
and let the ricotta fall into the cheesecloth. Put a plate under the colander, bring together
the ends of the cheesecloth to cover the ricotta, and let drain in the refrigerator for a few
hours or up to overnight, depending on the moisture content of the ricotta.

When the ricotta is firm, turn it out of the cheesecloth and place on a plate. It should form
a mound that is dense enough to slice like a cake. Bring to cool room temperature.

Cook the greens separately in abundant boiling salted water until tender. Drain each green to remove any excess bitterness. Bitter is good, but too bitter can be unpleasant.

Very coarsely chop the leaves, and cut the rapini into short lengths. Combine the four greens, fluffing them with a fork and mixing them to distribute evenly.

Toss the greens in olive oil and season with salt. Place a slice of ricotta on the side of the greens. Season the ricotta with olive oil, salt, and a generous grinding of black pepper.

※

FRESH PEAS WITH WILD FENNEL AND HOT RED PEPPER

[*serves 4*]

SET IN A SIMPLE BOWL ON THE OLD WOODEN TABLE IN THE CENTER OF THE KITCHEN, THE TABLE COVERED WITH A FRESHLY IRONED TABLECLOTH FADED TO A FLOWERED PASTEL through years of washing, Signora Pantella's peas are superb. It is an honor to sit as a guest at that table, seated at one of the plain, old wooden kitchen chairs.

Freshly picked and the first of the season, the peas are meatier and less sweet than our English peas—more substantial. The licorice-like flavor of wild fennel lends the peas a sweet, aromatic quality.

1 medium onion, finely diced
1 tablespoon finely diced pancetta
3 tablespoons extra-virgin olive oil
Very small pinch of hot red pepper flakes
2 pounds unshelled peas (about ¼ pound shelled)
2 generous sprigs young wild fennel,
tender stems and feathery parts only
1 cup spring or filtered water
Sea salt
Grindings of black pepper

Cook the onion and pancetta in the olive oil in a small braising pan over medium-low heat until the onion is tender and the pancetta has rendered its fat. Add the red pepper flakes.

Stir in the shelled peas and fennel sprigs. Cook for 3 or 4 minutes. Add the water and a tiny pinch of salt. Cover the pot and simmer for about 15 minutes, or until the juices have reduced to a small amount of liquid. Taste and season with additional salt and black pepper.

FRIED YELLOW PEPPERS WITH
WILD MINT AND RED WINE VINEGAR

[serves 4 to 6]

I HAD THIS IN A DESERTED LITTLE TRATTORIA ON THE OUTSKIRTS OF A TOWN I WAS PASSING THROUGH ON MY WAY DOWN TO THE VERY, VERY TIP OF THE SALENTINE PENINSULA, the beautiful town of Santa Maria di Leuca.

Frying brings out the sweetness of peppers more than any other cooking technique. Yellow peppers turn to burnished gold. Just a few tiny leaves of the wild mint that grows profusely throughout this rocky landscape, sharply sweet, yet of the earth, was enough to create a powerful presence. Cultivated mint and a bit of earthy oregano will also serve to accentuate the honey sweetness of the peppers.

6 yellow bell peppers, fleshy, with deep yellow-gold color
About ¼ cup extra-virgin olive oil or as needed
Sea salt and grindings of black pepper
2 garlic cloves, sliced
¼ cup chopped spearmint
Pinch of dried Mediterranean oregano
2 tablespoons red wine vinegar or
enough to balance some of the sweetness

Stem and seed the peppers. Cut lengthwise into ½-inch-wide strips. Trim away the white ribs and membranes.

Place a large sauté pan with enough olive oil to cover the bottom over high heat. Add the peppers to the hot oil and stir once or twice to coat the pepper strips lightly. Turn the heat to medium, and sauté the peppers for about 10 minutes. Add salt and a few grindings of pepper, the garlic slices, mint, and oregano. Stir, and continue cooking until the peppers are tender and slightly browned on the edges.

Transfer the peppers to a serving dish and, while hot, sprinkle with red wine vinegar. Let cool to room temperature.

If you are preparing the peppers a day or two in advance, refrigerate, but bring back to room temperature before serving.

LA SIGNORA'S TINY BOILED POTATOES

THIS IS ANOTHER HANDY TIP FROM LA SIGNORA. THE SALENTO HAS THE FINEST POTATOES I'VE EVER TASTED—THE SOIL, THE SALTY SEA BREEEZES, THE VARIETIES CULTIVATED, ALL are contributing factors.

Signora Pantella boils a potful of potatoes, each potato no larger than an inch and a half and some of them smaller. Yellow-fleshed, flavorful, exquisitely dense with papery thin skins, the potatoes are at the ready for numerous preparations—salads, soups, pastas, and so forth.

Cook as many potatoes as you think you can consume over the course of a few days. Note that the potatoes go into boiling water, not cold water, the preferred cooking method of the Salento. This helps the potatoes cook more quickly and evenly, with less loss of flavor.

Spring or filtered water
Sea salt
Small potatoes, preferably yellow-fleshed
varieties such as Yukon Gold or
Yellow Finn, unpeeled and scrubbed

Bring a large pot of water to a boil. Add salt and plunge in the potatoes. Cook for about 5 minutes or until tender but firm. Use a thin wooden skewer to test one potato for doneness. Too much poking of too many potatoes splits the skins and turn the potatoes mushy.

Drain when cooked and let the potatoes cool. A nice first dish would be a simple potato salad with olive oil, vinegar, and dried oregano, and maybe a few chunks of tomatoes. Cover the rest of the potatoes and refrigerate. Use when needed, for up to three days.

POTATO "FOCACCIA"

[serves 6]

THIS FOCACCIA IS NOT A BREAD, BUT A GRATINLIKE POTATO DISH OF CREAMY PUREED POTATOES FILLED WITH A LAYER OF TANGY TOMATO, CAPERS, AND OLIVES. IT IS SERVED cut into squares or wedges.

This was one of the many extraordinary dishes served at the Sagra della Patata, or potato festival, that took place in the small town of Parabita.

2 pounds small Yukon Gold potatoes
1 cup grated pecorino cheese
3 eggs, lightly beaten
Sea salt and grindings of black pepper
3 medium onions, finely diced
½ cup dry white wine
¼ cup spring or filtered water
1 fresh bay leaf
2 tablespoons extra-virgin olive oil plus extra for the baking dish
4 medium, ripe tomatoes, peeled and cut into large chunks
½ cup pitted oil-cured black olives
2 tablespoons capers
½ cup bread crumbs

Heat the oven to 400 degrees.

Boil the potatoes until tender. Peel, and while still warm, put the potatoes through a ricer to make a smooth puree. Mix the grated cheese and eggs into the potato puree and season with salt and pepper.

Place the diced onions in a pot with the wine, water, and bay leaf, and cook over medium-high heat until the liquid almost completely evaporates and the onions are tender. Add more water as needed until the onions are thoroughly tender. The white wine imparts a refreshing tang to the dish and keeps the onions intact.

Add the olive oil, tomatoes, and a pinch of salt to the onions. Simmer over medium heat for 10 minutes or until the tomatoes thicken to a sauce. Add the olives and capers. Simmer for 3 minutes. Set aside.

Oil a glazed clay baking dish that measures about 8 inches in diameter, or a medium oval gratin dish (about 10 inches long). Sprinkle a few bread crumbs on the bottom.

Spread half of the potato puree on the bottom of the baking dish. Spread the tomato and onion filling over the layer of potatoes. Carefully spread the rest of the potato puree over the top. Sprinkle with the remaining bread crumbs and drizzle with olive oil.

Bake for 40 minutes or until the top is golden brown. Let cool for at least 10 minutes.

Serve the potato focaccia warm or at room temperature, cut into squares or wedges.

⁂

POTATO TIELLA INFUSED WITH WINTER SAVORY

[serves 4 to 6]

BAKING SLICED RAW POTATOES WITH INTENSE, EARTHY WINTER SAVORY AND GARLIC INFUSES THE MILD FLAVOR OF POTATOES WITH THEIR SCENTS. SINCE NO PRECOOKING IS involved, the essence of the potato flavor is intensified, rather than being attenuated by a preliminary cooking in boiling water.

Winter savory grows profusely in my garden all through the summer, so the name is a bit deceiving. If unavailable, substitute fresh thyme and a pinch of dried Italian oregano.

2 pounds Yukon Gold potatoes, of uniform size, preferably small
3 garlic cloves, chopped
2 tablespoons chopped winter savory leaves or a handful of sprigs
Sea salt and grindings of black pepper
¼ cup extra-virgin olive oil plus extra for drizzling
½ cup spring or filtered water

Heat the oven to 425 degrees.

Slice the potatoes about ¼ inch thick. Place in a bowl and toss with the garlic, winter savory, salt, and generous grindings of black pepper and the olive oil.

Transfer the ingredients to a medium gratin dish, preferably of glazed terra-cotta. Level the top. Add the water. Finish with a restrained drizzling of olive oil.

Cover the baking dish and cook for about 30 minutes. Uncover and continue cooking until the potatoes are tender but firm, about 15 minutes. If any water remains in the dish, continue cooking a bit longer to let it evaporate. If the water has evaporated and the potatoes are still not cooked, add a bit more hot water as needed to complete the cooking.

The potatoes should be fully cooked but intact, and a deep golden color.

SIGNORA PANTELLA'S BASIC ZUCCHINI

[makes enough to last 2 people for 3 days]

WHEN THE GARDEN ZUCCHINI ARE AT THEIR PERFECT STAGE OF READINESS—SMALL, VERY FIRM, WITH AN EVEN GREEN COLOR, LA SIGNORA COOKS UP A FEW POUNDS WITH the simple addition of water. The cooked zucchini are delicious as they are, simply eaten with the light, sweet juices that develop in cooking and no other embellishments whatsoever—a refreshing tonic.

But the finely julienned zucchini strips can also be added to pasta tossed with tomato sauce, as a side dish warmed with a bit of grated Parmigiano, or *all'insalata*—at room temperature dressed with flavorful olive oil and fragrant lemon juice.

This method of cooking zucchini is at its most successful using firm, young zucchini. Older, watery zucchini with developed seeds will fall apart in cooking—and there is always the risk of bitterness, which, of course, ruins everything.

3 pounds small zucchini, about 4 or so inches long
(not baby zucchini)
Spring or filtered water
Sea salt
Extra-virgin olive oil (optional)

Wash and wipe the zucchini well to remove all traces of grit. Trim the ends. Cut each zucchini crosswise into two sections. Then cut each half lengthwise into ¼-inch-thick strips. There should be green skin on one side of many of the strips; the skin helps prevent the zucchini strips from falling apart.

Add enough water to come up ¼ inch on the side of a large pot. Add the zucchini and a pinch of salt. Cover and cook over medium heat until the zucchini strips are just cooked through, about 4 to 5 minutes. They should be tender but hold their shape.

Transfer the zucchini and juices to a bowl. Eat some immediately, drizzled with a few threads of extra-virgin olive oil, if desired. Allow the remaining zucchini to cool to room temperature. Refrigerate and use in various ways, such as those suggested above.

ZUCCHINI FRITTI IMPANATI

[serves 4]

THICK SLICES OF DENSE-FLESHED SUMMER SQUASH—I LIKE TO USE TENNIS BALL—SHAPED ZUCCHINI OR CHAYOTE (SURPRISINGLY, GROWN IN SOUTHERN ITALY) FOR THIS, but any firm, super-fresh zucchini that you can slice into thick rounds work well.

Cast aside any unfortunate memories of soggy fried breaded zucchini chips or strips. The egg and flour form a thin crust that seals the exterior of the zucchini slices when they hit the hot oil, keeping the flesh tender and moist, and not a bit oily.

2 pounds zucchini
Extra-virgin olive oil
2 eggs, lightly beaten
Sea salt and grindings of pepper
A mound of unbleached all-purpose
flour on a dinner plate

Clean, trim, and dry the zucchini well. Slice into ½-inch-thick rounds. Place rounds on a clean kitchen towel to absorb moisture from cut surfaces.

Pour enough olive oil to come about ½ inch up the side of a medium sauté pan and place it over medium-high heat.

Season the eggs with salt and pepper to taste.

Using a fork, and working a few at a time, dip each zucchini slice into the beaten egg, letting excess drain back into the bowl. Do not puncture the zucchini with the fork—just use it to lift the slices out of the egg. Coat both sides of zucchini with flour by immersing in the mound of flour and shaking off the excess so that only a fine film of flour remains.

Slip a few slices of zucchini into the bubbling hot oil, making sure not to crowd the pan. When golden on one side, carefully turn each slice over with a flipper and cook until the other side is also golden.

Drain on several layers of kitchen paper or paper towels, seasoning each batch fresh from the hot oil with salt to taste.

Serve immediately.

ANTONIETTA'S ZUCCHINA DA PERGOLA

[serves 4]

IN SOUTHERN ITALY, THIS DISH WOULD BE MADE WITH A TYPE OF VERY LONG, NARROW, AND SOMEWHAT TWISTED PALE GREEN ZUCCHINI THAT GROWS DANGLING FROM LEAFY pergolas. Seed catalogs here in America call this variety *tromboncino*—"little trombone"—because the zucchini are as long and convoluted as the instrument.

Since that variety is not easily available in markets, the best substitute is either pale green Italian zucchini, a little plumper than our regular zucchini, or one of the small round squashes: fluted scaloppine squash or the little squashes that are smooth and round and the approximate size of a tennis ball, called global zucchini. These come closest to the sweet, mild flavor and dense flesh of the Italian trombones.

1½ pounds Italian-style zucchini
2 tablespoons extra-virgin olive oil
½ medium onion, thinly sliced
1 large ripe red tomato, peeled, seeded,
and cut into coarse chunks
A few basil leaves
1 cup spring or filtered water
Sea salt
Grindings of black pepper (optional)

Cut zucchini into 1-inch dice.

Place the olive oil and onion in a medium braising pan and cook over low heat for about 10 minutes or until tender and starting to turn light gold. Add the chopped tomato, zucchini, basil leaves, water, and salt to taste.

Cover and cook over medium-low heat until the zucchini is meltingly tender. There should be a small amount of sweet juices remaining in the saucepan.

Before serving, add one or two grindings of black pepper, if desired. Serve either warm or at room temperature.

ANTONIA'S LIGHTLY BRAISED ZUCCHINI BLOSSOMS

[serves 4]

FRIED ZUCCHINI BLOSSOMS ARE DELICIOUS, BUT THIS SUBTLE PREPARATION REALLY ALLOWS YOU TO TASTE THE TRUE ESSENCE OF THE FLOWER.

The large, golden male blossoms of the zucchini plant, as large as a big lily, are abundantly available in Italy during the summer months. You can buy as many as you want and they will be perfectly fresh, picked that morning.

Here, it is not so simple. Don't be fooled by the little flowers still attached to young zucchini. These are female vegetable-producing blossoms, and they lack flavor and substance. The male flowers do not produce zucchini. If you grow your own zucchini, you'll have some to pick. And farmers' markets are a source.

Here is a recipe to adapt to however many you are fortunate enough to lay your hands on, producing a dish that is as pure and sweet as any vegetable dish could dream of being.

By the way, Antonia was my great-grandmother.

12 male zucchini blossoms in pristine condition
2 tablespoons extra-virgin olive oil
1 medium onion, finely chopped
Sea salt
1 cup spring or filtered water

Remove the orangey gold pistils from the zucchini flowers. Dip the blossoms, one at a time, in a bowl of cold water to clean and refresh them. Drain on clean kitchen towels.

Place the olive oil in a sauté pan just large enough to contain all the zucchini blossoms in one layer. Heat the oil and onion over low heat and sauté until the onion is tender and translucent, but not golden.

Arrange the zucchini blossoms over the onion. Season with salt to taste, and add the water. Turn the heat to medium-low. Cover and cook until the blossoms are tender, about 5 minutes.

Serve in shallow pasta bowls, distributing the broth among the dishes. If desired, top each serving with a few drops of raw olive oil.

FRIED ZUCCHINI FLOWERS WITH
HOT RED PEPPER BREAD STUFFING

[serves 4 to 6]

USE THE MALE FLOWER ONLY—A SHOWY GOLDEN BLOSSOM THAT WOULD LOOK RIGHT AT HOME IN A VASE IN THE LIVING ROOM. THE BLOSSOMS MUST BE SUPER-FRESH, PREFERably picked in the morning to be eaten that day since they are very fragile.

Signora Pantella made these for me one day, and she used a similar stuffing for baby artichokes on another occasion.

12 zucchini blossoms

FOR THE STUFFING

2 cups fresh bread soaked in about ⅓ cup whole milk, squeezed dry
1 egg, lightly beaten
1 small garlic clove, finely chopped
Hot red pepper flakes, to taste
2 tablespoons finely chopped Italian parsley
2 tablespoons freshly grated Parmigiano-Reggiano cheese
Sea salt and grindings of black pepper

BATTER FOR FRYING ZUCCHINI FLOWERS

1 egg, lightly beaten
1 cup unbleached all-purpose flour
Sea salt
Enough water to thin to consistency of cream, 1 to 1½ cups

Extra-virgin olive oil for frying
Sea salt

Remove the orangey gold pistils from the blossoms. Check for any insects lurking within. Dip each blossom gently in a bowl of cold water and carefully shake dry. Drain on clean towels.

Combine the ingredients for the filling and mix until it forms a soft paste. Gently stuff each flower with a tablespoon or so of the filling and fold flower edges to seal.

Mix the ingredients for the batter, adding enough water to form a smooth batter.

Heat the olive oil in a medium sauté pan with the oil measuring about 1 inch up the side of the pan until a small piece of bread dropped into it sizzles.

Dip a flower in the batter to coat it completely. Let excess drain back into bowl containing batter. Fry the zucchini flowers, a few at a time, for about 30 seconds on each side until crisp and golden brown. Let excess oil drip back into the pan. Drain the fried flowers in one layer on paper towels. Sprinkle with salt while they are piping hot. Serve immediately.

᪣

STUFATO
CONCETTA'S SUMMER GARDEN STEW
[*serves 6 to 8*]

I CAN REMEMBER SO CLEARLY HOW THE SMALL WHITE BOWL OF VEGETABLE STUFATO LOOKED WHEN IT WAS BROUGHT TO THE TABLE AT CUCINA CASARECCIA, CONCETTA'S well-known trattoria in Lecce. It was golden. Gold potatoes looking even more golden from the very light fresh tomato cooked down to a bit of sauce. Gold from the yellow pepper, and then, shades of zucchini green, and maroon from the squares of eggplant with small dark patches of skin. The flavor lived up to its beauty.

This type of stew is a balancing act—overcooking turns the vegetables to mush; too little time on the stove keeps the vegetables separate but doesn't allow for intermingling of flavors.

You have to feel your way through this recipe to get it just right. I've attempted to be as specific as possible about the quality of the vegetables used, cooking times, signposts along the way, but ultimately the real satisfaction comes from finding your own rhythm.

2 small eggplants, dark, firm and shiny, each weighing a little less than ¼ pound

Sea salt

1 medium onion, very firm

6 smallish Yukon Gold potatoes, weighing a total of 1¼ pounds

½ cup extra-virgin olive oil

*1 each yellow and green bell pepper, medium-large,
fleshy, firm, deeply colored, and without soft spots*

*2 medium zucchini (about ¼ pound) very firm,
preferably the pale green Italian variety that has dense,
almost seedless flesh and a sweet, light vegetal flavor*

1 pound red ripe tomatoes with dense, red flesh and not an excess of seeds

Spring or filtered water as needed

Grindings of black pepper

Grated pecorino cheese

(CONTINUED)

Cut the unpeeled eggplants into medium dice, a little smaller than ¾ inch. Layer the eggplants in a colander set on a plate, salting each layer as you go. The salt causes the eggplants to expel any bitter juices, as well as preventing the eggplants from becoming mushy during cooking. Weigh the eggplants down with heavy plates. Let rest for about an hour.

Meanwhile, cut the onion in half through the root end, then thinly slice. Peel the potatoes and cut them into scant ¾-inch dice.

Heat ¼ cup of the olive oil in a large braising pan, preferably of glazed terra-cotta, over medium heat. Add the potatoes and onion to the oil, add salt to taste, and stir. Stir frequently to prevent sticking. Cook until the potatoes are al dente and the onion is golden and tender, about 20 minutes.

While the potatoes cook, core and seed the peppers and cut into strips about 3 inches long and ½ inch wide. Cut the zucchini into 1-inch dice. Peel and seed the tomatoes. Cut into rough dice.

When the potatoes have finished their initial cooking, stir in the tomatoes. Cook until the tomatoes break down into a very light sauce, about 10 minutes, stirring often, and always with a wooden spoon.

Press down on the plate weighing down the eggplant to express any last lingering juices. Quickly rinse the eggplant under cold running water, then drain well on paper towels, or cloth kitchen towels, which are much more absorbent, gently squeezing out moisture.

Add the remaining olive oil to a large sauté pan over medium heat. Toss in the eggplant and stir. Cook for about 5 minutes, stirring frequently. Stir in the peppers and cook for an additional 5 minutes. Finally, stir in the zucchini and cook for 5 minutes. Taste and season with salt as needed.

Add the vegetables to the braising pan. Cook over medium-low heat until the vegetables are tender but not too soft, and the flavors have mingled, about 15 minutes. Check to make sure there is enough moisture. If the vegetables are sticking to the bottom of the pan, add spring or filtered water, a half a cup at a time, as needed to complete the cooking. The finished dish should not be dry but have some thickened juices at the bottom of the pot. Season with grindings of fresh pepper.

Serve warm or at room temperature. If desired, sprinkle pecorino cheese over the top.

SPRING VEGETABLE FRITTATA

[serves 1]

THIS VERY THIN FRITTATA, WHICH FEATURES A MOSAIC OF ALL THE MOST TENDER SPRING VEGETABLES, MAKES A SUPERB SIMPLE LUNCH OR DINNER FOR ONE PERSON.

Of course, you can also enjoy it for breakfast. But this wouldn't be very Italian. Italians rarely eat eggs in the morning. Frittatas usually appear later in the day and are served as a main course for a light meal, or cut into small squares or slices as an antipasto offering.

1 very small zucchini, about 4 inches long
1 very small, slender carrot with just a
short tuft of young green stems left on top
3 or 4 thin asparagus spears
A small handful of shelled new fava beans or peas
2 or 3 eggs, preferably cage-free organic
1 tablespoon milk
Sea salt and grindings of black pepper
¼ cup chopped dark green celery leaves
2 green onions, trimmed and thinly sliced, white parts only
1 to 2 tablespoons extra-virgin olive oil, or as needed
A few slices of fresh mild goat cheese

Heat the oven to 350 degrees.

Clean and trim the zucchini, carrot, and asparagus as needed for each vegetable. Boil the vegetables, including the favas or peas, separately in lightly salted water until tender. Drain in a colander.

When cool enough to handle, cut the zucchini into a few long strips. Cut the carrot lengthwise, right through the green stems, in half or into quarters.

Use a fork to lightly beat together the eggs and milk. Add salt and pepper to taste. Stir in the celery leaves and green onions.

Heat enough olive oil to cover the bottom of a small ovenproof sauté pan over medium heat. When the oil is hot but not smoking, add two thirds of the egg mixture. Lower the heat to medium-low and cook for a few minutes, stirring the eggs a bit with a fork in the beginning to evenly expose the egg mixture to the heat.

When the frittata starts to firm up a bit, arrange the vegetables over the top in a pattern of your choice (spokes of long vegetable strips and a scattering of favas or peas is easy and pretty), and distribute the cheese in the spaces between the vegetables. Top with the remaining egg mixture.

Transfer the pan into the hot oven and let cook until the frittata is just firm, a matter of a few minutes. Browning the eggs or even overcooking them slightly toughens the frittata.

Serve warm or at room temperature.

PASTA E RISO

pasta and rice

ALONG WITH A MASSIVE AMOUNT OF VEGETABLES, THE PEOPLE OF THE SALENTO EAT PASTA, PASTA, PASTA. IT FORMS THE BASIS OF THEIR WAY OF EATING: PASTA with tomato sauce; pasta with cultivated or wild greens; pasta with shellfish; pasta with tomato and veal sauce; pasta with zucchini; and pasta with just about any other vegetable you can think of.

The pasta of only one artisanal producer from the Salento is available here in America. Benedetto Cavalieri makes fabulous pasta of the highest quality that goes exceptionally well with the sauces of the region. (Williams-Sonoma carries the brand.) But other types of dried pasta from Italy also work well—other small producers such as Martelli and Rustichella d' Abruzzo, and second best, but also good, mass-produced pasta of high-quality from Barilla and De Cecco. Stock your pantry with various shapes, shop at the farmers' market or a good produce store, and you will never be at a loss for dinner.

Often, Signora Pantella sent a dish of hot pasta to my house, wrapped in a clean dishtowel to insulate it. She might send pasta made with her own home-bottled tomato sauce or pasta with her spicy tomato sauce. She would send over *pasta al forno* and simple lasagne. Her generosity always amazes me.

In this chapter I've included some cooking tips that Signora Pantella taught me. But mostly, I hope the recipes capture her spirit.

Rice also makes its way into the *cucina* of the region. Some say it was during Spanish domination that southern Italians learned to enjoy rice. The *tiella*, so much a symbol of Puglia and the Salento, may be based on the Spanish dish, paella. But I'd so much rather leave these historical musings to food anthropologists. The fact of the matter is that several well-known Pugliese dishes are based on rice. I've included them because, although they are not numerous, the rice dishes are an integral part of the repertoire.

Signora Pantella's Canned Tomato Puree

A NARRATIVE

EVERY SUMMER, SIGNORA PANTELLA PUTS UP JAR AFTER JAR OF TOMATO PUREE THAT LASTS the family through the winter, spring, and beginning of summer, until the next season's tomatoes are ripe. The tomatoes come from the family gardens and are watered, if it were possible, with an eye dropper of water—I've watched how little water is used and I've tasted the results! The less water given a tomato plant, the stronger the flavor, the denser the flesh.

The canning process is time-consuming and ends up involving the whole family. It is especially difficult since the ripening of the tomatoes, the small Leccese variety, corresponds with a time of tremendous heat in the region. One must start very early in the morning, at dawn, to survive the process—I'm sure I'd faint dead away.

Signora Pantella prepares the tomato puree flavored simply with basil leaves. She doesn't add salt since she feels it is easier to control when added to the pasta sauces she makes using her bottled *passato*.

Naturally, I'm grateful *la famiglia Pantella* has the stamina to produce this incredible tomato puree. It has served as the base for all manner of delectable dishes I've enjoyed during my summers in Italy.

As one who has never canned a single thing in my life, nor even watched the process, I'd rather not give a secondhand account. Canning must be done with absolute and complete confidence in one's expertise, or else—*disastro!*

So, instead of a recipe for canning the typical one hundred kilos of tomatoes, something very few of us would attempt, I offer a brief description of the many ways in which she utilizes the finished bottled tomato puree.

La Signora varies a basic tomato sauce she makes in countless ways. She'll top the freshly tossed pasta with a farm-fresh fried egg, or she'll add some fillets of her own roasted eggplant (see page 100) if she has some on hand. Signora Pantella might add some of the family's sweet home-grown zucchini. She might incorporate some fresh ricotta in the tomato sauce. Or she might stir in a discreet teaspoon or two of *ricotta forte,* an extremely pungent double-fermented ricotta considered a delicacy in the Salento—and what I might not so genteelly describe as a bit smelly and strange upon first tasting. Still, I've grown to appreciate it. Only a dab is used, literally a dab. In restaurants, *ricotta forte* is served dolloped, a teaspoonful at most, on the outside rim of a dish of hot pasta—there to be stirred in by the diner to taste.

The list of additions goes on and on, depending on the garden, the season, what the neighbor has brought by as a gift, what is in the pantry. But having mentioned so many variations, I offer two tomato sauces, always adorned with a flurry of grated cheese, that la Signora prepares often. I love them and know I could never tire of eating them! The recipes follow.

TOMATO SAUCE WITH OR
WITHOUT HOT RED PEPPER

[serves 4 to 6]

THIS IS SIGNORA PANTELLA'S BASIC TOMATO SAUCE, TO WHICH SHE OFTEN ADDS MINCED FRESH HOT RED PEPPER. I'VE ADAPTED IT USING A CAN OF SAN MARZANO plum tomatoes. It is a sauce that appears often during the week in the Pantella home.

3 tablespoons extra-virgin olive oil
¼ medium onion, very finely diced
2 garlic cloves, finely chopped
1 small fresh hot red pepper, finely chopped,
or ¼ teaspoon hot red pepper flakes (optional)
1 28-ounce can San Marzano plum tomatoes
2 large fresh basil leaves
Sea salt
1 pound pasta shape of your choice
Freshly grated pecorino cheese
Fresh basil leaves for topping

Heat the oil in a large sauté pan over medium heat. Add the onion, lower the heat, and let cook until onion is very tender. Add the garlic and optional red pepper and cook for another 2 or 3 minutes.

Meanwhile, drain the liquid from the tomatoes, reserving the juices. Cook the tomatoes with the basil leaves and salt to taste in a saucepan over medium heat for 15 to 20 minutes.

Remove the basil leaves and discard. Pass the tomatoes through the medium disk of a food mill to eliminate seeds and create a finely textured sauce. Alternatively, puree the tomatoes in a food processor and strain through a fine-mesh sieve to remove seeds.

Add the tomato puree to the ingredients in the sauté pan and cook for an additional 10 to 15 minutes to blend flavors. If the sauce becomes too dense, add some of the reserved tomato juices to the pan.

Cook any pasta shape you desire, such as spaghetti or penne rigate, in abundant salted boiling water. Drain when al dente. Toss the pasta with the tomato sauce and top with a generous handful of grated pecorino cheese and fresh basil cut into slivers.

TOMATO VEAL SAUCE

[serves 4 to 6]

SIGNORA PANTELLA MAKES THIS LIGHT, ELEGANT SAUCE BY USING THE TINIEST DICE OF VEAL AND JUST THE RIGHT AMOUNT OF FRAGRANT HERBS AND FINELY CHOPPED VEG-etables. Tossed with a ruffled very narrow lasagna shape, topped with a flurry of grated cheese, and sprinkled with tiny tender basil leaves, the results are truly sublime.

3 tablespoons extra-virgin olive oil
¼ medium onion, finely diced
1 small carrot, peeled and finely diced
1 small celery stalk, tough strings removed, finely diced
2 tablespoons chopped Italian parsley
1 bay leaf, preferably fresh, torn in half
Scant ½ pound boneless veal sirloin or shoulder, trimmed of fat
and connective tissue, cut or snipped with kitchen shears into ¼-inch dice
Sea salt
1 28-ounce can San Marzano plum tomatoes
2 large fresh basil leaves
1 pound lasagnette or egg fettuccine
Freshly grated Parmigiano-Reggiano cheese
Small handful of very small fresh basil leaves

Place the olive oil in a medium braising pan and turn the heat to medium-low. Add the onion, carrot, celery, parsley, bay leaf, and veal. Sauté over low heat for about 20 minutes, adding salt to taste. Stir frequently to prevent sticking.

Meanwhile, drain the juices from the can of tomatoes and reserve the juices. Cook the tomatoes with salt to taste and the basil leaves in a medium saucepan over medium heat for 20 minutes.

Remove the basil leaves and discard. Pass the tomatoes through the medium disk of a food mill to remove seeds and create a finely textured puree. Alternatively, puree the tomatoes in a food processor and pass through a fine-mesh sieve to remove seeds.

Add the tomato puree to the braising pan. Cover and cook over medium-low heat for from 30 to 45 minutes or until the veal is fork-tender. If sauce becomes too dense, add some of the reserved tomato juices.

Cook the pasta in abundant salted water until al dente. Drain well.

Toss the pasta with the sauce. Top with a handful of grated cheese and a sprinkling of small basil leaves.

❧

SUMMER PASTA AL FORNO

[serves 4 to 6]

THIS SAUCE IS ONE OF THE EASIEST SINCE THE TOMATOES REQUIRE NO PEELING OR SEED-ING, AND ALL THE INGREDIENTS ARE ASSEMBLED IN THEIR RAW STATE. NO STANDING over a hot stove either, since the cooking takes place in the oven. Naturally, the pasta itself requires cooking—but that is the extent of time spent in front of the burners.

The kitchen will heat up, but since everyone in the Salento lives in their *cortile,* or court-yard, or on their terraces, or at the beach all day, and eats outside, it doesn't pose too great a threat to everyone's comfort.

Baking evaporates the water from the sliced tomatoes in a manner very different from sautéing on the stove. The flavor deepens—think of sun-dried tomatoes. Different from a traditional sauce, the tomato slices stay somewhat separate from the olive oil so you encounter nice large pieces of meltingly soft tomato among the strands of golden spaghetti.

6 medium tomatoes, red and ripe
3 whole salt-cured anchovies or 6 large anchovy fillets in olive oil
4 tablespoons extra-virgin olive oil
Sea salt
2 large garlic cloves, thinly sliced
¼ teaspoon hot red pepper flakes
Handful of basil leaves
3 tablespoons coarsely chopped Italian parsley
1 pound thick spaghetti, artisanal if possible

If available, place a baking stone in the oven. Heat the oven to 450 degrees for 30 minutes.

Slice the tomatoes horizontally. Layer the slices in a colander and let drain briefly.

Rinse the salt from the anchovies. Gently use your fingers to separate the fillets and remove the spine and any other little bones sticking out. If using oil-cured anchovies, drain. Cut each anchovy into three or four pieces.

(CONTINUED)

Pour a little of the olive oil into the bottom of a medium *tiella* or an 8-inch square baking dish. Arrange half the tomato slices in one layer on the bottom of the dish. Season lightly with salt. Scatter half the anchovies, garlic, red pepper flakes, and all the basil leaves over the tomatoes. Top with another layer of tomatoes, the remaining seasonings, except the parsley, and drizzle with the remaining olive oil.

Bake, uncovered, until the water evaporates from the tomatoes and the oil separates, about 30 minutes. Remove the baking dish from the oven, sprinkle the parsley over the top, and with a wooden spoon, stir the ingredients once or twice to break up the tomatoes into rough pieces.

Meanwhile, cook the spaghetti in abundant salted boiling water until al dente. Drain well. Toss with the sauce. Serve immediately. No cheese is required.

❧

PASTA WITH TWELVE WILD HERBS

[*serves 4 to 6*]

THIS PASTA IS THE PRODUCT OF A TALENTED, ECCENTRIC CHEF IN LECCE WHO REFUSES TO DIVULGE THE TWELVE DIFFERENT HERBS HE USES. BUT ANYONE RAMBLING THROUGH the intensely fragrant *macchia*, the coastal scrub, can figure out most of the components, especially if your guide is an expert in local flora—which is how I came to know and love the *macchia*.

Although we can't reproduce the sauce exactly, we can assemble it in spirit, using wild herbs that are available, growing others ourselves, or just using the freshest cultivated herbs available. Remember that the herbs of the *macchia* are strongly aromatic and a little goes a long way. Here, we have to increase amounts. A light tomato sauce forms the base. All the herbs are used fresh, not dried.

4 tablespoons extra-virgin olive oil
3 wild or cultivated garlic cloves, finely diced
1 small onion (in Puglia they would use a
wild bitter onionlike flower bulb, soaked in water
for 24 hours to remove bitterness), finely chopped
Very small pinch of hot red pepper flakes
2 wild or cultivated bay leaves, torn in half

1 teaspoon chopped wild or cultivated thyme

1 teaspoon chopped wild or cultivated rosemary

2 teaspoons chopped wild or cultivated winter savory

1 teaspoon chopped wild or cultivated oregano

1 teaspoon chopped wild or cultivated marjoram

2 teaspoons chopped wild mint or cultivated spearmint

1 tablespoon finely chopped wild fennel tops or fennel bulb

1 28-ounce can imported San Marzano plum tomatoes,
seeds squeezed out of tomatoes, juices reserved

Sea salt

Large handful of wild or cultivated
arugula leaves, stemmed and chopped

1 tablespoon wild or cultivated salt-cured capers,
rinsed and finely chopped

1 pound imported orecchiette or penne rigate

Freshly grated pecorino cheese

Place the olive oil in a large sauté pan. Add the garlic, onion, and red pepper flakes. Cook over low heat until onion is tender and transparent.

Add all the herbs and warm in the olive oil for a few minutes to release the fragrances. Add the tomatoes to the pan, crushing them in your hands as you add them. Working over the sauté pan, strain the juices remaining in the can through a fine-mesh sieve to remove any seeds. Add salt to taste. Raise the heat to medium-low. Cook until tomatoes break down into a sauce, 15 to 20 minutes.

A few minutes before the sauce is ready, add the arugula and capers. Cook until the greens are tender.

Meanwhile, cook the pasta in abundant salted boiling water until al dente. Drain well. Toss with sauce. Serve sprinkled with a few spoonfuls of grated cheese.

PENNETTE WITH FRESH RICOTTA
AND PECORINO CHEESE

[serves 4 to 6]

WHEN THE RICOTTA IS FRESH AND MADE BY HAND IN SMALL BATCHES, FROM AN ARTI-SANAL PRODUCER, THIS IS ONE OF THE BEST PASTA DISHES IMAGINABLE. THE SAUCE requires no cooking—only a few tablespoons of hot pasta water to turn the ricotta into a dense cream.

In the Salento, I always have fresh ricotta tucked away in my little refrigerator. It is made from sheep's milk rather than cow's milk, which gives it a slight tang. I buy it in the mornings at a little nearby market, the curds still warm from the cauldron.

Look for producers of artisanal ricotta to enjoy this sauce the way it tastes in Italy. Since it will probably be made from cow's milk, stir in some fresh goat cheese or grated ricotta salata to add a bit of the almost lemony tang derived from sheep's milk.

1 pound pennette

Sea salt

¼ to 1 pound fresh ricotta, at room temperature

3 tablespoons extra-virgin olive oil

Grindings of black pepper

½ cup freshly grated pecorino cheese plus extra for the table

Cook the pennette in abundant salted boiling water until al dente.

Meanwhile, place the ricotta in a small bowl. Add enough boiling pasta water to form a dense cream. Add 2 tablespoons of olive oil and salt and pepper to taste. Keep warm on the stove near the boiling pasta.

When the pasta is al dente, drain, reserving some pasta water in case it's needed to thin the ricotta further. Toss the pasta with the ricotta cream, ½ cup of grated pecorino cheese, and the remaining 1 tablespoon olive oil. Add a few tablespoons of hot pasta water or more if the pasta seems dry. Top with generous grindings of pepper. Serve with lots of extra grated pecorino at the table.

THICK SPAGHETTI WITH
FRIED "WHITE" ZUCCHINI

[serves 4 to 6]

THIS CLASSIC DISH OF SOUTHERN ITALY IS AN EXAMPLE OF EXEMPLARY FRESH PRO-
DUCE MATCHED WITH ARTISANAL PASTA TO PRODUCE A GREAT DISH.

I use an Italian zucchini that is a little plumper than our narrow zucchini and very sweet. It is pale green, with a few darker green striations. Look for it in farmers' markets. If it is unavailable, I turn to scallopine squash, the small flying-saucer-shaped squash. It is all a question of sweetness and dense flesh: the narrow green zucchini in markets can sometimes be extremely bitter and watery, and destroy the whole dish of pasta—reason enough to send a whole family into a deep funk.

Whenever you purchase zucchini, seek out very firm ones that have no softening at the stem ends. Smaller is better, but not those little embryonic zucchini that haven't had a chance to develop flavor.

Artisanal spaghetti has a surface texture that is much more satisfying when you bite into it. It tends to be a bit thicker and holds its al dente firmness longer. For this dish, the spaghetti must be quite al dente.

1½ pounds zucchini
4 tablespoons extra-virgin olive oil
Sea salt
3 garlic cloves, peeled and thinly sliced
1 pound spaghetti
A handful of bright green fresh basil leaves
Freshly grated pecorino cheese
Grindings of black pepper

Wash the zucchini well to free it of surface grit. Trim the ends. Slice into thick coins.

Place the olive oil in a large sauté pan. Heat the oil over medium-high heat. Add the zuc-
chini coins, one layer at a time, and cook until golden brown on both sides, turning each coin over with a fork or little spatula. The zucchini should be meltingly tender. It will probably involve cooking the coins in three separate batches. When each batch is golden, transfer

(CONTINUED)

coins to a plate, first letting any excess oil drip back into the sauté pan. Season each batch with salt.

When all the zucchini is cooked, add the garlic to the hot oil and sauté until golden.

Meanwhile, cook the spaghetti in abundant salted boiling water until quite al dente. Drain, reserving a little of the pasta water, and toss with the zucchini and the oil in which it has fried and the garlic. If the pasta seems dry, add a few tablespoons of the hot pasta water at a time to slightly thin the oil. Scatter the basil leaves over the top, tearing them into large fragments over the pasta. Add a few tablespoons of grated cheese and some black pepper and quickly toss the pasta once or twice.

Serve immediately with extra cheese at the table. But remember, too much cheese will obliterate the sweetness of the zucchini.

ORECCHIETTE WITH RUCOLA, GOLD POTATOES, AND HOT RED PEPPER

[*serves 4 to 6*]

ARUGULA IS EMBLEMATIC OF THE SALENTO, AT LEAST FOR ME. IT GROWS WILD JUST ABOUT EVERYWHERE: IN THE COUNTRYSIDE, OF COURSE, BUT ALSO IN LITTLE NOOKS AND crannies along roads, in empty lots, in the cracks between stones in a *cortile*.

Orecchiette, a Pugliese specialty, catches the meltingly tender potato in its little pasta cups as it is tossed together with the sauce.

1 pound orecchiette

Sea salt

*½ pound Yukon Gold potatoes,
peeled and sliced medium-thin*

*1 pound arugula with large leaves,
stems trimmed, leaves chopped*

1 tablespoon chopped garlic

Pinch of hot red pepper flakes

3 tablespoons extra-virgin olive oil

Freshly grated pecorino cheese

Add the pasta to a big pot of generously salted boiling water. Stir well. After 5 minutes, add the sliced potatoes. Continue cooking the pasta and potatoes at a boil until the orecchiette are al dente.

A few minutes before the orecchiette are at the right stage of doneness, plunge the arugula into the boiling water.

Meanwhile, in a small sauté pan, heat the garlic and red pepper flakes in the olive oil until the garlic colors lightly.

Drain the pasta and vegetables. Toss with the flavored olive oil, breaking up the potato slices to form a coarse puree. Sprinkle with a generous handful of grated cheese.

Serve immediately with additional grated cheese at the table.

ORECCHIETTE WITH
RAPINI AND HOT RED PEPPER

[serves 4 to 6]

ONE CAN CLAIM THIS DISH OR ANOTHER AS THE CLASSIC DISH OF PUGLIA. BUT THIS ONE REALLY DOES EMBODY THE AREA LIKE NO OTHER—FROM THE UNIQUE ORECCHIETTE pasta to its companion bitter greens and the touch of fiery hot red pepper.

The following is the best method for making the dish with purchased dried pasta, which is what most people in the Salento use. Not that many Grandmas are interested in making this pasta by hand; they'd rather relax after a lifetime of hard work and watch a soap opera or one of Italy's truly zany game shows!

In the Salento, there is the option of buying orecchiette fresh at one of the little pasta shops specializing in hand-crafted pasta, and of course, nothing can compete with it. But a great amount of skill is required or the results are stodgy. Our best bet is buying an artisanal pasta imported from Puglia, such as the exemplary Benedetto Cavalieri pasta.

Sea salt
1 pound orecchiette
1 pound rapini, fresh and green without yellow blossoms,
thick stems trimmed, leaves and tender stems coarsely chopped
½ cup extra-virgin olive oil
3 garlic cloves, peeled and chopped
Hot red pepper flakes to taste
6 anchovy fillets
Pinch of Mediterranean oregano (optional)

Bring a large pot of salted water to a boil. Add the orecchiette and stir. When the water returns to a boil, add the rapini.

In a very large sauté pan, heat together over low heat the olive oil, garlic, and red pepper flakes. When the garlic colors lightly, add the anchovies. Stir with a wooden spoon until the anchovy pieces melt into the olive oil. Set aside.

When the orecchiette are al dente, drain the pasta and greens, leaving them just a little "wet." Add the pasta and greens to the sauté pan along with the optional oregano and toss briefly over high heat for about a minute. Taste and add salt if needed.

No cheese is served with this pasta since the anchovies provide a salty tang to the dish.

PASTA WITH ARTICHOKES, PEAS, AND FAVA BEANS

[serves 4 to 6]

THIS SUPERLATIVE ENSEMBLE OF VEGETABLES—EACH ENHANCING THE OTHER TO CRE-ATE A MEMORABLE WHOLE—IS AT ITS BEST IN SPRING, WHEN THE INGREDIENTS ARE young and tender.

Add pasta to the mix and it becomes one of the finest dishes of pasta you'll ever eat.

4 medium artichokes
A bowl of water with the juice of ½ lemon
4 tablespoons extra-virgin olive oil plus extra as desired
Sea salt
1 pound pasta such as penne rigate
1 cup shelled young, sweet fresh peas (about 1 pound unshelled)
1 cup shelled tender, green fava beans (about 1 pound unshelled)
Freshly grated pecorino cheese

Trim the artichokes of all tough, inedible parts. Sliver the artichokes and place in the bowl of lemon water (this keeps the artichokes from discoloring). When all the artichokes are cleaned and slivered, drain in a colander leaving a little water clinging to the surface of the artichoke pieces.

Sauté the artichoke slivers in 2 tablespoons of the olive oil and salt to taste over medium heat for about 8 minutes, letting the artichokes color a bit here and there.

Meanwhile, begin cooking the pasta in a big pot of salted boiling water.

Add a ladleful of the hot pasta cooking water to the sauté pan with the artichokes, and cook for a few more minutes. Add the peas and fava beans and cook until tender, about 8 minutes or so, adding more pasta water as needed. The vegetables should cook in a small amount of water to create flavorful juices.

When the pasta is al dente, drain, reserving a bit of pasta water. Toss with the vegetables and their juices, the remaining olive oil (add more if you'd like), and a sprinkling of grated pecorino cheese. Taste for salt. If the pasta seems dry, add a little of the reserved pasta water until the sauce loosens up a little.

Serve immediately with extra grated cheese at the table.

SPAGHETTINI WITH
A MOUNTAIN OF TINY CLAMS

[serves 4 to 6]

THIS IS SERVED IN EVERY SEAFOOD TRATTORIA UP AND DOWN THE SALENTINE COAST, ALWAYS MADE WITH THE VERY SMALL CLAMS CALLED VONGOLE VERACI THAT ARE RICH with briny flavor. The closest we come to that type of clam are the small Manila clams. Unfortunately, they just don't have the intensity of flavor that comes from living in the salty Mediterranean sea, but they are a more than adequate substitute. Littleneck clams, hard-shelled bivalves with clam meat that usually ends up as tough as a rubber band, are totally unacceptable.

On one of my forays out to the extreme *scoglia*, the rocky bluffs by the sea, my wild-food guide pried off a clam imbedded on the side of a rock, a clam as small as the nail on a dainty little finger, and with his trusty knife, opened the little clam and offered it to me to eat raw. It was tender and delicious, full of the taste of the sea. These, I was told, make a superb sauce for spaghettini, the only problem being that about three hundred of the diminutive clams are needed for the sauce!

3 pounds fresh Manila clams
Sea salt
½ to ¾ cup extra-virgin olive oil
8 garlic cloves, finely chopped
1 teaspoon hot red pepper flakes
2 cups dry white wine
½ cup chopped Italian parsley
1 pound imported spaghettini

Carefully place the clams in abundant cold salted water to soak for ½ hour. The kitchen sink works well for this. The soaking encourages the clams to open slightly and release any sand in their shells. Lift them out of the water, a few at a time, and rinse under cold running water. Place in a bowl.

Clean the sink of sand and repeat the process, gently adding the clams to the water so as not to break the shells. After ½ hour, lift the clams out of the water and rinse under cold running water. Place the clams in a bowl, discarding any with cracked shells, any that are open but do not clamp shut when gently tapped against the side of the bowl, or any that feel heavy for their size (they are probably filled with mud although I must admit I've never encountered one in that sorry state).

Heat the olive oil in a large sauté pan. Add the garlic and red pepper flakes, and cook briefly over low heat. Carefully add all the clams, the white wine, and parsley. Cover the pan and turn the heat to high. Gently shake the pan back and forth every few minutes. Check the clams after about 4 minutes. Be careful to not overcook them. They are ready the second the clams open.

Remove the clams as they open with a slotted spoon, letting juices flow back into the sauté pan, and transfer to a covered bowl to keep them warm.

Meanwhile, cook the spaghettini in salted boiling water until al dente. Drain the pasta and add to the sauté pan. Cook quickly over high heat for a moment or two to allow the spaghettini to absorb some of the juices. Taste and correct the seasonings.

Immediately serve the pasta and juices topped with the warm clams and all the juices they have released.

❧

LINGUINE WITH TOMATO AND MUSSEL SAUCE

[serves 4 to 6]

THE MUSSELS FOUND IN THE MEDITERRANEAN ARE EVER PRESENT IN THE COOKING OF ITALY. THROUGH PERSONAL OBSERVATION, I WOULD HAVE TO SAY THAT MOST OF THEM seem to end up eaten by the people of Puglia! They eat mussels by the sackful, and for good reason—they are plentiful and delicious. Cultivation of mussels is on a large scale around Taranto, but some small seaside trattorias up and down the coast have their own contraptions for harvesting mussels, and they haul the mussels straight from the briny sea for your dish of *pasta con le cozze.*

Look for mussels that are of medium size, and ask your fishmonger if the meat within is plump and tender. Little bits of shriveled mussel meat won't add up to a very tasty sauce. The farmed mussels available nowadays are pretty much grit-free and can be cooked directly in the tomato sauce.

2 pounds mussels

1 small onion, finely diced

3 garlic cloves, thinly slivered

4 tablespoons extra-virgin olive oil

¼ cup chopped parsley (reserve a big pinch for garnish)

A few very fresh basil leaves

8 very ripe plum tomatoes, peeled, seeded, and chopped, or 8 canned
San Marzano plum tomatoes, drained, seeded, and quartered

½ cup dry white wine

Sea salt

1 pound imported artisanal linguine

Scrub the mussels well to remove surface grit and debeard them if necessary. Discard any shells that are open or cracked.

Cook the onion and garlic in the olive oil in a medium sauté pan over low heat until the onion is lightly golden and very tender. Add the parsley and basil leaves and stir into the olive oil mixture for a few minutes. Add the tomatoes and wine, stir briefly, and raise heat to high. When the sauce comes to a boil, lower the heat, add salt to taste, and simmer for 15 minutes or until the tomatoes break apart to form a sauce. In the final few moments of cooking, add the mussels. Cover and cook just until the shells open. Correct seasonings if necessary.

Meanwhile, cook the linguine in abundant salted boiling water. When the pasta is al dente, drain well and gently toss with the sauce so as not to crack the shells. Garnish with the reserved parsley. Serve immediately.

SPAGHETTI ALLO SCOGLIO

[*serves 4 to 6*]

THIS SAUCE IS ANOTHER STAPLE IN EVERY SEASIDE RISTORANTE AND TRATTORIA. WHAT MAKES IT ALLO SCOGLIO IS THE FACT THAT THE SAUCE IS COMPOSED OF SHELLFISH that live either on the rocks or near the rocky coastal bluffs, called the *scoglio*.

Just a touch of dense, reduced tomato paste, or better yet, but unavailable here as far as I know, *estratto*, a sun-dried tomato paste, is all that is required. Anything more would interfere with the fresh briny flavors.

The shellfish must be cleaned scrupulously before adding them to the sauce or the finished dish will end up gritty—as disastrous for pasta as it is for cooked spinach or lettuce salads.

2½ pounds mixed shellfish such as small
Manila clams, mussels, and bay scallops
(scallops are more often available here already shelled)
5 tablespoons extra-virgin olive oil
3 to 4 garlic cloves, finely chopped
Sea salt and grinding of black pepper
1½ cups dry white wine
2 tablespoons imported Italian tomato paste (the type in the tube)
1 pound imported artisanal spaghetti
2 heaping tablespoons chopped Italian parsley

Clean the clams as directed on page 132. Scrub the mussels well and discard any that are open or cracked. Rinse the scallops in a colander under cold running water and let drain.

Heat the olive oil and garlic in a large sauté pan over fairly low heat until the garlic is golden brown. Season with salt and pepper. Pour in the wine and let bubble for 2 or 3 minutes. Add the tomato paste and stir to combine. Add all the shellfish to the sauté pan and stir gently to distribute evenly. Cover and cook over medium heat until the clam and mussel shells open, a matter of a few minutes. Remove pan from the heat the second they open so that the seafood doesn't toughen.

Meanwhile, cook the spaghetti in abundant salted boiling water until al dente. Drain well and transfer the pasta to the sauté pan with the sauce. Gently toss for 2 to 3 minutes to meld flavors. Serve immediately, sprinkled with parsley.

The Big Sunday Lunch

THE "BIG SUNDAY LUNCH" REPRESENTS, ALMOST MORE THAN ANYTHING ELSE I CAN think of, the essence of the Italian experience, an image emblazoned in everyone's mind as the key to happiness in life. Long, leisurely hours spent at the table of life, simply enjoying food and wine in the company of family and friends. It is a humanizing experience, making us all feel more alive and less alone.

When I was a child growing up in southern California, my family always had a Big Sunday Lunch upon returning from church. My mother's mother was the family tomato sauce expert, and early Sunday morning she would begin cooking.

I remember waking up to the smell of onions cooking in olive oil, surely one of the great perfumes on earth. She diced the onions very fine, and cooked them over the lowest possible heat. By the time I roused myself from bed and peered into the pot, the onions had positively melted into the oil, turning into a barely textured cream. Fast-forward to adulthood, and the only other fragrance that even remotely compares is when someone you love brings you a freshly brewed cup of sugary espresso in bed when you are just waking up.

Next, Nonna stirred in chopped garlic and parsley, waited a few minutes, then added the tomatoes. This she did in the time-honored method of an Italian *casalinga*, or housewife, lifting each tomato out of the can and squeezing it through her fingers to break it down into a coarse puree—an efficient and effective method of getting the cooking in motion, since breaking down the tomatoes into a sauce is the goal. A bit of salt and pepper, and on would go the lid, slightly ajar. Meanwhile, we children would have breakfast: coffee and milk, buttered toast, and on occasion, a frittata.

Then it was off to church, my sisters and my two grandmothers, all dressed in our finest clothes, our fancy hats, and even gloves for the holidays. My Italian father was, very atypically, an atheist, so he stayed home and read the Sunday paper from the first page to the last. He was an avid reader of history, philosophy, economics, and that ever-present newspaper that seemed to always be directly in front of his face! My mother busied herself preparing the rest of the Big Sunday Lunch.

By the time my father picked us up after Mass, the lunch was almost ready. The smell of tomato sauce wafted through the breezeway of our suburban house and kept on going right down the block. A salad was assembled but not yet dressed, a vegetable cooked. A chicken was usually roasting in the oven. The table was set. Bread and wine were in place, as were small dishes of olives or pickled vegetables, *giardiniera*, as a simple antipasto. Elaborate antipasti are not a traditional part of meals at home, even for the Big Sunday Lunch. In Italy, a multitude of antipasti is the domain of restaurants only.

We hurriedly changed out of our church finery, since by then we were famished after all that kneeling and standing and praying. In those days Mass was said in Latin so I didn't understand a word of it, but I always loved the ritual—the mysterious incantations, the smoky incense, the martyred saints, the beatific expression on the faces of the lucky saints, the compellingly gruesome Christ figure on the cross, the grief-stricken Mary, mother of God.

At about one o'clock the meal would begin, with everyone at the ready once the pasta was immersed in the big pot of boiling water, since pasta waits for no one. Then the warm wheat smell of the cooking pasta would rise and mingle with the scent of tomato sauce and roasting chicken. When the pasta was at the right point of doneness, it was quickly drained and tossed with the sauce and a handful of grated cheese.

Thus would begin the Sunday meal and we wouldn't rise from that table for at least two hours. Each course was given its due consideration, a succession of dishes that offered few surprises, but delivered complete and total pleasure and satisfaction.

With the chicken, we would have a simple vegetable accompaniment. Sometimes Nonna would make one of her two specialties from Palermo—her special caponata, or her winter squash *agro-dolce,* marinated in a mint, sugar, and red wine vinegar reduction. If my father's mother cooked the vegetable, it was a dish of wild greens she'd collected from the empty meadows of mustard greens that still dominated our neighborhood at that time, or wild mushrooms she collected with the surety of a countrywoman. Of course, these wild *funghi* scandalized my mother and her mother, born

and bred in the city of Palermo, but the mushrooms were seductively fragrant as they cooked and we all lived to comment on their succulence and flavor.

Next came the salad and, depending on the season, it might be an all-lettuce salad or a summery salad with tomatoes and cucumber. The salad was always dressed at the last moment. The green salad was drizzled with olive oil and fresh lemon juice, and sprinkled with salt. The mixed salad, since it contained tomatoes, replaced the lemon juice with red wine vinegar. I sopped up the remaining juices from the bottom of the salad bowl with a crust of bread—this mopping up was always reserved for me because I suppose I was the most passionate, or greedy, about it.

After the salad came fruit from the big cut-glass punch bowl that was always filled to the brim with an assortment of fruits in season. This fruit was eaten with a fork and knife—peeled or pitted, cored, and cut up by each person.

My father would sometimes bring out a bottle of sweet Marsala wine, his favorite—after all, he was a true Sicilian in his tastes—and we children would have little sips from the grown-ups' tiny cordial glasses. The meal lasted forever, time slipping by in slow motion. Since on any other day assembling for a long lunch was impossible or impractical, Sunday was our only chance, the one special day of the week, to truly revel in our Italianness.

In Italy, the Big Sunday Lunch is still an event and, when possible, all generations gather. I've sat in on many of these lunches, and the sense of well-being derived from them has no rival. High spirits prevail, a feeling of time held in suspension, of living forever, of peace and playfulness, teasing and flirting, and babies being kissed and bounced on knees, all merging with the scents of food and a bit of giddiness brought on by wine. All that matters is the moment, the forkful, the feeling of togetherness.

It seems to me that Sunday is the one day in America when this type of meal can be celebrated—a long Sunday lunch, every Sunday. What could be more important or meaningful? And it need not be just real relatives; it can be an improvised extended family of friends and neighbors. The group could take turns assembling at each other's homes.

Set the table. Put out a basket of good bread—it's the one thing no self-respecting Italian would fail to have at the table, on Sunday or any other day of the week: bread, bread, and more bread!—a carafe of wine, and a bottle of mineral water. Make a large serving of a simple pasta dish or perhaps the *pasta al forno* on page 142, the ultimate togetherness dish, if possible served from a big, round earthenware cooking vessel placed at the center of the table.

Afterwards, a roasted chicken or whole fish—something that is whole rather than in bits and pieces to reenforce the feeling of sharing. But it could also be a stew cooked ahead of time or whatever is easy to prepare. The important point is, don't let a dread of having to make the Big Sunday Lunch into a performance enter into whether or not you embark upon these Sunday meals.

A seasonal vegetable, simply prepared—as far as I'm concerned any seasonal vegetable is delicious by merely adding a drizzling of raw extra-virgin olive oil and a scattering of sea salt to the cooked vegetable—can be served with the meat or fish or stew.

Then serve a simple salad—keep the number of ingredients to a minimum since this is the moment to slow down and refresh the palate. Remember, many salad ingredients including raw lettuces, celery, and fennel act as aids to digestion, which is why tradition calls for serving them at the end of the meal.

Finish with a bowl of fruit, the fruits rinsed in cool water just before placing the bowl on the table, and provide a clean plate and knives and forks to do justice to the fruit. Naturally, for festive occasions bring out a cake purchased from a local Italian bakery, or make one of the simple ones found in the pages of this book, such as Maria's Torta Squisita on page 198, and offer some freshly brewed espresso for the adults.

Then sit back and reflect on all the joy flooding the room, whether it be your suburban kitchen or big-city dining room. And if you want to watch that joy grow by an additional increment or two, bring out a few *digestivi* or liqueurs to add one last lingering flavor to the meal, to prolong the feeling of *benessere,* or well-being. By initiating this ritual you've brought the spirit of Italy into your own home.

SUNDAY MEAT SAUCE

[serves 4 to 6]

THIS EXCELLENT MEAT SAUCE HAS A DEPTH AND RICHNESS OF FLAVOR THAT OFFERS PROFOUND SATISFACTION.

3 tablespoons extra-virgin olive oil

1 large onion, finely diced

1½ pounds assorted boneless veal, pork, beef, and lamb,
not ground but cut with scissors or a sharp knife into small pieces
or dice (ask your butcher to do this; most will happily oblige)

Sea salt and grinding of black pepper

Pinch of hot red pepper flakes

1 fresh bay leaf

½ cup red wine

1 pound very ripe tomatoes, peeled and diced

Spring or filtered water, as needed

1 pound imported artisanal pasta (almost any shape
works with this sauce except very delicate ones,
but ruffled lasagnette pasta is a particularly fine match)

Freshly grated pecorino or Parmigiano-
Reggiano cheese, or a mixture of the two

Heat the olive oil and onion in a braising pan or soup pot. Cook over low heat until the onion is golden and tender. Add the meat and brown over medium heat for several minutes.

Add the salt and pepper to taste, hot pepper flakes, bay leaf torn in half, and red wine. Let the wine bubble until it evaporates.

Add the tomatoes, stir, and cook, covered, over low heat for 1½ hours, stirring regularly, until the flavors develop fully. Check often and add water as needed to prevent scorching.

Cook the pasta of your choice in abundant salted boiling water. When al dente, drain well and toss with the sauce. Generously sprinkle with a handful of cheese and toss again before serving. Serve with extra cheese at the table.

PASTA WITH TOMATO SAUCE FLAVORED WITH A LITTLE PORK AND RED WINE

[serves 4 to 6]

SIGNORA PANTELLA HAS GIVEN ME MORE HOURS OF HAPPINESS AT THE DINNER TABLE THAN I CAN COUNT. THE SIMPLICITY, FRESHNESS, AND INTEGRITY OF THE RAW MATERIALS she uses are second nature to her. Every slight change of ingredients creates yet another utterly wonderful pasta dish.

Here, pork ribs, each diced no larger than a champagne cork, each containing a little piece of bone, contribute a rich flavor. Red wine adds additional depth to the sauce.

As usual, the piping hot pasta would arrive at my door wrapped in clean dishtowels tightly tied in a topknot in order to seal in the heat. Upon opening the fragrant package, I could always count on seeing la Signora's final touch—a big handful of grated cheese thickly strewn over the top.

3 tablespoons extra-virgin olive oil

*⅓ pound lean pork ribs, trimmed of fat, cut into 1-inch pieces
(have your butcher do this for you)*

3 garlic cloves, chopped

½ medium onion, finely chopped

¼ cup chopped celery leaves (darker leaves have more intense flavor)

¼ cup chopped Italian parsley

Pinch of dried Mediterranean oregano

1 fresh bay leaf

Sea salt and grindings of black pepper

Pinch of hot red pepper flakes (optional)

½ cup red wine

*2½ pounds peeled and coarsely chopped ripe tomatoes,
preferably juicy dense-fleshed Romas, or 2 28-ounce cans
imported whole peeled San Marzano plum tomatoes*

Spring or filtered water, as needed

1 pound penne rigate, rigatoni, spaghetti, or other sturdy pasta of choice

Grated Parmigiano-Reggiano or pecorino cheese

Place the olive oil in a large braising pan. Warm it over medium heat, then add the pieces of pork, turning them over briefly in the hot oil to lightly sear the exterior, just long enough to remove the raw appearance.

Add the aromatics—garlic, onion, and herbs—and stir together to combine ingredients. Add salt and pepper, and a bit of red pepper flakes, if desired. Cook over medium-low heat until the onion is golden and tender. Add the wine and let it evaporate completely.

Add the tomatoes. Bring to a boil, cover, and cook over moderate heat for 45 minutes to 1 hour, or longer. If the sauce becomes too thick, add water as needed. During the final few minutes of cooking, taste and add salt and pepper as needed.

Cook the pasta in abundant salted boiling water. When al dente, drain thoroughly and toss with the sauce including the small pieces of pork.

Serve immediately, with grated cheese on the side. Watch out for any bones that may have separated from the meat!

ANGIULINO'S ULTIMATE PASTA
AL FORNO WITH TEENY MEATBALLS

[serves 6]

ANGIULINO'S PLACE—TRATTORIA IS TOO FANCY A NAME FOR THIS SIMPLE ESTABLISHMENT—
IS ONE OF THE OLDEST STILL-FUNCTIONING HOLE-IN-THE-WALL PLACES IN LECCE. YOU WALK
down narrow cobblestone streets with marvels of southern Italian baroque architecture on
either side of you—not the overly ornate and ponderous style we think of immediately
when the word *baroque* is mentioned. Here in the Salento, the baroque buildings are exu-
berant, yes, but it is a happy exuberance—nothing tortured or sinister about it, just fruits
and flowers and decorative elements combined on the lighthearted façades carved from
regional golden limestone.

Angiulino's place has the simple foods I love: steamed mussels, cooked greens, thin
breaded cutlets, and, of course, his *pasta al forno*, a dish that is soul-satisfying right down to
your toes. And don't forget the red wine, preferably a light, fresh red wine like the one
Angiulino pours for everyone.

SIMPLE TOMATO SAUCE

3 tablespoons extra-virgin olive oil

1 medium onion, finely diced

1 tablespoon chopped garlic

1 fresh bay leaf

¼ cup coarsely chopped Italian parsley

*2 28-ounce cans imported whole peeled
San Marzano plum tomatoes*

Sea salt

POLPETTINE

½ pound freshly ground beef

½ pound freshly ground pork

*About 2 cups dried country bread,
soaked in water, then squeezed dry*

1 egg, lightly beaten

¼ cup grated pecorino cheese

1 garlic clove, finely chopped

¼ cup chopped Italian parsley

Generous grindings of black pepper

1 pound rigatoni, preferably artisanal
Drizzles of extra-virgin olive oil
1 pound fresh mozzarella in water,
drained and coarsely shredded
1 ½ cups grated pecorino cheese
1 cup bread crumbs

Heat the olive oil and onion in a large sauté pan over low heat until the onion is tender and transparent. Add the garlic, bay leaf, and parsley, and cook for an additional few minutes.

Add the tomatoes and their juices, first squeezing out the seeds from the tomatoes or gently scooping them out with your fingers. Season with salt. Simmer for 15 minutes or until the tomatoes break down into a sauce. Use a wooden spoon to break up the tomatoes as they cook. Taste for salt. Set aside.

Combine the ingredients for the polpettine until amalgamated. Wet your hands lightly with water. Shape the mixture into very small meatballs the size of marbles, and not any larger.

Lightly oil a baking sheet. Arrange the meatballs on the sheet, allowing space between the polpettine. Cook the meatballs under a broiler set on low for about 4 minutes, shaking the baking sheet every so often to evenly distribute the heat. Drain the meatballs on paper towels.

Heat the oven to 400 degrees. It must be very hot when the pasta goes in.

Cook the pasta in abundant salted boiling water. Drain when half cooked, about 5 minutes or so, and toss with a few drops of olive oil to prevent pasta from sticking.

Moisten the inside of a large baking dish with olive oil. The baking dish of choice is a *tiella*, a glazed ceramic vessel, one measuring 12 to 14 inches in diameter. Or use a 10 x 14-inch gratin dish.

Toss the rigatoni with the tomato sauce, polpettine, mozzarella, and 1 cup of the grated pecorino cheese. Sprinkle the top evenly with bread crumbs and the remaining grated cheese. Drizzle with a few fine threads of olive oil.

Bake uncovered for 45 minutes or until the top is golden brown. Let rest for 10 minutes, or up to 20 minutes if you can bear waiting, to allow the ingredients to adhere. Serve it forth, cut into wedges that usually fall apart very appealingly.

RICE WITH "FORAGED" GREENS

[*serves 4*]

NATURALLY, THIS SIMPLE RICE DISH CAN BE MADE WITH CULTIVATED LEAVES, BUT THE TRADITION IS TO USE THOSE GATHERED IN THE WILD. FARMERS' MARKETS ARE A GOOD source for unusual greens such as arugula and borage, although usually they are the cultivated variety. Or grow the greens yourself; being weeds by nature, arugula and borage are easy as pie to grow.

Aside from being delicious, this dish is an excellent tonic for the body.

¾ pounds stemmed tender young
arugula (tangy) or borage leaves (mild)
1½ cups arborio rice
3 to 4 tablespoons extra-virgin olive oil
plus extra for seasoning
Sea salt
Freshly grated pecorino cheese (optional)

Boil the greens in a little salted water until tender, 10 to 15 minutes. Drain well and chop rather finely.

Cook the rice in a generous pot of salted boiling water. When tender but still a little al dente, save about 1 cup of the cooking water, then drain the rice, leaving it "wet."

Place the rice in a bowl and add the cooked greens and olive oil. Stir well to distribute the greens evenly, seasoning with salt to taste. Add enough of the reserved cooking liquid to the bowl to create a moist but not liquid dish.

Taste and correct the seasonings, adding more olive oil or salt as needed. Serve hot in shallow pasta bowls.

You could season the dish with grated cheese, a tempting thought no doubt. But it is so tasty on its own, and more of a tonic, you might enjoy it cheeseless. Try it both ways and decide which you prefer.

RICE WITH ARTICHOKES
AND FAVA BEANS

[*serves 4*]

COOKING ARTICHOKES AND FAVA BEANS TOGETHER CREATES AN UNFORGETTABLE FLAVOR—SUBLIME AND EARTHY, DEEPLY SATISFYING. BOTH ARE SLIGHTLY BITTER WITH a trace of sweetness. Both have a certain density of flesh. Both create delectable juices. Together, along with rice to absorb some of the intriguing intermingled mineral essences, this simple dish rises to great heights.

The freshest baby artichokes have leaves that snap off crisply. The pods of fava beans are an indicator of their freshness: the greenest, tenderest pods that look almost dewy contain the freshest beans.

Please do not be tempted to peel the individual fava beans since a great deal of the flavor is in the skin. As long as the bean is green, from brilliant green to lighter green, and not yellowish, cook it unpeeled straight out of the pod. Big starchy beans require an entirely different cooking method.

½ lemon
12 baby artichokes
3 tablespoons extra-virgin olive oil
3 whole garlic cloves
1 tablespoon chopped fresh winter savory
(if unavailable, replace with fresh thyme)
Sea salt and grindings of black pepper
2 cups arborio rice
1 cup shelled fava beans (about 1 pound unshelled)
3 cups boiling spring or purified water
Freshly grated pecorino cheese (optional)

Squeeze the juice of the lemon half into a big bowl of cold water and throw in the lemon rind. Set aside.

Remove the outer dark green leaves of each artichoke and trim the tips of the stem end. Quarter the artichoke and cut into thin wedges. As you finish trimming and slicing each artichoke, toss it immediately into the lemon water to prevent discoloration.

Place the olive oil in a braising pan and turn the heat to medium. Drain the artichoke

(CONTINUED)

145

slices and add to the pan along with the garlic cloves and winter savory. Stir to coat the artichoke slices in the oil. Sauté until the artichoke slices are tender and slightly golden, seasoning with salt and pepper to taste.

Meanwhile, cook the rice in a large pot of salted boiling water for 5 minutes and drain. Add the rice and raw fava beans to the artichokes and stir together with a wooden spoon.

Add the boiling water, a little at a time, stirring often, until the rice is nicely al dente and the fava beans, including the peel, are completely tender. Taste and add salt and pepper as needed.

Transfer to a terra-cotta dish, cover, and let rest on a kitchen counter for 10 minutes to let flavors merge. This last technique comes from Patience Grey's *Honey From a Weed*.

If desired, you can serve the rice sprinkled with grated pecorino cheese, but this is entirely optional and many would argue the flavor of the cheese intrudes a bit too aggressively. Try it both ways and see which you prefer.

TIELLA WITH RICE, MUSHROOMS, AND GOLDEN POTATOES

[*serves 4 to 6*]

IN THIS VARIATION ON THE THEME OF TIELLA COOKERY, THE MAIN INGREDIENTS ARE LAYERED WITH A SPRINKLING OF PARSLEY, GARLIC, AND GRATED CHEESE BETWEEN each layer. It is quite a delicious dish—different textures, rich flavor—and as a bonus, it is completely simple and straightforward to prepare. Just pop the *tiella* in the oven and let the oven's heat work its magic.

Serve this as a first course, main dish, or side dish, depending on what else you have planned for the meal.

4 tablespoons extra-virgin olive oil plus a bit more
1½ pounds Yukon Gold potatoes, peeled and cut into thin slices
Sea salt and grindings of black pepper
4 garlic cloves, finely chopped
½ cup chopped Italian parsley
¾ cup grated pecorino cheese
*¾ cup arborio rice, boiled in a generous
amount of salted water until al dente, drained well, and
tossed in a few drops of olive oil to prevent sticking*

*Small handful of dried porcini mushrooms, soaked in
1 cup warm water (omit if using fresh porcini)*

*1 pound flavorful mushrooms such as cremini,
portobello (black gills on underside removed), or, if you are
lucky to find them, very fresh porcini mushrooms, sliced*

2½ cups cold spring or filtered water, more or less

½ cup homemade bread crumbs made from dried-out rustic bread

Heat the oven to 450 degrees.

Oil a large 10-cup baking dish about 4 inches deep, preferably round and made of glazed terra-cotta, with 2 tablespoons extra-virgin olive oil. Arrange the raw potato slices on the bottom of the dish. Season with salt and pepper. Sprinkle with approximately one third each of the garlic, parsley, and grated pecorino.

Arrange the al dente rice in a layer over the potatoes and season with salt and pepper. Again, sprinkle with one third of the garlic, parsley, and grated pecorino.

If using, drain the dried porcini mushrooms, reserving the soaking liquid. Pass the liquid through a triple layer of cheesecloth to remove any grit released by the mushrooms. Coarsely chop the rehydrated mushrooms. Mix with the sliced raw mushrooms. Arrange the mushrooms on the top layer. Season with salt and pepper and sprinkle with the remaining garlic, parsley, and grated cheese.

Drizzle the remaining 2 tablespoons of olive oil over the surface of the baking dish. Add the cold water and the strained porcini water to the *tiella* and allow the water to filter down through the ingredients. The water should lightly moisten all the ingredients up to or near the level of the potatoes. Sprinkle the top generously with bread crumbs and moisten with a few threads of olive oil.

Cover the *tiella* and bake for about 30 minutes. Uncover and continue cooking until the potatoes are tender, the water has evaporated, and the bread crumbs are golden, 20 to 30 minutes. Use a thin wooden skewer to check if potatoes are done.

Serve hot or at warm room temperature directly from the baking dish.

COZZE AL RISO

[*serves 6*]

HERE IS ANOTHER DISH THAT TREATS RICE LIKE PASTA. A FINAL COOKING TOGETHER WITH THE SAUCE, JUST FOR A FEW MINUTES, INFUSES THE RICE WITH THE FLAVORS OF mussels, tomato, and golden brown garlic. Delicious and so much simpler than making risotto, this style of cooking rice is one to remember and use frequently, since it is as adaptable as pasta with different sauces.

Buy mussels from a reputable source. Mussels with scrawny meat lack succulence and are devoid of flavor.

3 pounds mussels (about 4 dozen)
½ cup dry white wine
½ cup spring or filtered water
2 pounds ripe tomatoes
Sea salt
2½ cups arborio rice
3 tablespoons extra-virgin olive oil plus a bit more
3 garlic cloves, peeled and crushed
½ cup chopped Italian parsley
Grindings of black pepper

Wash the mussels in a colander under cold running water. Most mussels are farmed nowadays and come to the market very clean. If necessary, scrub and debeard the mussels.

Place the mussels in a large, deep sauté or braising pan. Add the wine and water. Cover and cook over high heat until the mussels open. Check after a few minutes. Remove from the pan the second they open or the mussel meat will toughen. Reserve the cooking juices.

Working over the sauté pan, remove the mussel meat from each shell, allowing any juices to drain into the pan with the cooking liquid. Strain the cooking liquid through a colander lined with several layers of dampened cheesecloth.

Cut the tomatoes into large, thick chunks. Cook in a saucepan with salt to taste for about 10 minutes. When the tomatoes break down, put them through the medium disk of a food mill to remove seeds and skin. Set puree aside.

Cook the rice in abundant salted boiling water for about 10 minutes, or until quite al dente. Drain and set aside, tossed with a few drops of olive oil to prevent sticking.

Meanwhile, heat the olive oil and garlic until the garlic is lightly browned. Add the tomato puree and the strained mussel cooking liquid. Simmer over medium heat for 5 minutes. Stir in the parsley.

Add the rice and cook over low heat until the rice is al dente. Add the mussels just long enough to warm them; any longer and they will toughen. Serve immediately, topped with generous grindings of black pepper.

RICE WITH TOMATO VEAL SAUCE
AND TINY GOLDEN POTATO DICE

[serves 4 to 6]

THIS, ANOTHER OF SIGNORA PANTELLA'S DISHES, DISPLAYS ALL THE FINESSE OF HER COOKING, EMPLOYING SIMPLE INGREDIENTS AND TREATING THEM IN A DELICATE AND precise manner.

Different from risotto, the rice is cooked in salted boiling water until al dente, just as you would cook pasta. This method of rice cookery is more common in the south of Italy than the risotto technique of northern Italy. As with pasta, most of the surface starch is removed when the rice is drained in a colander. The creaminess of risotto is replaced by rice grains that are more distinct and separate—equally delicious and as adaptable as pasta.

2 cups arborio rice

Sea salt

1 recipe Tomato Veal Sauce (page 122)

¼ pound Yukon Gold potatoes, boiled until
cooked but firm, peeled, and cut into small dice

A few basil leaves (optional)

Freshly grated Parmigiano-Reggiano or pecorino cheese

Boil the rice in abundant salted water. While the rice cooks, gently heat the prepared sauce in a large sauté pan. Add the diced potatoes to the sauce and stir.

When the rice is just short of al dente, drain, reserving a cup or so of the water to use if the rice mixture becomes dry.

Immediately toss the rice with the tomato sauce. Add the optional basil leaves, torn into fragments, and simmer over low heat until the rice is al dente and most of the sauce has been absorbed. If needed, add the reserved rice water, a little at a time. The finished dish should not be "saucy": the rice should be lightly colored by the sauce and the rice grains should remain intact. (Fluffy rice with each grain completely separate is not the goal.)

Serve hot, generously strewn with grated cheese.

PESCE E FRUTTI DI MARE
fish and shellfish

WARM SEAFOOD SALAD "SEA SHACK" STYLE

[*serves 4*]

VARIATIONS OF THIS SIMPLE SALAD ARE AVAILABLE AT EVERY RUSTIC TRATTORIA LIN-
ING THE COAST OF ITALY. DOWN IN THE HEEL OF THE BOOT, THE SALAD INVARIABLY
contains octopus and *totani*, a type of squid unavailable here, and sometimes just those
two ingredients.

The simplest seafood salads are often the most pleasing—just lots of tender, or nicely
chewy, pieces of seafood with nothing to interfere with the pleasure of eating it—no shells,
peels, or added ingredients such as capers or olives.

But, if desired, you can certainly add a few freshly cooked mussels to the salad at the
last moment.

6 tablespoons extra-virgin olive oil

5 tablespoons lemon juice

½ small garlic clove, very finely diced

*Small amount of finely diced hot red pepper
or small pinch of hot red pepper flakes (optional)*

Sea salt

*1 pound cleaned small squid, body cut into rings,
tentacles cut into small pieces*

½ pound bay scallops

½ pound medium shrimp, shells on

Very small amount of chopped Italian parsley for garnish

Thick wedges of lemon

(CONTINUED)

Choose a shallow serving bowl large enough to contain all the ingredients. Combine the olive oil, lemon juice, garlic, optional red pepper, and a pinch of sea salt. Beat lightly with a fork to combine, not emulsify, the ingredients.

Cook the squid in a pot of salted boiling water until opaque and tender. Check after 3 minutes and, if necessary, continue cooking until squid is meltingly tender. Drain in a colander. Place in the serving bowl and toss.

Meanwhile, cook the scallops in a fresh pot of salted boiling water for about 2 minutes. Drain and when cool enough to handle, cut each scallop in half horizontally. Add to the bowl and toss.

Devein the shrimp by making a shallow cut along the curved edge of the shell, and, if present, rinse away the black vein. Cook in salted boiling water for 2 minutes. Drain. When cool enough to handle, remove the shells and cut each shrimp into three chunks. Combine with other seafood and toss.

Taste and season with sea salt as needed. Stir in the chopped parsley. Serve accompanied by thick wedges of lemon. The salad is equally delicious served after resting for an hour or so, covered, in a cool spot in the kitchen. If making well in advance, refrigerate and then return to room temperature.

THIN SWORDFISH STEAKS THE ITALIAN WAY

[serves 6]

IN ALL MY TRAVELS IN ITALY, I DON'T BELIEVE I'VE SEEN SWORDFISH SLICED ANY THICKER THAN ABOUT ¹/₂ INCH. AND FOR GOOD REASON. SWORDFISH DRIES OUT EASILY when overcooked. A thicker steak requires much more time on the stove. By the time the inner flesh is cooked properly, the outside has hardened. Follow this recipe and you'll never have to worry about overcooking swordfish again.

Find a purveyor of superior swordfish. I've had a few bad experiences lately with swordfish that was strangely tough and stringy, truly *schifoso*—quite digusting.

> *2 pounds fresh swordfish steaks sliced no thicker than ½ inch*
> *½ cup bread crumbs made from dried country bread*
> *¼ cup chopped Italian parsley*
> *1 small garlic clove, finely chopped*
> *Sea salt*
> *3 tablespoons extra-virgin olive oil plus extra for frying*
> *Thick lemon wedges*

Drain the swordfish well.

Stir together the bread crumbs, parsley, garlic, and sea salt on a plate.

Place 3 tablespoons of olive oil in a bowl. Moisten each steak on both sides with a brush dipped in the oil. Lightly sprinkle each side with the bread crumb mixture, gently patting it in so it adheres.

Pour in enough oil to cover the bottom of a large sauté pan and heat it over medium heat.

Cook the swordfish steaks over medium-low heat for about 2 to 3 minutes on each side. Transfer to a platter and season with a sprinkling of salt.

Serve with lemon wedges.

TUNA SCALOPPINE, LIGHTLY GRILLED

[serves 6]

TUNA AND SWORDFISH SHARE A TENDENCY TOWARD DRYING OUT DURING COOKING. THE SAME PRINCIPLE APPLIED TO SWORDFISH IN THE PREVIOUS RECIPE IS AT WORK HERE.

The thinner the slice, the easier it is to control the cooking. Find a fish purveyor to slice the tuna even a little thinner than ½ inch, since tuna is that much more susceptible to over-cooking. A preliminary soak in a bit of olive oil will further protect the delicious flesh.

Leave raw tuna to sushi enthusiasts. Here, it should cook almost all the way through to a uniform color, with just a touch of pale pink at the center.

2 pounds fresh tuna, each slice a little less than ½ inch thick
Extra-virgin olive oil for the marinade and for grilling
Sea salt
1 large crushed garlic clove, thickly sliced
Dried Mediterranean oregano
Grindings of black pepper
Thick lemon wedges

Place the tuna in a shallow glass or ceramic dish. Drizzle with olive oil and season with salt. Turn over the steaks in the oil and salt, sprinkling on the garlic slices throughout. Set aside for 30 minutes or so.

Meanwhile, fire up a grill or turn on the broiler. When the temperature is quite hot, remove the garlic slices from the tuna and grill or broil the steaks close to the heat source for 1 to 1½ minutes per side.

Transfer to a platter and sprinkle sparingly with oregano and a grinding of pepper. Serve with lemon wedges.

POACHED HALIBUT AL MODO MIO

[*serves 4*]

MY FAVORITE WAY TO POACH FISH DOES NOT INVOLVE IMMERSING THE CREATURE IN WATER. INSTEAD, YOU MIGHT CALL IT SHALLOW-POACHING SINCE JUST A SMALL AMOUNT of water is used. The water turns into a delicious little broth to spoon over the warm fish.

I prefer to keep the seasonings to a minimum—I want to taste the fish. Just a few aromatics are called for, and a little sweet, pure water. And, of course, an all-important final drizzling of the finest raw extra-virgin olive oil!

4 halibut fillets of uniform thickness
Spring or filtered water to come ½ inch
up the side of a large sauté pan
Extra-virgin olive oil
Sea salt
2 fresh bay leaves, torn in half
3 or 4 sprigs Italian parsley plus extra
coarsely chopped parsley to sprinkle on top
1 garlic clove, thinly sliced
3 or 4 thin lemon slices
Grindings of black pepper
Thick lemon wedges

Place the halibut fillets in a sauté pan large enough to contain the fillets in one layer. Add the water and a few drops of extra-virgin olive oil, season with sea salt, and sprinkle with the bay leaves, parsley sprigs, garlic, and lemon slices.

Poach the fish over medium-low heat, covered, until the fish is just cooked all the way through.

To serve, use a slotted spatula to lift each fillet out of the hot liquid and place in individual shallow pasta dishes. Sprinkle the fish with sea salt and a light grinding of pepper. Top with a few big tablespoons of the fish broth and a drizzling of olive oil. Garnish with a bit of chopped parsley. Serve with lemon wedges on the side.

WHOLE FISH BAKED WITH
LOTS OF ANCHOVY AND BREAD CRUMBS

[serves 4]

BAKING A WHOLE FISH IS A SURE-FIRE, FUSS-FREE WAY OF COOKING FISH TO A MELTING TENDERNESS. HERE, BREAD CRUMBS, PARSLEY, AND ANCHOVIES LITERALLY BLANKET the fish, protecting it from drying out as well as infusing it with rich flavor.

Use the fish suggested below or any very fresh white fish locally available. If whole fish is hard to come by, this method works quite well with fish fillets or fish steaks.

1 cleaned and gutted 2½-pound striped bass,
or similar whole white-fleshed fish
2½ cups bread crumbs made from dried country bread
½ cup chopped Italian parsley
Sea salt and grindings of black pepper
4 tablespoons extra-virgin olive oil
4 large anchovy fillets cured in salt,
wiped clean, or 1 can anchovies in olive oil, drained
2 juicy lemons

Heat the oven to 400 degrees.

Open the fish out as flat as possible so that both sides benefit from the seasonings. Place the fish skin side down in a lightly oiled large baking dish, preferably of glazed terra-cotta.

Cover the fish with half the bread crumbs and half the parsley and season with sea salt and grindings of pepper to taste.

Heat the olive oil in a small sauté pan. Add the anchovies and cook over lowest heat until they start to break down into a puree. Pour the warm mixture evenly over the fish. Distribute the remaining bread crumbs and parsley over the top.

Bake for 20 minutes for a large fish or as needed for the fish you are using.

To serve, carefully spoon the topping off to one side of the baking dish. Remove the spines and any other remaining bones from the fish. Spoon the topping back on the fish and spread it evenly over the fillets. Drizzle lightly with the remaining olive oil and the juice from the lemons.

Serve by dividing the fish into equal portions, making sure each portion gets its fair share of topping and juices from the baking dish.

WHOLE GRILLED FISH IN
AN OLIVE OIL AND HERB MARINADE

[serves 6]

MAYBE NOTHING THAT COMES FROM THE SEA IS AS IMPRESSIVE AND SATISFYING AS A WHOLE GRILLED FISH. IT IS SIMPLY MAGNIFICENT. COOKING THE FISH WITH ALL ITS bones where they are supposed to be, and enrobed in its own skin, creates a flesh of melting tenderness and great flavor.

There is really nothing much to add, except possibly some chopped herbs and garlic to an olive oil marinade as I've done here. The real trick is finding a very fresh whole fish. You can use a four-pound fish or six individual small whole fish. The basic cooking technique is the same.

1 4-pound whole fish, such as red snapper
or striped bass, gutted and scaled, with head left on
1 sprig rosemary
1 sprig winter savory or thyme
1 sprig sage
1 sprig fresh Italian oregano
4 sprigs Italian parsley
1 large garlic clove
Sea salt
½ cup extra-virgin olive oil
A big, juicy lemon
Fresh bay leaves (optional)
Lemon wedges

Wash the fish inside and out, and dry well.

Strip the leaves from the herb sprigs. Finely chop together the herb leaves and garlic clove.

Open the fish and spread just a little of the chopped mixture inside the cavity of the fish. Season lightly with salt.

Combine the remaining herb mixture with the olive oil, the juice of the lemon, and a pinch of salt. Place the fish in a large, deep enamel or ceramic platter. Pour the marinade over the top. Let marinate for about an hour, turning the fish over every so often.

(CONTINUED)

Heat a charcoal or gas grill until very, very hot and lightly oil it. Remove the fish from the marinade and let the excess drip back into the dish. Lay the fish on the grill. Cook until a thin crust forms on the skin, which causes the skin to naturally separate from the grill. Turn the fish over once, using a large fish spatula. As the fish cooks, brush the exterior with the marinade. It should cook approximately 15 minutes per side. Check the flesh for doneness and adjust cooking time as needed.

Transfer the fish to a platter and garnish with a few fresh bay leaves, if available. Bring the whole fish to the table and bone it or enlist someone to do so. It simply involves lifting off the spine from each fillet and removing any fin bones or miscellaneous inedible bits and pieces.

Serve portions of flesh with the crispy skin still attached. Place a bowl of thick lemon wedges on the table to squeeze over the fish.

BATTERLESS FRIED PINK SHRIMP

[*serves 4*]

I ATE THESE WONDERFUL MORSELS AT A SUMMER RELIGIOUS FESTA IN THE TOWN OF GALLIPOLI ON THE IONIC COAST. IN THE SULTRY CHURCH, THE BEAUTIFUL YOUNG CHOIR, their faces shiny with sweat and religious joy, and their strong, sweet voices, made me feel *molto emozionata.*

Then, in the hot night air, alongside the church situated right next to the port, men wearing those ubiquitous white paper caps started frying up the tenderest, sweetest shrimp, fresh from the sea. A big serving of a heap of shrimp, burning hot and fragrant from the oil, could be purchased for the equivalent of a few dollars. The light red wine, almost a *rosato,* common in this area and perfect on that hot, humid night, was poured for a few pennies a glass.

1 pound small shrimp, preferably fresh, unpeeled,
preferably with heads and tails still attached
Extra-virgin olive oil
Unbleached all-purpose flour
Sea salt and grindings of black pepper
Lemon wedges

Rinse and dry the shrimp well on paper towels.

Heat enough olive oil to come ½ inch up the side of a large sauté pan.

Dredge a few of the shrimp at a time in the flour. Shake off the excess flour.

When the oil is very hot but not smoking, slide in, one at a time, a handful of shrimp, making sure not to crowd the pan. Cover with a splatter shield. Cook for 1 minute on one side. Carefully turn each shrimp over with a spatula and fry for another 30 seconds. Lift each one out of the oil with a slotted spatula, letting excess oil drain back into the pan.

Drain on paper towels or brown kitchen paper, seasoning the shrimp while still piping hot with a generous sprinkling of sea salt, and, if desired, grindings of black pepper. Eat immediately, with lemon wedges on the side to squeeze over the shrimp.

"FLATTENED" GRILLED SHRIMP

[*serves 4*]

I DON'T RECALL WHERE I ATE SHRIMP PREPARED IN THIS MANNER, BUT I DO KNOW THE RESULTS WERE MEMORABLE. FLATTENING THE SHRIMP, ACTUALLY WEIGHTING THEM down while cooking, shortens the cooking time, and since the flesh is very thin and even, they cook uniformly. Also, the shells turn golden brown and crisp, and are infused with the taste of the grill since they are pressed so hard against it. Sucking on the shells is almost as delicious as eating the shrimp.

Come to think of it, it is the same technique as for *pollo al mattone*—chicken cooked under the weight of a brick.

1½ pounds large shrimp
Extra-virgin olive oil
3 garlic cloves, lightly crushed
Sea salt and grindings of pepper
Lemon wedges

Arrange the shrimp in a shallow bowl. Drizzle with enough olive oil to lightly coat the shrimp. Scatter the slices of garlic over the shrimp and stir to distribute them among the shrimp. Generously season with salt and pepper.

Cover and set aside the shrimp in a cool place to marinate for about an hour.

Meanwhile, heat up a charcoal or gas grill, or a stovetop grill, until very hot. Using tongs, lift the shrimp out of the marinade, letting excess oil drip back into the bowl. Remove any slices of garlic that cling to the shrimp. Place the shrimp on the hot grill and weigh them down with clean bricks or a large, heavy skillet, the bottom wrapped in foil, weighted with large cans.

Cook for about two minutes per side, turning once and placing the weights again on top of the shrimp. The shells should be crisp and golden brown, and the shrimp flesh moist and tender.

Off the grill, season the shrimp again with salt and grindings of pepper. Serve immediately with lemon wedges on the side.

WHEN LUNCHTIME ROLLS AROUND, A HUSH DESCENDS ON CITIES; IN SMALL TOWNS, COMplete silence prevails. The only sounds are the muffled rattling of forks and knives, and the faraway clanging of dishes. Each family or individual is focused on consuming the most important meal of the day, and in that moment, or more precisely during those hours, nothing else in the world matters.

Pranzo—lunch—when done properly, is a time-consuming affair. When dining at home, the basic courses include a *primo*, or first course, which consists of a pasta, rice, or polenta dish, or a *minestra*, a soup. A small serving of meat or fish comes next and is called the *secondo*, or second course. It is accompanied by a *contorno*, a vegetable dish. A small salad follows, a simple mixed salad, or an *insalata verde*, green salad. The dressing is invariably olive oil and red wine vinegar or olive oil and lemon juice. To finish the meal, the fruit is brought out. Then, espresso for the adults.

This is how the average Italian family eats at home. Rarely is there an antipasto course— except for special occasions. Desserts as we know them do not make an appearance, again, except for special occasions. Bread is always, always on the table, as are wine and mineral water.

Antipasti before the *primo piatto* and deserts after meals are more the province of restaurants and trattorias, which gives someone traveling in Italy a distorted idea of Italian eating traditions. If you don't dine with an Italian family in their home, you might come to the conclusion that lunch is an endless feast.

Instead, a family lunch is a complete, satisfying dining experience, but wholesome and simple, the course offerings rather small (except for pasta!), and moderation is a given. Rarely does anyone overindulge, in wine or any of the other offerings. An Italian meal is modulated, the eaters pace themselves, a skill that seems inborn but is learned at the table starting from the tenderest years of childhood, and is based on observation and following conventions.

After this meal, a bit of repose is in order. Some take a nap; others simply relax awhile. Then the second part of the day begins as people return to work for the second shift, so to speak, refreshed and renewed.

MENU FOR A SUMMER PRANZO

[*recipe follows*]

Light Red Wine
Mineral Water
*Signora Pantella's Red Peppers
al Forno (page 162)*
Pasta alla Sangiovanniello (page 163)
Pepate di Cozze (page 164)
Summer Fruits
Espresso

SIGNORA PANTELLA'S RED PEPPERS AL FORNO

[serves 4]

LA SIGNORA PREPARED THESE DELECTABLE PEPPERS WHEN I DINED AT HER HOME ONE SUMMER EVENING AND SERVED THEM STREWN WITH LOTS OF BIG GREEN OLIVES.

This is a simple dish to assemble. Baking the pepper strips in a *tiella* tenderizes the skin so there is no need to peel them first. And the baking process concentrates the peppers' sweetness—they almost taste candied. Bread crumbs absorb the syrupy juices that the peppers give forth. All that vegetal sweetness is balanced by big tangy capers and briny green olives.

4 big, deep-red bell peppers (thin-fleshed frying peppers
will yield less good results than thick-fleshed, heavier peppers)

4 tablespoons extra-virgin olive oil

½ cup homemade coarse bread crumbs

2 garlic cloves, thinly sliced

2 heaping tablespoons big capers cured in salt, rinsed well

Sea salt

Big green olives cured in brine, drained, and unpitted

Heat the oven to 375 degrees.

Clean the peppers of seeds, core, and thick white membranes. Cut the peppers into thick strips.

Toss the pepper strips in a bowl with the olive oil to coat them. Stir in the bread crumbs, garlic, and capers. Add salt to taste.

Transfer the ingredients to a medium baking dish, preferably of glazed terra-cotta. It should be large enough to contain the mixture about 3 inches up the side of the dish. Spread the mixture evenly.

Bake for about 45 minutes or until the peppers are tender and juicy. Serve the *tiella* warm, but even more delicious, at room temperature, strewn with green olives.

PASTA ALLA SANGIOVANNIELLO

[serves 4 to 6]

IT IS SUMMER IN THE SALENTO AND EVERYONE CONSUMES PASTA WITH TOMATO SAUCE ONCE, BUT MORE LIKELY, TWICE A DAY. IN MY SUMMER APARTMENT, I DON'T NEED A clock to tell me what time it is: I base it on when I begin to detect the fragrance of tomato sauce being cooked by everyone in town, for lunch and for dinner.

Since the combination of pasta and tomato sauce is basic to life in all the south of Italy, hundreds, maybe thousands, of subtle variations on the theme have been devised.

Here, the tomatoes are peeled and chopped and the sauce is cooked quickly on the stove. A few anchovies, the addition of capers, no basil, just parsley are some of the distinguishing nuances. Tossed with lasagnette, an inch-wide ribbon pasta with a curly edge, or wide fettuccine, and grated pecorino cheese, it assumes its own unique persona.

3 tablespoons extra-virgin olive oil
2 garlic cloves, finely chopped
2 whole salt-cured anchovies, rinsed, split, and boned,
or 4 oil-cured large anchovy fillets, drained
1½ pounds ripe tomatoes, peeled, seeded, and very coarsely chopped
Sea salt
2 tablespoons capers, rinsed and squeezed dry
A small piece fresh hot red pepper or a pinch hot red pepper flakes
2 heaping tablespoons coarsely chopped Italian parsley
1 pound lasagnette or wide fettuccine
Grated pecorino cheese

Place the oil in a large sauté pan. Turn the heat to medium-low. Add the garlic and cook until lightly gold. Add the anchovies and with a wooden spoon, stir the pieces until they break down in the oil to a creamy consistency.

Add the tomatoes, salt to taste, the capers, red pepper, and parsley. Cook over low heat for 15 minutes or until it just forms a sauce.

Meanwhile, cook the pasta in salted boiling water. Drain when tender but still a little firm to the bite. Toss with the grated cheese and the sauce. It should be lightly sauced. Pass additional cheese at the table.

PEPATE DI COZZE

[serves 4]

BIG HEAPING PLATTERS OF STEAMED MUSSELS ARE ONE OF THE GREAT TREATS OF SEASIDE DINING. IN PUGLIA, THE STEAMED MUSSELS ARE GIVEN A BLAST OF HEAT AND perfume from abundant freshly ground black pepper, creating a very lively flavor. Another version replaces black pepper with chopped fresh hot red peppers. Serve with sturdy bread to sop up the spicy juices, and a nice, light rosato or cool white wine.

4 pounds mussels
¼ cup extra-virgin olive oil
3 garlic cloves, minced
¼ cup chopped Italian parsley
1 cup dry white wine
1 tablespoon freshly ground black pepper

Wash and scrub the mussels well, being careful not to crack the delicate shells. Discard any that are open or cracked. Remove the beards by pulling them free or cutting them off.

Select a sauté pan large enough to contain the mussels no more than two or three layers deep.

Place the olive oil, garlic, and parsley in the pan and sauté over low heat. Add the white wine and bring to a boil. Stir in the black pepper. Add all the mussels, cover, and cook over high heat. As each mussel opens (or several may open at the same time), use a slotted spoon to transfer it to a large shallow serving bowl, letting excess juices drain back into pan. By removing them as they open, the mussels remain plump and tender and do not dry out from overcooking.

When all the mussels have opened and are in the bowl, continue to cook the liquid until it is reduced to about ½ cup. Pour the spicy juices over the mussels and serve.

MUSSEL AND POTATO TIELLA

[*serves 6*]

HERE'S A DISH THAT SPEAKS OF PUGLIA—ONE YOU'RE NOT LIKELY TO EASILY FIND ELSEWHERE. THE LAYERING GIVES IT AWAY, AND THE COOKING VESSEL—GLAZED EARTH-enware. This particular *tiella* is especially of the region since mussels are used abundantly in numerous preparations.

4 pounds mussels, cleaned and debearded
2 pounds medium-small Yukon Gold potatoes of uniform size
1 pound fresh, small zucchini
Extra-virgin olive oil as needed
1½ cups bread crumbs
2 medium onions, cut in half through the root end and thinly sliced
1 cup grated pecorino cheese
Large handful of parsley leaves, chopped
Sea salt and grindings of black pepper

Heat the oven to 375 degrees.

Steam the mussels open in a large sauté pan in about 1 cup of water. Remove from the heat when the mussels are barely open. When cool enough to handle, remove the top shell, leaving the mussels on the half shell. Strain the juices through several layers of damp-ened cheesecloth.

Peel the potatoes and thinly slice them. Cut the zucchini into strips (see page 110 for Signora Pantella's method).

Lightly oil the bottom of a large baking dish, preferably of glazed terra-cotta. I use my prized 12-inch *tiella* for this dish. Sprinkle ½ cup of the bread crumbs over the bottom. Layer half the potato slices over the bread crumbs, then layer the zucchini over the pota-toes, and end with a layer of onion. Sprinkle with ¼ cup of the cheese and half the pars-ley. Season with salt and pepper to taste. Layer half the mussels on top.

Layer the remaining potatoes, zucchini, and onions in the way described above to create an additional layer. Top with the remaining mussels. Sprinkle the rest of the cheese, bread crumbs, and parsley over the mussels. Pour the reserved mussel juice over the top.

Cover with foil and bake for 30 minutes or until the potatoes are tender.

Let rest for 10 minutes before serving.

CALAMARI FRITTI

[serves 4]

IT WOULDN'T BE ITALY WITHOUT FRIED CALAMARI. THE SCENT OF THEM FRYING IN OLIVE OIL HAS A POWERFUL PULL FOR ME—IT IS UNBEARABLY HARD FOR ME TO RESIST.

Calamari fritti were part of my childhood as we sat around the family kitchen table while batch after batch was fried; part of my first trip to Italy, spent mostly in Palermo and the seashore visiting friends and relatives; and have been part of many subsequent trips to Italy, as well as the North Beach neighborhood where I have my office. It always brings me back to the Mediterranean: the salt air, the aquamarine water, sand and rocks, prickly pear cactus growing on the cliffs.

The flavor of squid matches its provocative aroma. Just a light dusting of flour is sufficient to protect the squid from high heat. Nowadays, all sorts of breading are used, but all that crusty, thick coating totally obscures the flavor of the squid; it could be rings of just about anything white in there. Dipping sauces are also the rage. I guess you could call me a purist, but I like my fried calamari with just a squeeze of lemon, or nothing at all.

Small fresh squid are incredibly tender and delicate, with a unique flavor all their own. If at all possible, find a source for fresh squid, the smaller the better.

2 pounds cleaned small squid
Extra-virgin olive oil to come 1 inch up the side of the pan
About 1 cup unbleached white flour
spread on a large plate or waxed paper
Sea salt
Thick wedges of lemon

Cut the squid into ¼-inch-thick rings and the tentacles into two or three pieces. Dry the squid thoroughly.

Heat the oil in a medium sauté pan over high heat. When the oil is hot, dip a few squid pieces in the flour and shake off the excess from each piece. Slip into the bubbling hot oil. Continue in this manner without crowding the pan. Cover with a splatter shield to protect from oil burns. When golden on one side, carefully turn over each piece and cook until the other side is golden.

Transfer the fried squid onto several layers of paper towels or brown kitchen paper to drain. Season with salt while hot. Serve immediately with lemon wedges.

BIG SAUTÉ OF TINY CLAMS AND MUSSELS

[*serves 4 to 6*]

PICTURE A ROCKY SCOGLIERA ON THE MEDITERRANEAN, A SEASIDE TRATTORIA PERCHED AMONG THE ROCKS. A MOUNTAIN OF TINY CLAMS AND SHINY MUSSELS ARRIVE IN A shallow pasta bowl, the shellfish emitting the briny fragrance of the sea situated right below your feet. Overhead, an awning shields you from the sun. The sea is sparkling, blindingly bright. Your pleasant task—to shell and devour every last clam and mussel set before you and drink up the juices from one of those huge Italian soup spoons.

3 pounds smallest Manila clams
3 pounds mussels
¼ cup extra-virgin olive oil
1 small onion, finely chopped
4 garlic cloves, finely chopped
Pinch of hot red pepper flakes
1 cup dry white wine
¼ cup chopped Italian parsley
Grindings of black pepper
Lemon wedges

Soak the clams in a basin of cold water. Lift them out, leaving behind the sand they release. Clean the sink and repeat the procedure two or three more times, or until no traces of grit remain in the sink.

Scrub the mussels well but gently under cold running water until the shells are clean and smooth. Gently slide the beard, or tuft of fibers imbedded in the shell, back and forth until it gives way. Or simply cut it off.

If using a terra-cotta braising pan, set a cast-iron heat diffuser on the burner of the stove since the terra-cotta will crack if placed directly on the burner. If not using a terra-cotta braising pan, the heat diffuser is not necessary.

Place the olive oil in a large braising pan of your choice.

Turn the heat to low and add the onion. Let it color lightly. Add the garlic and red pepper flakes, and sauté for a few more minutes.

Add the clams, mussels, and white wine. Turn the heat to high and cook until the shells

(CONTINUED)

are just beginning to open. Add the parsley and generous grindings of black pepper. Cover and cook until the shells are just open. Overcooking is ruinous for clams and mussels.

Ladle clams and mussels into individual bowls along with the juices. Have a large bowl at the table for all the empty shells. A plate of thick lemon wedges is almost always a welcome addition when seafood of any type is being served.

⁂

MAURO'S SOPHISTICATED CALAMARETTI "SOUP"

[*serves 4*]

NOT REALLY BROTHY LIKE OUR SOUPS, THIS HAS JUST A SMALL AMOUNT OF LIQUID IN THE FINISHED DISH, A WONDERFUL CONCENTRATION OF SEA ESSENCE. CHERRY TOMATOES are popular these days in Italy, so their presence signifies a dish that is up to the minute.

2 pounds very small squid, cleaned

3 garlic cloves, chopped

*A tiny bit of fresh finely diced hot red pepper
or small pinch of hot red pepper flakes*

3 tablespoons extra-virgin olive oil

½ cup dry white wine

3 cups fish broth, or spring or filtered water

Sea salt

*½ basket sweet, tender-skinned red cherry tomatoes,
or a combination of red and yellow, stemmed*

Coarsely chopped Italian parsley leaves for garnish

Thin slices country bread, grilled and rubbed with garlic (optional)

Wash the calamaretti well and let drain thoroughly.

Sauté the garlic and red pepper in olive oil in a medium braising pan over low heat for several minutes. Add the wine and let bubble over medium heat until reduced by half.

Add the calamaretti, stir to blend flavors, and let cook over medium-low heat for 5 minutes. Add the broth or water and salt to taste. Continue to cook over gentle heat.

A few minutes before the squid is tender, add the whole cherry tomatoes. Continue cooking without stirring so as not to crush the tomatoes, until the squid is done.

Ladle the calamaretti stew into shallow pasta bowls. There will be a small amount of broth. Garnish with parsley and serve. Serve with optional grilled bread on the side.

PESCE IN BRODO

[serves 2]

ANOTHER EXAMPLE OF POACHING FISH (SEE PAGE 155), ALTHOUGH THIS REQUIRES QUITE A BIT MORE WATER SINCE A WHOLE FISH IS BEING COOKED.

The pure-tasting fish broth is served as a first course with a handful of pastina cooked in the broth. The fish is the second course, flavors brightened by a light sprinkling of finely chopped Italian parsley and raw freshest garlic.

A drizzle of extra-virgin olive oil
8 to 10 cups spring water, or enough to barely cover the fish
¼ cup chopped Italian parsley
2 garlic cloves, finely chopped
2 tablespoons fresh lemon juice
Sea salt and grindings of black pepper
1 2-pound whole fish or 2 smaller whole fish each
weighing about 1 pound, such as red snapper or rock cod

THE PRIMO PIATTO
¼ cup small pastina, small pasta shapes for soup
A light sprinkling of chopped Italian parsley

THE SECONDO
Sea salt and freshly ground pepper
Extra-virgin olive oil
Finely chopped Italian parsley
Finely chopped garlic
Lemon wedges

Place everything except the fish in a braising pan large enough to contain the fish. Estimate the amount of water needed. Bring to a gentle simmer.

Add the fish. Check the water level to make sure the fish is just covered with water. Add more liquid if necessary. Cover and simmer for about 10 minutes.

Carefully turn the fish over and continue simmering until cooked, an additional 10 minutes. Remove the fish from the broth, set on a platter, and cover to keep fish warm.

(CONTINUED)

Strain the fish broth through a colander lined with several layers of dampened cheese-cloth. Bring the fish broth to a boil in a medium soup pot. Add the pastina and cook until tender but still slightly al dente. Drain, reserving the hot fish broth.

Divide the pasta betweeen two shallow soup bowls and ladle enough fish broth over the pasta to make a lightly brothy soup. Reserve remaining broth for another use such as a fish soup. Garnish the pastina with a little freshly chopped parsley. Serve without cheese.

For the *secondo,* place the whole fish on a serving platter or place the individual fish on two dinner plates. Season the fish with salt and black pepper to taste. Top with a drizzle of olive oil and a sprinkling of finely chopped parsley and garlic. Fillet the fish at the table. If serving two small fish, let each diner fillet his or her own. Serve with lemon wedges on the side.

❧

MIXED SEAFOOD SPIEDINI WITH LEMON LEAVES

[serves 4]

AN EASY, ATTRACTIVE WAY TO SERVE AN ASSORTMENT OF SEAFOOD. GRILLING ALWAYS DOES WONDERS FOR THE FLAVOR OF SO MANY CREATURES FROM THE SEA. HERE, THE seafood threaded on the *spiedini,* skewers, is interspersed with fresh lemon leaves or bay leaves and lemon slices to lend a wonderful perfume to the finished dish.

I think it was in Amalfi at a wonderful trattoria called Da Gemma that I tasted skewered calamari, or squid, intertwined with lemon leaves and cooked over hot coals. For those of you who have never smelled a fresh lemon leaf, you'll be amazed by its aromatic properties. Just tear a fresh leaf in half to release its aromatic oils, and smell deeply next to the torn edge.

1½ pounds cleaned squid

½ pound medium scallops, about 8

½ pound medium shrimp, unpeeled, about 8

½ pound swordfish, cut into 8 squares

Extra-virgin olive oil

Sea salt and grindings of black pepper

1 or 2 large lemon leaves or bay leaves per skewer,
each leaf torn into large fragments

1 lemon, thickly sliced

Lemon wedges

Rinse the squid thoroughly inside and out until perfectly clean. Cut the squid body so that it lays out in one flat piece, then cut into ½-inch strips. Cut the tentacles in half or thirds depending on size.

Combine the squid and remaining seafood in a bowl. Drizzle with olive oil and toss so that each piece is lightly coated. Season generously with salt and pepper. Let marinate for about 1 hour in a cool spot in the kitchen.

Using four metal skewers, or eight sturdy wooden skewers first soaked in water, begin threading the ingredients, alternating them so that each skewer gets its fair share, and placing a fragment of lemon leaf or bay leaf, and, more randomly, lemon slices, between the seafood pieces. To skewer the calamari, impale them on the skewer lengthwise and then push the strips together loosely like closing an accordian.

Baste the skewers with the olive oil marinade and season with salt and pepper.

Place the skewers over a hot grill or under the broiler, and using tongs, carefully turn them occasionally so that all sides are exposed to the heat. Baste the skewers as they cook. The seafood should cook about a total of 5 minutes or until all the components are cooked through but still tender.

If desired, place the skewers on a platter lined with a small spray of fresh lemon or bay leaves, and surround with lemon wedges.

Serve hot.

ZUPPA DI PESCE

[serves 4 to 6]

THIS IS A CLASSIC, BUT ONE THAT HAS VARIATIONS UP AND DOWN THE COAST OF ITALY. WE CAN PRODUCE A REALLY GREAT FISH SOUP WITH OUR OWN LOCAL FISH, AS LONG AS it is as fresh as possible.

Notice the soup is a bit spicy. I've used a pasilla pepper that has some of the qualities of the hot green peppers I've tasted in Puglia—spicy but not burning hot. If unavailable, substitute a pinch of hot red pepper flakes.

1 pound small Manila clams

1 pound mussels

½ pound cleaned squid

Extra-virgin olive oil

4 large garlic cloves, coarsely chopped

A few large green celery leaves, chopped

¼ pasilla pepper, seeded and diced,
or a pinch of hot red pepper flakes

4 ripe Roma plum tomatoes or 1 large red ripe
dense-fleshed tomato, peeled, seeded, and chopped to a puree

1 pound large shrimp, deveined, with shells left on

1 pound rock cod, cut into 2-inch dice

3½ cups fish broth (see page 84 or 169)

A little chopped Italian parsley

Sea salt

Clean the clams by soaking them several times in a basin of cold water. Let the sand settle to the bottom and after 15 minutes, lift the clams out of the water. Repeat the process until the water is free of grit. Throw away any clams that are open or have cracked shells.

Clean the mussels by scrubbing them well under cold running water. Tug off the beard, the tuft of fibers that are sometimes found imbedded in the side of the shells, or cut it away. Discard any mussels with open or cracked shells.

Wash the squid well inside and out. Cut the body sac into ¼-inch-thick rings. If small, leave tentacles whole, or, if larger, cut into two or three segments.

Choose a large glazed terra-cotta braising pan or any nonreactive metal braising pan. If using a terra-cotta pan, place a heat diffuser on the burner or the pan will crack.

Add enough olive oil to come ¼ inch up the side of the pan. Cook the olive oil, garlic, celery leaves, and the pasilla or red pepper flakes over low heat for several minutes. Add the fresh tomato puree and let simmer for about 5 minutes.

Add the clams, mussels, and shrimp. Cover and cook just until the shells of the mussels and clams open. Add the squid, fish, fish broth, and parsley. Cook briefly over low heat until the fish and squid are tender.

The shellfish and broth should provide enough salt. Taste the soup, and if needed, add salt to taste.

This *zuppa* is often served ladled over a piece of grilled bread, and in fact the word implies that the soup is served over bread. But I find the bread tends to soak up all the broth. I prefer experiencing the pure flavor of the broth here, but if you'd like, you can line the bottom of each serving bowl with a thin slice of grilled bread rubbed with a bit of raw garlic. Or serve the grilled bread on the side. Or simply serve with good rustic bread at the table, my top choice.

❧

"BROWN PAPER" SEAFOOD FRITTO MISTO

[*serves 4 to 6*]

MY FAVORITE FRITTO MISTO COMES FROM THE "SEA SHACK" ON THE IONIC COAST OF THE SALENTO WHERE I LOVE TO GO FOR SEAFOOD, AND SEAFOOD IS WHAT THIS PLACE is all about.

I truly do not know the name of the place. It is so unassuming, no sign advertises its name and no menu has ever been presented to me. The napkins are paper and the wine comes to your table in an old, not cute, pitcher. The tables are cement and the chairs anonymous. It is completely open-air in the sense that there is no indoor seating. When the weather changes, the place shuts down. There are big basins in back where the seafood is washed as it is brought in from the sea. In fact, mussel beds lie just below the shack, on the rocky coast.

Anything I order here is fresh and wonderful. And the prices are ridiculously low. You can really have a seafood feast without even putting a dent in your budget.

The *fritto misto* is hot and crispy, always accompanied by a good-sized bowl of enormous chunks of home-grown lemons, enough to satisfy the most ardent lover of lemon on their seafood. The perfect accompaniment is cool white wine and nothing else.

½ pound shrimp, preferably with
their heads still on, deveined but in the shell
½ pound medium sea scallops, tough muscle removed
½ pound cleaned small squid, cut into ¼-inch rings
½ pound firm white fish, cut into small squares
Unbleached all-purpose flour
Extra-virgin olive oil
Sea salt
Thick lemon wedges

Rinse the seafood and dry it well on kitchen paper or clean kitchen towels.

Pile enough flour on a large dinner plate to create a mound.

Pour in enough oil to come about 3 inches up the side of a heavy medium braising pan. Heat the oil to 375 degrees.

Quickly dip a handful of seafood at a time into the flour. Place in a fine sieve and gently shake off the excess. Slip the pieces into the oil (if the oil bubbles rapidly the temperature is correct). With a metal spoon, move the seafood in the oil to disperse it evenly, turning the pieces so they color uniformly. When golden, use a slotted spoon to transfer the seafood to a thick stack of paper towels to drain, first letting excess oil drain back into the pan. Season with salt while the seafood is very hot. Keep warm but uncovered while cooking the remaining seafood.

Serve on a platter lined with brown kitchen paper or napkins. Accompany with lemon wedges. A cantaloupe cut into wedges makes the ideal dessert.

CARNE E POLLAME
meat and poultry

A PLATE OF PROSCIUTTO FOR DINNER

[serves 1]

IT HAS BEEN A NUMBER OF YEARS NOW THAT WE'VE BEEN ABLE TO EXPERIENCE THE PLEASURE OF REAL ITALIAN PROSCIUTTO—BEFORE, IT WAS RATHER INEXPLICABLY denied entry into America.

A plate of choice prosciutto and a small green salad, on a separate plate, makes a superb dinner for one. Or two or three, or more for that matter.

A trattoria near my home in San Francisco seems to have a direct pipeline to the best prosciutto this side of the Mediterranean. Good prosciutto must not be dark or dried out; it must be sliced expertly, not too thick or it becomes tough, and not too thin or it ends up in tatters no matter how gently it is handled. It should be primarily lean, not veined with excessive fat; and the fat left around the circumference should be meltingly soft and white.

The two types of prosciutto available: Parma prosciutto, sweet and buttery, is lightly veined with creamy white fat; San Daniele, which is more full-flavored, is leaner but still moist and tender when it is at its peak of perfection.

The best way to serve prosciutto is on its own separate plate, with the slices just barely overlapping. No condiments are needed. Simple fresh rustic bread, or bruschetta, slices of grilled bread rubbed with raw garlic and drizzled with olive oil, complete the picture.

6 to 8 slices imported Italian prosciutto for a single serving
Rustic bread or bruschetta (see above)
Salad of tender greens, mixed sweet and bitter
(see below)

(CONTINUED)

Purchase prosciutto *crudo*, raw-cured, as opposed to prosciutto *cotto*, which is cooked ham. Plan to use it the same day, if possible. Keep it tightly wrapped until just before serving. The flavors are more pronounced if the prosciutto is served at room temperature, so remove the package, if refrigerated, at least a half hour before serving.

Arrange on an individual plate, barely overlapping the slices. The entire plate should be covered with gorgeous slices of rosy pink prosciutto. Serve with either of the breads suggested above.

Follow with a simple salad. My current favorite comes from the garden—radish thinnings with leaves and tiny radishes, and rustic arugula, both from my garden, mixed with the crisp, green leaves of an incredible variety of Italian butter lettuce grown by my generous San Francisco neighbor, Signor Giovanni.

Please, no balsamic vinegar on this and most salads. It completely overpowers the lovely flavors of the salad greens. Simply dress with extra-virgin olive oil, sea salt, and a few drops of lemon.

Cena

DINNER

DINNER IN ITALY IS A MUCH MORE SUBDUED AFFAIR THAN PRANZO, LUNCH. ALTHOUGH TIMES are changing, historically dinner was a light meal, and it continues to have a lesser importance than the midday meal. Eating dinner out in Italy may offer a skewed version of this very important piece of the puzzle of Italians and how they really eat. And here, I'm talking about how Italians eat at home.

I'll never forget my surprise on that fateful first trip to Italy when I was twelve, visiting my father's relatives in the small town of Bompietro in the Madonie mountains of Sicily. We dined with my father's elderly cousins. The meal seemed so meager, as though it had been a careless afterthought. Just a bit of this and that placed on the dining table. A cooked vegetable, a salad, a bit of frittata or boiled eggs, a small plate of cheeses—I can't recall all the specifics but it was not the abundant meal I was used to in America. It seemed strange to me, coming as I did from the land of excess. Later, I came to realize that this was the customary way of eating dinner in Italy. Since the main meal was at midday, dinner was the equivalent of the amount of food we might eat for lunch here in America.

Cena reflects a winding down of the fueling of our bodies. It should provide just enough food to take one through the rest of the evening, since the workday has come to a conclusion.

Cena is served at about nine o'clock or a bit later, when the second half of the workday has ended. In the dog days of summer, dinner might not be served until ten or sometimes even later while Italians wait for a hint of cool breeze to bring on an appetite.

Back at home, we might want to put into practice the concept of eating light at night. Here in America, as obsessed with dieting and weight loss as we are, we sadly suffer from the extreme problem of an overweight population. A light evening meal offers a sensible step toward achieving a normal weight.

Naturally, this light evening meal only makes sense as a healthful style of eating if you've had an adequate amount of food at midday. Once you've figured out how to accomplish this (see page 63 for an essay on "A Civilized Lunch During the Workday"), then a light evening meal is really the ideal. See the menus at the back of the book for examples of what you might serve for a light evening meal.

After dinner, especially during the months of summer, a *passeggiata* is in order—a long, leisurely stroll through town with no particular destination in mind. Except possibly a certain special *gelateria* that makes its own ice cream, since what could be more Italian than a final gelato to end a hot summer day!

So, keep it light at night and see how much better you feel in the morning, energetic and ready for a caffè latte and biscotti or piece of bread to send you out into the world to begin a new day.

LIGHTLY BREADED CHICKEN SCALOPPINE

[serves 4]

THIS SIMPLE BUT EXTREMELY FLAVORFUL WAY OF COOKING CHICKEN IS A STAPLE IN MOST ITALIAN HOUSEHOLDS. THE TWO IMPORTANT ASPECTS TO PROPERLY PREPARING scaloppine—cutlets—are: make sure the raw chicken is very thin and of uniform thickness; and perform the simple task of making bread crumbs at home with dried high-quality rustic bread. Packaged so-called seasoned—or unseasoned, for that matter—bread crumbs are full of additives and preservatives that mar the delicate flavor of the chicken; all you taste are the jarring flavors of stale dried herbs and a slight rancidity.

When done correctly, with truly fresh ingredients, this is one of the finest ways of preparing chicken breast I know since the bread crumbs and egg protect the delicate meat from toughening.

2 eggs, preferably organic and free-range

*1 cup homemade bread crumbs (dried bread reduced to crumbs
in a mortar, hand-cranked cheese grater, or food processor)*

Sea salt

Extra-virgin olive oil for frying

*2 whole chicken breasts, preferably free-range, split,
skinned, boned, butterflied, and gently pounded to an
even ¼-inch thickness (ask your butcher to do this)*

Grindings of black pepper

Lemon wedges

Lightly beat the eggs in a shallow bowl. Season the bread crumbs with salt. Mound the bread crumbs on a dinner plate. Pour enough olive oil to measure ¼ inch up the side of a large sauté pan. Heat the olive oil until hot but not smoking. Dip one chicken breast at a time, first in the egg, letting excess drip back into bowl, and then in the bread crumbs, shaking off excess.

Sauté the chicken in the bubbling hot oil until golden on both sides, 4 to 5 minutes per side. Drain well on kitchen paper. Season with salt while the scaloppine are hot. Add a grinding of pepper if desired.

Serve hot, warm, or at room temperature, with lemon wedges on the side.

GRILLED GAME HENS AL MATTONE

[serves 4]

CRISP, DEEP GOLDEN BROWN SKIN AND MOIST, TENDER FLESH RESULT WHEN COOKING CHICKEN UNDER A HEAVY WEIGHT, SUCH AS BRICKS. THE KEY HERE IS OPENING UP THE chicken flat so that it cooks quickly and evenly.

For home cooks, I've found that using fresh Cornish hens is a bit more manageable. The flesh, which is richer than that of chicken, holds up quite well against the rigors of intense heat. The recipe below is for the smaller creatures, but a whole large chicken done in this manner and successfully prepared is also quite a feast for the eyes and taste buds.

4 fresh Cornish hens, split lengthwise through
the breast bone and opened flat (easy to do, but I prefer
asking the butcher to perform such tasks)
Extra-virgin olive oil
Sea salt
Generous grindings of black pepper
Thick lemon wedges

The hens can be cooked on an outdoor grill, on a cast-iron ridged stovetop grill, or even in a very hot oven. Create a very hot medium in which to cook the hens.

Season the hens on both sides with extra-virgin olive oil and a generous sprinkling of salt. Lay the game hens, flattened open and skin side up, on the grill. Weight down the hens with anything you can think of that is heavy and heat-resistant: a baking stone, clean large bricks, or a heavy cast-iron skillet, the bottom wrapped in heavy foil, filled with cans.

Cook for approximately 10 minutes. Turn the hens over and replace the weights. Cook for about 10 minutes more. The hens should be dark brown and crusty, and cooked through, but very juicy and tender. Adjust cooking times as needed.

Off the heat, season the hens again with salt and an abundance of black pepper. Serve with lemon wedges.

SIGNORA PANTELLA'S POLLO IN UMIDO

[*serves 4 to 6*]

SMALL CHUNKS OF CHICKEN ON THE BONE, YELLOW POTATOES CUT INTO SMALL DICE, AND AN ABUNDANCE OF FLAVORFUL, LIGHTLY SPICY AND NICELY THIN JUICES MAKE this braised dish distinctive. What might normally be considered hearty or heavy, in the hands of Signora Pantella becomes exquisitely delicate.

A fresh bay leaf adds its special perfume hinting of vanilla and lemon.

6 small Yukon Gold potatoes or other yellow-fleshed variety (about 1 pound)
5 tablespoons extra-virgin olive oil
1 3½-pound free-range chicken, cut up (see Note)
Sea salt and freshly ground black pepper
¼ cup dry white wine
1 medium onion, cut into small dice
1 28-ounce can peeled whole tomatoes, preferably San Marzano
¼ teaspoon hot red pepper flakes
1 fresh bay leaf, torn in half
½ cup spring or filtered water

Cook the potatoes in salted boiling water to cover. When al dente, drain. Peel when cool enough to handle.

Place 2 tablespoons of olive oil in a large frying pan. Lightly brown the chicken pieces over medium heat just a few minutes on each side to seal in the juices. Don't crowd the pan. It is better to do it in two or three batches depending on the size of the pan. Transfer the chicken pieces to a platter, season well with salt and pepper, and keep warm.

Drain off the fat from the pan and return it to the stove. Add the wine and over low heat, stir to scrape up any browned particles stuck to the bottom of the pan. Add the remaining olive oil and the diced onion. Sauté over medium-low heat until the onion is tender.

Using a slotted spoon, lift the tomatoes out of the juices in the can and add to the pan. Reserve the juices for another use.

Use a knife and fork to cut the tomatoes into small pieces in the pan. Add the red pepper flakes and bay leaf. Season with salt and pepper. Cook for about 5 minutes over medium heat.

Add the chicken pieces to the pan, spoon the light tomato sauce over the chicken, and add ½ cup water. Cover and cook for about 20 minutes.

Cut the potatoes into ½-inch dice. Add to the chicken and stir gently to combine, spooning juices over the potatoes. Cook for about 5 minutes, or until the potatoes are tender but still hold their shape. The juices should be rather thin. Add more water, a little at a time, as needed.

Let rest for a few minutes. Serve in shallow pasta bowls, dividing the juices among the bowls.

NOTE: The chicken needs to be cut into small pieces before cooking. Ask your butcher to cut each breast into three pieces, to divide the drumstick and thigh, and to cut each thigh in half. Reserve wings and back for broth.

❧

BEEF TAGLIATA WITH BABY ARTICHOKES

[*serves 6*]

SCALLOPS OF BEEF LOIN—POUNDED THIN AND COOKED IN A FLASH IN A RED-HOT SKILLET— REQUIRE ONLY A DRIZZLE OF RAW EXTRA-VIRGIN OLIVE OIL AND A SPRINKLING OF SEA salt for seasoning, and perhaps a few drops of juice from a fresh, fragrant lemon.

But the variations are many. Sometimes a simple topping of chopped herbs and olive oil is brushed over the seared meat. A warm spoonful of fresh tomato sauce with hot red pepper takes it in a slightly different, but equally delicious, direction. Seasonal vegetables, thinly sliced and quickly sautéed, make for a superb finishing touch—asparagus, flavorful mushroom varieties, and small artichokes are especially well suited to the flavor of beef.

In the following recipe, trimmed artichoke slivers sautéed in that dynamic duo, Italian parsley and garlic, make an unbeatable topping for the beef scallops.

1 small juicy lemon, cut in half
12 baby artichokes
3 tablespoons extra-virgin olive oil plus a little extra
3 garlic cloves, chopped
¼ cup chopped Italian parsley
Sea salt and grindings of black pepper
2 pounds beef tenderloin, trimmed of all fat and sinew,
each cut into 3-ounce medallions and pounded to approximately ¼-inch
thickness (a good butcher will make fast work of this)
Lemon wedges

(CONTINUED)

Fill a large bowl with cold water. Squeeze in the juice of the lemon and throw in the rinds.

Trim the artichokes of the tough outer leaves until only the pale green ones remain. Cut off the top third of each artichoke. Trim any dark areas from the base. Use a paring knife to strip off the tough fibers from the stem but leave the stem attached. As you finish each artichoke, plunge it into the lemon water to prevent discoloration. Top with a clean wet dishcloth to seal off air.

Heat the olive oil in a medium skillet over low heat. Add the garlic and cook for a minute or two, then add the parsley and stir. Cook for several minutes.

Meanwhile, drain the artichokes well. Thinly sliver the artichokes lengthwise. Toss the slivers into the sauté pan. Raise the heat to medium, season with salt and pepper, and cook the artichokes for several minutes, stirring often, until they are tender and a little golden along the edges, about 5 minutes. Set aside, and keep warm.

Warm a heavy skillet over high heat. Very lightly oil the pan with a clean kitchen cloth dipped in a bit of olive oil. There should be no excess oil in the pan or the meat won't brown properly.

Sear the beef scallops quickly on each side, a minute or so, just until the outsides of the scallops turn lightly brown. As each one is cooked, quickly place the cooked beef scallop on a platter, season with salt and pepper, and keep warm.

When all the meat is cooked, spoon the artichokes and any juices over the top. Serve with lemon wedges on the side.

SEARED PAPER-THIN BEEF SCALOPPINE

[serves 4]

SLICED TO A PAPER THINNESS AND CUT FROM THE TOP ROUND, THIS IS MORE OFTEN THAN NOT COOKED IN THE SAME WAY AS THE RECIPE FOR CHICKEN SCALOPPINE (PAGE 178), and it is delicious cooked in that manner. But I also like to quickly sear this larger, thinner slice of meat in a hot skillet using the same technique employed for Beef Tagliata (page 181).

As with tagliata, there is no time to walk away from the stove since the cooking is lightning fast. Count five seconds on each side and it is done. I prefer this simple, flavorful beef scaloppine served on its own, with sea salt, grindings of black pepper, and a bit of lemon.

But as with tagliata, a few pinches of a finely chopped herb—parsley, rosemary, basil, winter savory, or Italian oregano—and a touch of very finely chopped raw garlic are delicious additions. Or, for a spicy touch, try a few drops of Hot Red Pepper Olive Oil (page 77).

The scaloppine can also be added to a plate of pasta and fresh tomato sauce for a discreet protein boost; quickly cut the seared meat into strips and toss with the pasta.

1½ pounds top round, sliced paper-thin
Extra-virgin olive oil
Sea salt and grindings of pepper
Lemon wedges
Hot Red Pepper Oil (optional)

Lightly brush the beef slices with olive oil and season with salt and pepper.

Heat a large, very heavy skillet, preferably of cast-iron. Oil the skillet with a clean kitchen towel dipped in a bit of olive oil. It should be enough to just coat the bottom and there should be no excess oil.

Place a scaloppine or two, depending on the size of the meat and the pan, in the red-hot skillet. Count about 5 seconds, flip the beef over, and count to 5 again. Transfer the meat to a platter. Season lightly with additional salt and pepper. Keep warm and continue cooking the remainder of the scaloppine.

Serve with lemon wedges and a drizzle of spicy or plain olive oil, if desired.

BOLLITO DI MANZO
WITH GIARDINIERA SAUCE

[makes 4 to 6 servings of boiled beef and about 6 cups of beef broth]

I'VE ALWAYS LOVED THE IDEA OF BOILED BEEF BUT FOUND THE RESULTS TO BE RATHER DISMAL—GRAY AND TOUGH INSTEAD OF SUCCULENT AND TENDER.

But I didn't want to give up on it because, first of all, I am a big fan of good beef broth. When you boil a nice chunk of beef, even if the beef itself is disappointing, the broth never is. But also, I knew that it was possible to get the beef right.

In this recipe, you'll find that the beef is every bit as good as the broth. Serve the sliced beef hot, topped with a spoonful of colorful Giardiniera Sauce (a recipe follows). Once the beef cools, it can dry out and toughen. See recipe directions for keeping cooled beef tender.

2 quarts spring or filtered water
1 medium onion, peeled but whole
1 sweet medium carrot, peeled
1 celery stalk with many green leaves on top
1 small whole tomato
1 peeled potato (see Note)
5 sprigs Italian parsley with stems
3½ to 4 pounds beef brisket or beef chuck
Sea salt
Giardiniera Sauce (recipe follows)

Place the water and all the vegetables and parsley in a large stockpot and bring to a boil. Cook for 15 minutes to begin flavoring the broth.

Add the meat (it should be covered with water by about 2 inches), put a lid on, and bring to a boil over high heat. Skim off impurities that rise to the surface. Adjust heat to a gentle simmer. Cook beef for about an hour, then add a generous amount of salt, a tablespoon or two, depending on your personal preference. Cook an additional 1½ hours or longer, depending on the thickness of the meat. The beef is done when it is fork-tender.

Remove the meat from the broth. Let it rest a few minutes, then slice thinly. Serve with a piquant cold sauce such as the one in the recipe that follows. (If serving the beef later, thinly slice it while warm and generously dress with olive oil, salt, and pepper. Otherwise, the meat will become tough and dry.)

To serve the broth, first strain out all the vegetables. Cook a handful of pastina in the broth and serve with grated cheese. Or refrigerate and reserve broth for another meal.

NOTE: The potato is added to absorb some of the fat from the meat. The same technique is applied when making Hen Broth (page 85).

GIARDINIERA SAUCE

[*makes about 2 cups*]

THIS COLORFUL, TANGY SAUCE IS A FINELY CHOPPED MIX OF VEGETABLES PRESERVED IN VINEGAR, CALLED GIARDINIERA, AND OTHER PIQUANT CONDIMENTS AND FRESH HERBS. It is easy to put together and adds a nice jolt of flavor and color to the beef. It is also delicious on chicken, poached fish, and as a spread for sandwiches. But I like it best with the beef.

For a less vinegary and piquant sauce, stir in some very finely diced cucumber, first peeled and seeded. A hothouse cucumber or one from a farmers' market are the best choices.

1 16-ounce jar mild giardiniera (pickled vegetables),
without preservatives if possible, drained, rinsed, and finely chopped
2 heaping tablespoons capers, drained and coarsely chopped
¼ cup extra-virgin olive oil
¼ cup lemon juice, preferably from an
organic lemon, and the zest of the lemon
¼ small red onion, very finely diced (about ¼ cup)
Sea salt and grindings of black pepper
½ cup tightly packed finely chopped Italian parsley leaves
Chopped basil leaves in summer

Stir all the ingredients except the parsley and basil together in a small serving bowl. Just before serving, add the fresh herbs. Taste and correct seasonings.

LAMB SPIEDINI

[*serves 4*]

MORSELS OF HERBED LAMB GRILLED ON A SKEWER ARE VERY PRIMITIVE IN FEELING, WITH THE TASTE OF THE GRILL PERFUMING THE LAMB. NOT QUITE AS PRIMEVAL, BUT STILL delicious, is simply broiling the skewered meat.

The skewers can be served with a few fresh radishes and crisp, light yellow, inner leaves of escarole for a palate-freshening foil to the richness of the meat.

2 tablespoons extra-virgin olive oil
2 tablespoons very finely chopped herbs
(a mix of fresh thyme, marjoram, rosemary, and sage)
1½ pounds leg of lamb, cut into 1-inch cubes
Sea salt and grindings of black pepper
Lemon wedges

Combine the olive oil and herbs in a bowl. Stir the meat cubes in the herb mixture, seasoning with salt to taste. Let marinate for at least an hour.

Fire up the grill until medium-hot or turn on the broiler. Thread the meat cubes on metal skewers or sturdy wooden skewers (if using wood, first soak them in water).

Grill the skewers for 8 to 10 minutes, turning them regularly to brown all sides. Grind pepper over the meat. Serve with lemon wedges on the side. If desired, accompany with a small undressed salad such as the one described above.

LAMB AND POTATO TIELLA

[*serves 4*]

ANOTHER OF THOSE RUSTIC CASSEROLE-TYPE DISHES THAT REQUIRE LITTLE EFFORT
AND COME OUT TASTING SO DEEPLY SATISFYING.

1 pound leg of lamb, cut into 1-inch dice
Sea salt and grindings of black pepper
1 tablespoon chopped rosemary leaves
Extra-virgin olive oil
1½ pounds (about 4 medium) Yukon Gold
potatoes, peeled and thinly sliced
1 medium onion, cut in half through
the root end and thinly slivered
12 ripe, sweet, cherry tomatoes, quartered
3 garlic cloves, chopped
½ cup white wine
1 cup bread crumbs, homemade from dried
rustic bread, and unseasoned

Heat the oven to 375 degrees.

Season the lamb with salt and pepper. Add the rosemary and a tablespoon or two of olive oil and toss.

Lightly oil a medium gratin dish, preferably of glazed terra-cotta. Place one third of the sliced potatoes on the bottom and season with salt. Toss together the onion, tomatoes, and garlic. Moisten with a bit of olive oil and season with salt. Spread the mixture over the potato slices.

Distribute the lamb and its marinade evenly over the vegetables. Sprinkle the wine over the top. Arrange the remaining potatoes over the top, seasoning the potatoes with salt and pepper. Drizzle the potatoes lightly with olive oil. Top the potato slices evenly with the bread crumbs and drizzle generously with olive oil.

Cover the baking dish with foil. Bake for 30 minutes. Uncover, raise the heat to 425 degrees, and bake for an additional 30 minutes or until the potatoes and meat are tender and the bread crumbs are evenly browned.

ROASTED LEG OF LAMB WITH
ARTICHOKES, POTATOES, AND "WILD" MINT

[serves 6 to 8]

NOTHING MAKES A MORE APPROPRIATE DISH FOR AN EASTER DINNER THAN A MAGNIF-
ICENT ROASTED LEG OF LAMB. WITH SEASONAL ARTICHOKES AND GOLDEN POTATOES
baking alongside the lamb, most of the meal is basically cooked in one dish.

Wild mint would be a wonderful seasoning—its strongly aromatic properties, at once earthy and sharply sweet, make a good foil for the richness of lamb. Since it is not available here, I substitute a combination of fresh mint and dried Italian oregano, which helps repro-duce the complexity of the wild herb.

I've used a boned leg of lamb, which is so much easier to serve and cooks more evenly.

1 boned leg of lamb (about 5 pounds)
Sea salt and grindings of black pepper
1 bunch fresh spearmint leaves, chopped
1 heaping teaspoon dried Italian oregano
¼ cup chopped garlic
Juice of 2 lemons
¼ cup olive oil
1 cup spring or filtered water
8 baby artichokes, cleaned, trimmed, quartered,
and kept in lemon water to cover
10 small Yukon Gold potatoes

Heat the oven to 450 degrees.

Lay out the lamb flat. Season both sides of the meat with a generous amount of salt and pepper. Combine the mint, oregano, and garlic and press into both sides of the meat, cov-ering all surfaces. With the lamb still flat on the work surface, tie the meat with string as you would tie up a boxed package, wrapping it several times around its width and once around the length; this helps the meat hold its shape while cooking. Place in a roasting pan. Pour the lemon juice over the top and drizzle with 2 tablespoons of the olive oil.

Place the lamb in the oven and lower the temperature to 400 degrees. Roast for 30 minutes. Add the cup of water, lower the temperature to 350 degrees, and roast for another 30 min utes.

Drain the artichokes well. Toss the artichokes and potatoes in the remaining olive oil and season with salt. Arrange the vegetables alongside the lamb.

Continue roasting the lamb with the vegetables for about 30 minutes more or until a meat thermometer reads from 147 to 150 degrees for medium-rare with pink juices to 160 to 165 degrees for tender well-done with golden juices, and the vegetables are cooked. Let the meat rest outside the oven for 10 minutes before slicing.

Transfer the cooking juices from the pan. Heat the juices and pour over the sliced meat. Serve the lamb slices with the whole potatoes and artichoke slices. Correct seasonings.

❧

PINWHEEL SAUSAGES WITH SMALL TANGY SALAD

[serves 4]

IN THE ITALIAN NEIGHBORHOOD OF NORTH BEACH HERE IN SAN FRANCISCO, A SPECIAL BUTCHER SHOP IS THE SPOT FOR ITALIAN-STYLE CUTS OF MEAT AND SAUSAGES. FOR this recipe, I've used their Sicilian sausages, which the butchers season with white wine and fennel seeds. The sausages are neatly displayed in very slender one-pound coils. They remind me of a firework we used to hammer to a tree, light with a match, and watch spin wildly in fiery swirls.

Although it looked magnificent, this is not the cooking method I would propose for the sausages! Instead, a simple flat griddle or cast-iron pan works best. And if you have them available, throw in a few big fresh bay leaves.

As with all rich meats, I strongly suggest serving the sausages with a touch of green—some tangy leaves of arugula and tender radishes, a few inner leaves of endive or escarole, and a handful of tender celery leaves—to cut the richness of the meat and add a cleansing note.

2 1-pound coils of fresh, handcrafted slender
sausages purchased from a high-quality butcher

Salad greens, including any of the ones
suggested above, just a small handful per plate

Lemon wedges

Unroll each coil. Pinch the casing at the halfway point to separate the sausage into two equal pieces. Roll two small half-pound coils from each 1-pound coil. Or ask your butcher to perform this task.

(CONTINUED)

Heat a griddle or a heavy cast-iron pan to medium heat. Make sure the pan does not get too hot. Do not add any oil or other fats to the pan.

Cook the sausage coils on both sides for 4½ minutes per side, turning them over with a metal spatula. They should be thoroughly cooked and golden. (Cooking times will vary depending on the thickness of the sausages you purchase. Ask your butcher how long to cook the sausages you buy.) Do not prick the sausages while they cook or all the juices will escape.

Place a few tangy salad greens on individual plates. Place a coil of sausage next to the greens. Accompany with lemon wedges.

❧

BRAISED DANDELION GREENS
FLAVORED WITH LEAN PORK RIBS

[*serves 4*]

A RUSTIC DISH PREPARED BY SIGNORA PANTELLA. THE DANDELION GREENS COOK WITH A BIT OF PORK TO FLAVOR THE GREENS AND MAKE THE VEGETABLE DISH MORE SUBSTANTIAL.

The variety of greens she used is not available here, but dandelion greens make a superb substitute. Also, the fat must be trimmed from the pork ribs to produce the correct effect; the finished dish should be deeply flavorful but not in the least bit greasy or fatty.

⅓ pound meaty pork ribs, cut into 1-inch pieces
and trimmed of fat (ask your butcher to do this for you)
1 tablespoon extra-virgin olive oil
½ teaspoon hot red pepper flakes
Sea salt
1 cup spring or filtered water, or more as needed
1½ pounds dandelion greens, trimmed of any tough stems,
leaves cut crosswise into thick strips
Lemon juice to taste

Sauté the pork rib pieces in the olive oil and red pepper flakes in a medium soup pot until all traces of rawness on the surface of the meat are gone. Season with salt. Add the water and cook at a simmer for 30 minutes, with the lid partially covering the pot.

Add the greens to the pot and add salt to taste. When the greens have wilted somewhat, gently stir together the greens and pork rib pieces. Stir only once or twice during cooking; too much jostling in the pan will cause the meat to detach from the bones.

Simmer until the greens are tender and just a small amount of juices remains in the bottom of the pan, 8 to 10 minutes for tender greens. If needed, add more water to the pot until greens are cooked.

Squeeze in a little lemon juice to taste just before serving.

❧

ROAST PORK WITH WILD FENNEL

[serves 6 to 8]

PORK HAS A RICH, SWEET FLAVOR THAT REQUIRES STRONG FLAVORS TO STAND UP TO IT. HERBS, BOTH WILD AND CULTIVATED, ARE USED IN THIS RECIPE—A LARGE AMOUNT of chopped wild fennel, and smaller amounts of fresh rosemary and garlic—to create an extraordinary pork roast.

1 tablespoon chopped rosemary leaves
1 heaping tablespoon chopped garlic
⅔ cup chopped wild fennel tops and tender stems
(if unavailable, use 2 heaping tablespoons fennel seeds, coarsely ground)
Sea salt and grindings of black pepper
1 boned pork rib roast (about 4 pounds)
Extra-virgin olive oil

Heat the oven to 350 degrees.

Combine the rosemary, garlic, and wild fennel or fennel seeds. Season the herb mixture generously with salt and abundant grindings of pepper. Spread open the pork roast. Spread the herb mixture evenly over the meat, reserving about a tablespoon of the herbs.

Roll up the roast so that the white meat is in the center and the darker meat on the outside and tie it into a snug package. Rub the exterior of the meat with the remaining herb paste. Rub olive oil onto the surface of the exterior of the pork.

Roast the pork, uncovered, for about 2 hours or until it registers 170 degrees on a meat thermometer. While the roast cooks, baste it occasionally with its own juices.

Remove the roast from the oven and let rest for 10 minutes. Cut it into ½-inch-thick slices. Serve the pork with a bit of the pan juices. The pork, sliced a little thinner, is also delicious as a filling for panini.

{ A Bowl of Fruit }

THIS IS THE PRINCIPLE "DESSERT" SERVED AFTER MEALS IN ITALY, WHETHER IT IS A fancy dinner or a simple panino. It is as intrinsic a part of the meal as the meat or fish, as the pasta, the vegetables, or whatever else comes before it. It is the ideal, the quintessential nondessert dessert, the final refreshing taste in your mouth at the end of the meal before the final, final flavor—the espresso.

The bowl of fruit can be as simple as one type of seasonal fruit, such as fresh cherries, shiny and sweet, or it can be a mix of the best of the season—peaches and plums and other fruits that look particularly prime at the market.

A single fruit can also be slightly embellished. Peaches are sometimes sliced into the final few inches of red wine left in your wineglass. Strawberries might be flavored with a bit of lemon juice and sugar and left to macerate for a while in a cool spot. A splash of Maraschino liqueur can intensify fruit flavors without intruding upon them. For the most part, if a fruit is truly ripe and ready to go, nothing is needed to augment the flavor.

Don't refrigerate most fruits as this impairs their flavor and texture. The exception are melons. Watermelon, especially, is delicious served nice and cold—the perfect summertime refresher given its high water content, hence the name.

In Italy, fruit is served on a plate with utensils to help with the task of eating. For example, one peels one's apple before eating. Of course, oranges are peeled, and with practice, you, too, can remove the peel in one continuous ribbon when you become handy with your knife. Italians always peel figs before eating: two reasons for this that I've heard are (1) you can choke on the peel, and (2) it's always been done that way. I could add another reason which may sound a little frivolous but . . . the skin sticks to your teeth!

Italians devour enormous amounts of fruit. I personally witnessed an individual devouring twenty figs, one after another, as he plucked them from a tree loaded with fruit, first meticulously depriving each fig of its peel and cutting away the soft, cushiony pith with a small pocketknife.

I've seen this sort of thing often, such as the enormous wedges of watermelon, practically the size of half a watermelon each, being consumed at one sitting, the fruit offering of a particular trattoria on a certain summer day. In fact, I was one of those people on that summer day in that sweltering trattoria, osteria really, wielding my knife and fork until every deep reddish pink fragment of watermelon vanished.

In Italian restaurants one often sees fruit served in a bowl of water with a few ice cubes. This gives the fruit a slightly cool edge without refrigeration, which, as noted, can compromise the texture. It is a pleasure to eat this barely cool fruit on a warm day—and a wonderful way to cleanse the palate after a meal.

Always have fruit in your home: it promotes health, the sweet juices bring closure to a meal, the blushing colors bring pleasure. Fruit is probably the greatest edible gift we have from nature.

SOPRATAVOLA

SOPRATAVOLA LITERALLY MEANS ON THE TABLE. AND IT IS AT THE CENTER OF THE TABLE THAT A BOWL OF FRUIT IS OFTEN PROMINENTLY DISPLAYED. IN SOUTHERN ITALY, and most famously in Puglia, after-dinner fruit is often accompanied by a complementary raw vegetable. At first, this notion may sound strange to you. But it is in the eating that you understand the rightness of the offering.

Of course, not just any vegetable and fruit combination works. Certain raw vegetables are known to aid digestion; some have a high water content, refreshing in summer and serving to rehydrate bodies that have lost moisture through perspiration; others are naturally sweet and the sense of pairing them with fruit is inherent.

The following three combinations work well together—with a seasonal component to them. Serve with a knife and fork to perform the necessary peeling where appropriate.

In the Salento, the cucumbers served at the end of the meal are a bit different from ours in flavor and very different in appearance. These small, round cucumbers have a very slight melon flavor. But our cucumbers, when fresh and crisp and not overgrown and bitter, make a fine substitute.

- *In fall and winter, serve a basket of unpeeled oranges and tangerines, and wedges of trimmed raw fennel bulbs.*

- *A summer offering might be a platter of melon slices, such as cantaloupe or green honeydew, unpeeled figs, and peeled cucumber wedges.*

- *In autumn, serve small grape clusters, pomegranates cut in half, and tenderest inner celery stalks with leaves.*

SAVOIARDI

LADYFINGERS

[*makes about 18 cookies*]

IF YOU'VE HAD ONLY PACKAGED LADYFINGERS, YOU'LL BE AMAZED BY THESE TENDER, CRISP STRIPS OF COOKIE. NOT TOO SWEET, THEY GO WELL WITH AN ESPRESSO.

Unsalted butter and unbleached flour for baking sheets
½ cup unbleached all-purpose flour
¼ cup potato starch
Pinch of salt
4 eggs, warmed to room temperature
½ cup granulated sugar
1 teaspoon vanilla extract
Zest of 1 orange, preferably organic
Confectioners' sugar

Heat the oven to 400 degrees. Butter and lightly flour two baking sheets.

Stir together the flour, potato starch, and salt in a bowl.

Separate the egg yolks from the whites. In another bowl, beat together the egg yolks and 2 tablespoons of the granulated sugar until the mixture is pale yellow, thick, and creamy. Stir in the vanilla and orange zest.

In another bowl, beat the egg whites until foamy, then gradually beat in the remaining 6 tablespoons granulated sugar until the whites are glossy and hold stiff peaks.

Gently fold one quarter of the egg yolk mixture into the beaten egg whites. Then, alternating, gradually fold in half of the flour, the rest of the egg yolk mixture, and then the rest of the flour. The batter should be light and fluffy.

Spoon the batter into a pastry bag in which you have inserted a ½-inch plain tip. Pipe 4-inch-long strips of batter about 1 inch apart on the baking sheets. Sift a generous amount of confectioners' sugar over the tops of the cookies.

Bake for 8 to 10 minutes or until the cookies are golden. Remove the cookies from the baking sheets, transferring them to a cooling rack. Lower the oven temperature to 275 degrees. When the oven and cookies have cooled, place the cookies back on the baking sheets and bake an additional 10 minutes or until crisp.

Ladyfingers keep well in an airtight container for several weeks.

ANISE CAKE

[*serves 6 to 8*]

THIS WONDERFULLY TENDER AND MOIST CAKE IS STRONGLY FLAVORED WITH LICORICE-SWEET ANISE. SERVE IT DUSTED WITH CONFECTIONERS' SUGAR AND ACCOMPANY WITH little cups of espresso, either as an afternoon treat or for dessert.

A good keeping cake, it stays fresh for days wrapped in waxed paper and tucked away in the pantry.

Unsalted butter and unbleached flour for the pan
2¼ cups sifted cake flour
1½ cups sugar
1 tablespoon baking powder
1 teaspoon sea salt
½ cup unsalted butter, melted
6 eggs, separated
½ cup spring or filtered water
1 tablespoon anise extract
1 teaspoon grated lemon zest
½ teaspoon cream of tartar

Heat the oven to 350 degrees. Butter and flour a 9-inch springform pan.

Sift the flour, sugar, baking powder, and salt into a bowl.

Make a well in the center and add the melted butter, egg yolks, water, anise extract, and lemon zest. Mix with a rubber spatula or wooden spoon, making sure there are no lumps. Whip the egg whites with the cream of tartar until stiff but not dry. Gradually and gently fold the whites into the batter.

Pour the batter into the pan. Bake for 1 hour. To test for doneness, insert a thin wooden skewer into the cake; it should emerge fairly dry with a bit of moisture on it. Cool for 10 minutes. Run a thin, flexible knife along the edge of the cake. Remove the cake from the springform pan.

TORTA DOLCE DI OLIO D'OLIVA

[serves 6]

A SIMPLE, EXQUISITE CAKE APPROPRIATE AT ANY TIME OF THE DAY—FOR BREAKFAST OR AN AFTERNOON SNACK WITH COFFEE, AND A WONDERFUL "KEEPING" CAKE FOR WHEN guests drop by unexpectedly, since it stays moist and tender for up to a week.

If the use of olive oil in a cake sounds strange to you, remember that an olive is a fruit, and its oil is especially healthful and wholesome. You can use a full, rounded, fruity olive oil that will impart to the cake a slight trace of the olive flavor, or a soft, buttery-tasting oil that will remain fairly neutral.

If you're serving this for dessert, some wedges of fresh figs would make a fitting accompaniment.

1¼ cups unbleached all-purpose flour

1 cup sugar

1 tablespoon baking powder

½ teaspoon salt

5 large eggs, preferably free-range organic, whites and yolks separated

⅔ cup Moscato dessert wine

½ cup extra-virgin olive oil

Grated zest of 2 oranges, preferably organic

2 teaspoons vanilla extract

Heat the oven to 325 degrees.

Combine the flour, ⅔ cup of the sugar, the baking powder, and salt.

Whip the egg whites until foamy. Then beat in the remaining ⅓ cup of sugar and continue beating until soft peaks form.

Beat together the egg yolks, the Moscato wine, olive oil, orange zest, and vanilla in a large bowl. Add the flour mixture to the egg yolk mixture and stir until just combined.

Gently fold the egg whites into the egg yolk and flour mixture a little at a time.

Pour the batter into an ungreased 9-inch springform pan. Bake for 45 minutes. To test for doneness, insert a thin wooden skewer into the cake; it should emerge fairly dry with a bit of moisture on it. Cool completely on a wire rack. Run a thin, flexible knife around the rim of the springform pan to loosen the cake. Transfer the cake to a serving plate.

Best if not refrigerated. Simply store in an airtight cake tin or wrapped in waxed paper.

SEMOLINA CAKE

[serves 6]

ANOTHER OF THOSE WONDERFUL "KEEPING" CAKES, THIS IS VERY MOIST AND TENDER —REALLY A CROSS BETWEEN A CAKE AND A PUDDING—AND GOOD FOR SNACKING ON any time of the day.

To dress it up for dessert, use rum instead of orange flower water, add homemade or finest quality finely diced candied orange and citron rind in place of the orange zest, and, as a final touch, add a sprinkling of natural green pistachios.

If desired, dust the top with confectioners' sugar just before serving.

Unsalted butter and semolina for the springform pan
4 cups milk
Small pinch of sea salt
¼ cup semolina
1⅓ cups sugar
2 tablespoons orange blossom water
Grated zest of 2 oranges, preferably organic
4 eggs, lightly beaten

Heat the oven to 375 degrees. Butter an 8-inch springform pan. Sprinkle with some semolina and shake out the excess.

Place the milk and salt in a saucepan. Bring the milk to the brink of a boil over low heat. Add the semolina in a thin stream, whisking continuously with a sturdy wire whisk. Continue until the semolina thickens and begins to pull away from the sides of the pan.

Remove from the heat and continue stirring for 1 or 2 minutes. Let cool a little. Stir in the sugar. Add the orange blossom water and orange zest and stir until evenly distributed. Quickly stir in the beaten eggs.

Pour into the pan. Bake for 1 hour or until firm to the touch and lightly brown on top.

Remove from the oven and cool on a rack to room temperature.

Refrigerate to firm up the cake, about 30 minutes. Unmold. Serve cool or at room temperature. Store cake in refrigerator wrapped in waxed paper.

MARIA'S TORTA SQUISITA

[*serves 6*]

MY FRIEND MARIA SODINI, A LONGTIME NORTH BEACH RESIDENT, BROUGHT ME A SLICE OF HER SPECIAL CAKE TO TASTE. IT WAS THE MOST DELECTABLE CAKE I COULD IMAGINE. She gave me the recipe, but try as I might, I couldn't get it right—it didn't rise high enough, it wasn't as delicate, the crumb wasn't as tender. I kept trying, asking her for tips that might guide me, to no avail. Sensing my frustration, she invited me to her home so I could watch her prepare it and study her every move.

I walked up the shiny, immaculate terrazzo steps leading to her home, beautifully maintained plants placed on the steps to greet me along the way. I was accompanied by one of my sisters and my little niece.

Maria was ready. All the special bowls and measuring utensils she used for the cake were neatly arranged on the tiles. A huge, sweet lemon just-picked from her tree was on the counter. She offered us coffee and gave little Ava some of the fresh apricots she was eyeing that Maria had on a plate on the kitchen table where we sat. A freshly baked *torta* was on the counter. She offered us slices of the cake to go with our coffee and with Ava's apricots. As usual, the cake was *squisita*, exquisite.

We watched as Maria went through the steps, I with notebook in hand, something I have rarely done, since I usually intuit my way to a recipe. But I didn't want to miss a single nuance. I quietly asked a question or two as Maria worked in her precise manner.

Finally, it was time to fold the egg whites into the batter. We watched as she carefully and expertly performed this task without losing even a small fraction of an inch of volume—a marvel to watch; the fluffy mixture reached almost to the rim of the bowl. Into the oven went the cake and I knew it would be perfection.

I've tried to incorporate into the recipe every tip and suggestion offered by Maria. And I thank her for inviting us into her lovely home and offering us such warm hospitality *all'Italiana.*

A final note: For special occasions, Maria fills the center of the cake with strawberries and frosts the cake with freshly whipped cream. Maria also loves the cake for breakfast, sliced, toasted, and spread with peach jam.

2¼ cups sifted cake flour

1½ cups sugar

1 tablespoon baking powder

¼ teaspoon salt

½ cup canola oil

*6 extra-large eggs, preferably organic, at room temperature
(remove from the refrigerator at least 30 minutes before or immerse
in warm water for 5 minutes), yolks and whites separated*

*2 teaspoons pure vanilla extract in a 1-cup measuring cup
topped up with cold water to measure ¾ cup vanilla water*

*Grated zest of ¼ huge, sweet thick-skinned lemon
(Maria does this on the medium holes of a four-sided grater
and includes some of the sweet pith with the zest)*

½ teaspoon cream of tartar

Heat the oven to 325 degrees and place the rack on the middle shelf of the oven.

Very lightly oil the inside of a smooth-sided 10-inch pan with a removable tube. There should be the barest trace of oil.

Sift the flour, sugar, baking powder, and salt into a bowl. Make a well in the center and add the canola oil, egg yolks, vanilla water, and lemon zest. Use a whisk to mix the ingredients together until smooth.

Put the egg whites in a medium-large bowl. Sprinkle the cream of tartar over the top. Whip the egg whites with the cream of tartar until stiff but not dry. (Maria uses a hand-held beater, just like mine.)

Pour the batter over the top of the egg whites. Very gently fold in the batter with a spatula without stirring. There should be no loss of egg white volume!

Pour the cake batter into the pan. It should come four-fifths up the side of the cake pan. Bake for 50 minutes, raise the temperature to 375 degrees, and bake an additional 10 minutes or until the top is golden. Do not open the oven or puncture the cake to test for doneness. Its golden exterior will tell you when the cake is done.

Invert the cake pan over an empty wine bottle so that it is slightly suspended in the air. When the cake is completely cool, remove from the bottle and gently unmold the cake.

CHERRIES AND SUGARED RICOTTA

[serves 4 to 6]

HERE IS A FRUIT AND CHEESE OFFERING FOR DESSERT, ALTHOUGH RICOTTA IS TECHNI-CALLY NOT A CHEESE, BUT RATHER A BY-PRODUCT OF CHEESE-MAKING. USE VERY SWEET, ripe cherries or another seasonal fruit at its peak. Of course, seek out the best artisanal-style ricotta you can find.

1 pound ricotta, drained in cheesecloth if not firm
5 tablespoons sugar, or more as needed
½ pound cherries, pitted and cut in half
2 tablespoons Maraschino liqueur
Grated zest of ½ lemon, preferably organic

Combine the ricotta and 3 tablespoons of the sugar. Refrigerate for an hour or up to overnight.

In a separate bowl, mix the cherries, Maraschino liqueur, lemon zest, and remaining 2 tablespoons sugar. Let macerate for about an hour.

Just before serving, taste both mixtures and add more sugar if needed. They should not be overly sweet. Swirl the cherries and juices into the sweetened ricotta to create a pattern of white and red streaks.

Spoon into individual dessert cups or small goblets. Serve as soon as possible, or refrigerate briefly if combining the ricotta and fruit in advance.

❧

THREE COMPOSED OFFERINGS

SUPPLY FORKS, KNIVES, AND A PLATE FOR EACH PERSON, AND SERVE FORTH A COM-POSED OFFERING FOR DESSERT. IT COULD BE NOUGAT CANDIES, TOASTED ALMONDS, and fresh cherries; a tray of assorted very fancy chocolates, candied citrus peels, and fresh figs; or a wedge of fine Parmesan-Reggiano, fresh walnuts, and crisp persimmons.

This is a supremely simple way to end a meal, open to hundreds of variations, from rough and rustic to very chic and sophisticated.

- *A plate of oranges, whole unpeeled almonds, and broken chunks of dark chocolate.*

- *Fresh pineapple pieces, medjool dates, and Signorina Maria's Marzipan (page 201) in paper candy cups.*

- *Small apples, small pears, and a chunk of taleggio cheese.*

SIGNORINA MARIA'S MARZIPAN

[makes about 1½ pounds marzipan]

SIGNORINA MARIA, MY NINETY-TWO-YEAR-OLD LANDLADY AND DOWNSTAIRS NEIGHBOR IN THE SEASIDE TOWN IN THE SALENTO WHERE I SPEND MY SUMMER VACATIONS, GAVE me a gift of her homemade marzipan, which she brought to me on a pretty floral saucer. Marzipan stays fresh for months. Signorina Maria made her marzipan for Easter, and when she brought me some in June, it was still quite fresh. Her little touch was to sprinkle some Marsala on the marzipan to compensate for a bit of dryness that had crept into the paste.

Homemade marzipan has an entirely different taste and texture from the store-bought variety. The result is a slightly granular, lighter texture far more interesting than the thick, leaden paste available in stores. The taste is strongly of almonds rather than glucose.

In Italy, a very few almonds from a variety of almond tree that produces bitter almonds only are added to the sweet almonds to produce the characteristic flavor of real marzipan. One day on a drive through the Salentine countryside, out of curiosity, I nibbled on a bitter almond picked from a tree where we sat under its shade. Even though the amount I tasted was no bigger than the head of a pin, I don't think I've ever tasted anything quite so bitter in my entire life. I spit it out, but the horrible taste lingered. I had to eat a handful of figs from a nearby tree and drink copious amounts of bottled water to clear my palate of the acrid taste.

These bitter almonds, which contain a trace of some poisonous element, are not allowed into America. I've used apricot kernels as a substitute. The flavor they impart to marzipan is amazingly similar to that of bitter almonds, but they also require a preliminary baking, since they, too, contain a trace of poison. Nowadays in Italy, apricot kernels are used in place of bitter almonds quite frequently. Just look at the label on a tin of amaretti cookies.

On a less poisonous note, I tasted a wonderful marzipan "candy" sprinkled with shiny sugar crystals that I bought from a small pastry shop in one of those sleepy towns in the Salento. It was composed of two layers of marzipan, one plain and one coffee-flavored, dark brown, almost black. I've attempted to duplicate this by simply kneading espresso beans ground to a fine powder into a portion of the almond paste until it turns a dark coffee brown. Try it yourself; the flavor should be a pleasant balance of coffee and almond. I'm not sure how the professional confectioners do it, but it probably involves espresso extract, available to the trade and used to heighten coffee flavor.

(CONTINUED)

12 apricot kernels, found in specialty food markets
2 cups whole sweet almonds, unpeeled
2 cups granulated sugar
⅓ cup spring or filtered water
¼ teaspoon vanilla extract
Confectioners' sugar for dusting

Blanch the apricot kernels in boiling water for a few seconds to loosen the skins. Slip off the skins. Place in a 275-degree oven for 10 minutes, which eliminates any minuscule amounts of toxins found in the kernels.

Blanch the almonds in boiling water for a few seconds. Slip off the peels. Dry almonds briefly in an oven on the lowest setting.

Grind both the almonds and apricot kernels very finely using a hand-cranked grinder, or, second best, in small batches in a food processor. The result should be tiny flakes, almost the size of grated Parmesan cheese. If you process the almonds, add a little of the sugar to the almonds to prevent the almonds from releasing their oils.

Combine the ground nuts and apricot kernels, the remaining sugar, the water, and the vanilla in an electric mixer or processor. Mix or process until a smooth but lightly textured paste forms.

Transfer the marzipan to a work surface of marble or wood sprinkled with a little confectioners' sugar. Knead the marzipan briefly by hand. Roll into logs. Wrap tightly in plastic wrap and refrigerate.

❧

GELATO DI ZUPPA INGLESE

[makes 4 to 6 servings]

THIS IS THE CLASSIC ITALIAN GELATO PREPARATION, MADE WITH A CUSTARD BASE. THE FLAVORINGS ARE THOSE FOUND IN THE DESSERT CALLED ZUPPA INGLESE. CONTROVERSY has swirled around the origin of the name, roughly translated as "English Soup," and it does bear a resemblance to English trifle. But the popularity of Italian *zuppa inglese* has never wavered.

Originally, *zuppa inglese* was tinted a deep rose from the addition of a liqueur called Alkermes, the color derived from dried powdered cochineal insects (well, at least it's natural!). Nowadays, synthetic dyes are used for the red color.

The *gelato di zuppa inglese* that I enjoy when in Italy has omitted the red liqueur. Among the components you will find are rum, mixed candied fruit cut into infinitesimal dice, and possibly an additional *goccia*, "drop," of a favorite liqueur such as Maraschino—clear, strong, cherry flavored, but not cloyingly sweet. Other possible ingredients include bits of dark chocolate and chopped toasted almonds. To add or not to add, the choice is yours.

2 cups whole milk
4 egg yolks
½ cup granulated sugar
2 tablespoons dark rum
A few drops of Maraschino liqueur (optional)
Pinch of salt (about ¼ teaspoon)
¼ cup very finely diced highest quality mixed candied
fruit, especially candied orange rind, or all candied citrus rind,
the candied fruits made without preservatives or dyes

Warm the milk in a small saucepan over medium heat until it is at the brink of a boil. Off the heat, let the milk cool for 10 minutes.

Combine the egg yolks, sugar, rum, and optional liqueur in a bowl. Beat until mixture forms ribbons. Very gradually add the milk to the bowl, stirring as you add the liquid.

Place the custard in the top half of a double boiler. When the water in the lower pot begins to boil (remember, the water level should not touch the bottom of the upper pot), start stirring continuously for 2 or 3 minutes. Do not allow the custard to boil.

Pour the custard into a bowl. Stir in the candied fruit and any other optional ingredients. Refrigerate until the mixture is very cold.

Process the ice cream according to the manufacturer's directions. Serve immediately or transfer the gelato to a plastic or metal container with an airtight lid and let it firm up in the freezer for an hour or so. It should not be rock-hard, but creamy and luscious.

GELATO DI MELONE

[makes 4 servings]

DURING MY SUMMERS IN ITALY, I, ALONG WITH EVERY SINGLE ITALIAN, YOUNG AND OLD, LIVE ON ICE CREAM. IT ISN'T CONSIDERED DECADENT OR INDULGENT TO EAT GELATO. It is simply one of the rituals involved with eating and living and being Italian.

Maybe it is because Italian ice cream tends to be less dense that it is perceived as more of a refreshment than the path to dietary destruction. Or maybe it is just that hot climates require the frequent consumption of cooling foods. Or maybe it is just that gelato tastes so damn good!

Cantaloupe gelato and snacking on the divine little local cucumbers, called *cocomeri*, saw me through a particularly torrid summer by the sea.

½ cup sugar
¼ pound peeled and diced ripe,
fragrant cantaloupe (about 2 cups)
¼ cup milk
¼ cup heavy cream
½ teaspoon vanilla extract
3 extra-large egg yolks
2 or 3 drops pure lemon extract, preferably organic

Sprinkle ¼ cup of the sugar over the diced cantaloupe and let macerate in the refrigerator while preparing the custard base.

Stir together the remaining ¼ cup sugar with the milk and cream in a heavy-bottomed saucepan. Bring the liquids to just below a boil over medium-low heat. Stir in the vanilla. Remove from the stove.

Beat the egg yolks until they turn a creamy yellow color.

Off the heat, very gradually whisk the beaten egg yolks into the milk and cream. Turn the heat to medium-low, and whisking constantly, cook the custard for about 5 minutes or until it lightly coats the back of a spoon. Transfer to a bowl. Let cool and refrigerate. Or, to speed things up, cool custard in a big bowl of ice, stirring often as it chills.

Drain all liquid from the cantaloupe (I like to drink it). Add lemon extract to the cantaloupe and puree until smooth.

Add puree to cold custard and blend together with a rubber spatula.

Process the gelato according to manufacturer's directions. Serve immediately. Or transfer to a metal or plastic container with an airtight lid and let firm up for an hour or so in the freezer. The ice cream should not be frozen hard, but be lush and creamy.

Ordering Gelato Like an Italian

IN ITALY, THE CUSTOM IS TO ORDER A FEW FLAVORS IN ONE ICE CREAM CONE OR CUP, rather than a scoop of just one flavor as we often do here in America.

Sometimes a serving of ice cream will have so many different flavors, little pats of this flavor and that, that it looks almost psychedelic. But that's the way it's done in Italy.

Italians mix and match according to their preferences. It makes ordering ice cream more of a challenge, since the various flavors need to meld, or should I say melt, together successfully. Often, a little dab of unsugared freshly whipped cream is the crowning touch.

Here are a few of my favorite combination *gelati* "scoops," which I always have in a *coppa*, or cup, rather than a cone. But with so many choices, it is always a delightful form of torture to make the final decisions.

* *Peach, coconut, and zuppa inglese*

* *Dark chocolate, crema, custard cream, and hazelnut, with a dab of whipped cream*

* *Strawberry, lemon, and cantaloupe (all gelati, not sorbets)*

CIBO SELVATICO
wild food

FERAL, STRONG—THE REAL THING. WILD FOOD IS THE ORIGIN OF ALL FOOD. WILD FOOD OFFERS ITSELF SPONTANEOUSLY FROM THE EARTH. GIFTS FROM NATURE. When we eat wild foods, we feel a stronger connection with nature; when we forage, we learn about nature's seasons and cycles.

Beginning with my first book, I've talked about the importance of wild food, the thrill of it: a bowl of wild arugula salad in Rome; a grilled porcini mushroom the size of a dinner plate in Bologna. But these were all restaurant experiences, albeit sublime ones.

My trips to the Salento set my passion for wild food on fire and make me want to learn more and more about them. Day after day in the Salento, I ate wild foods I and my friends gathered during forays into nature—from the *macchia*, the scrub by the sea, from fields, and from the waters of the Mediterranean.

Free for the picking are intensely fragrant herbs: pungent wild oregano, wild savory, and sea thyme perfumed by salt spray; caper bushes cascading from the stones of abandoned castle walls—unopened flower buds to pluck and preserve in salt, caper leaves to preserve in brine; needle-thin wild asparagus; and masses and masses of wild fennel.

Along the rocky coast, tiny clams no bigger than a baby's fingernail cling to the cliffs, to be pried off the rock and eaten raw. And sea urchins, ink purple and brown, covered with sharp spikes, clench the rocks beneath the sea. You dive for these, and with the wide, strong blade of a diving knife pry them from the shallow waters. But do this only with someone who knows the sea intimately, who will find the bay and coves that are impeccably clean and free of pollutants.

Back on land, or should I say rock, you crack open the shells, clean away the inedible part, leaving a briny-tasting coral star that you eat with just a bit of bread as a utensil to scoop up the sea urchin. Perhaps you might add a drop of lemon juice.

Italy itself is in the process of losing the art of foraging—fewer people do it and it's mostly the old folks.

Although some still enjoy going mushrooming, or having a sea urchin feast on the cliffs, the old-style forager searched to survive, to provide food for the family, or to sell for much-needed money. Foraging can be difficult work—time-consuming, backbreaking, tedious.

In the Salento especially, it appears to me that foraging is still a way of life. I often see foragers bent over, with knives and plastic bags or woven baskets, carefully studying the earth and sea, and gathering all manner of wild foods—wild mushrooms and asparagus, a type of snail to cook in tomato sauce, or the tips of a specific seaweed to eat in a salad with tomatoes. It is still part of the ritual of life, the foods they crave.

In Italy, you can buy certain wild foods at outdoor markets, but at a premium; they are expensive, since many of these foods are difficult to gather and clean, the season is short and ephemeral, and the product itself can be highly perishable.

Here in America, I've noticed wild foods popping up at farmers' markets—wild greens and a selection of wild mushrooms, to name two; we, too, had a tradition of foraging that had been lost but is now being revived.

Wild foods have a power and mystery about them. You can tell by the intense flavors that there's been no meddling by human hands. Wild foods have special properties—they heal and nurture and help the body maintain health.

I have no intention of offering a scientific cataloging of the wild foods I've eaten, nor of dwelling on these foods as cures. Since many of these foods have cultivated counterparts—cultivated purslane, cultivated capers, cultivated blackberries—you can adapt the recipes in the book for use with domesticated ingredients and wait until you travel to Italy or find yourself at the right farmers' markets to try the wild variety. Just knowing that wild foods continue to thrive is a hopeful sign for the planet.

But I have to say that just being in nature, real nature, makes my thoughts run freer and my heart beat a little faster. For me, eating wild greens, tiny raw clams, or wild *corbezzole*, a strange little fruit that grows on a scrubby tree in the high *macchia*, has been one of the most exciting parts of my Italian odysseys.

{ Dishes with Wild Ingredients }

HERE IS A LIST OF SOME OF THE DISHES CON-
TAINING WILD INGREDIENTS THAT I'VE ENJOYED
in the Salento—some that I've prepared myself,
some prepared by others for me to taste, and a
few I've eaten at simple trattorias. They're here
as inspiration. You'll be able to re-create some
of them with cultivated counterparts. Or, better yet, travel to the Salento and sample them
in their place of origin.

* *Bread morsels with wild sea urchin and lemon*

* *Pickled wild sea fennel salad, served at a seaside trattoria*

* *Pickled wild caper leaves, served as part of an antipasto at a seaside trattoria*

* *Frittata of wild asparagus*

* *Pickled spicy wild fennel blossoms, as a component of a potato salad at the potato festival*

* *Wild snail salad with wild arugula, cucumber, green tomato, and wild oregano*

* *Tomato salad with wild oregano and wild garlic*

* *Dried fava puree with cicorielle, a small, tender, slightly bitter wild green*

* *Spaghettini with a sauce of tomato and miniature clams*

* *Spaghettini with wild fennel and hot red pepper*

* *Spaghetti with sea urchins*

* *Thumbnail-sized wild lumache, snails, gently braised with sea thyme*

* *Wild dandelions with grated pecorino*

* *Grilled lampascioni—referred to as wild onions, but actually the bulb of a wild hyacinth; bitter, but delicious*

* *A handful of small wild blackberries*

QUANDO NON SI SENTE BENE

foods for when you are not feeling well

EVERY COUNTRY HAS ITS REMEDIES FOR COLDS, INFLUENZA, FEVER, UPSET STOM-ACH, AND GENERAL INDISPOSITION—MALESSERE, THEY CALL IT IN ITALY. IN SUCH cases, Italians advise *una dieta in bianco*. Although this literally translates as a white diet, and many of the foods are indeed white or light in color, its larger meaning embraces foods that are easy to digest, mild rather than highly seasoned, usually cooked without tomato or other acid foods, and most important, prepared with great simplicity.

Beef broth is a classic component of a *dieta in bianco*. It is Italy's version of our chicken soup, and is considered to be restorative and nutritious. The beef broth must be absolutely clear, strained of every impurity and completely free of fat. Often a little pastina is added to the broth—small shapes such as tiny stars, orzo (which means "barley"), and other delicate shapes such as capellini. My favorite pastina is anellini—small, thin rings of pasta—but this shape for pasta can be difficult to locate. A little grated Parmigiano-Reggiano cheese is the broth's only seasoning.

Pasta is also used in a water-based cross between a soup and a sauced pasta. Thin pasta—capellini is particularly well suited—is cooked in a generous amount of water, then drained, leaving behind enough moisture so the pasta is a little soupy. The cooked pasta and the pasta cooking water are placed in a shallow pasta dish, and tossed with a little unsalted butter and *un velo*, a thin veil of grated Parmigiano-Reggiano cheese. The butter and cheese are always added to the pasta off the stove in order to keep the dish as light and easily digestible as possible.

When a little more nutrition is called for, a small amount of very fresh ricotta can be placed in the serving bowl and thinned with some of the hot pasta water before the pasta is added. The ricotta melts to a creamy consistency. Again, the topping is simply

Parmigiano-Reggiano cheese. To achieve the right degree of creaminess from the ricotta, look for small producers of ricotta that cater to an Italian clientele.

Rice is another basic food of a *dieta in bianco*. The rice is cooked in the same way as pasta, then drained of most, but not all, of its water and mixed with sweet butter and freshly grated Parmigiano-Reggiano cheese, or ricotta as above.

Although the thought of using the water in which pasta or rice has cooked may seem odd, cooking with high-quality unprocessed rice and imported hard-wheat durum pasta produces cooking water that possesses flavor and nutrition, and not just an overabundance of starch. The water, in addition to lightening the dish in general, helps to extend the flavor of the butter or cheese, allowing you to use less of the richer ingredient and still flavor an entire dish, making it easier for the stomach to digest.

Poached fish is another dish highly regarded by proponents of the all-white school of cookery for the infirm. Poached in a little water flavored with a few of the most basic seasonings—sea salt, Italian parsley, lemon slices—the fish is served with some of the tasty poaching liquid, a touch of extra-virgin olive oil, and, if desired, a few drops of lemon juice. Any firm-fleshed white fish can be used. Just ask your fish vendor to suggest varieties that are particularly appropriate for poaching. Needless to say, only the freshest of fish should be used.

Aside from its role here as the perfect light and digestible high-protein food, fish poached Italian style is a wonderful way to truly appreciate the subtle flavor of impeccably fresh fish. The fish poaching liquid, if abundant enough, can be served separately as a soup into which you can throw a small handful of pastina, again using only the thinnest and most delicate shapes. Grated cheese is never used with fish or fish broth.

Zucchini cooked *in bianco*, tender and sweetly vegetal, is also advised for the indisposed. The zucchini is cut into strips or dice, then gently simmered in water. The finished dish is seasoned simply with a few drops of olive oil and a touch of sea salt. The cooking juices are part of the dish, a sweet, light broth that requires, above all, starting with very fresh small zucchini.

The water in which leafy wild or cultivated greens have cooked—as well as the greens, of course—is considered very healing and beneficial to one's health. In the Italy of the past, small shops, floors and walls lined in clean white tiles, offered various different hot liquids in which specific greens were cooked as cures for ailments. Patrons would drink the broth "prescribed" by the broth specialist from tall glass mugs or bring bottles to be filled and taken home to the ailing.

In a famous Italian cookbook, *La Scienza in Cucina e L'Arte di Mangiare Bene (Culinary Science and The Art of Eating Well)*, written in 1890, Pellegrino Artusi gives a recipe he calls Broth for the Sick. The recipe was given to him by a highly esteemed doctor who was attempting to cure a friend of the author who was seriously ill. As part of his cure, the doctor prescribed this specific broth.

The recipe involves layering thin, lean slices of veal or beef, adding just enough water to cover, then covering the pot with a plate filled with water and replenishing the water in the plate as it evaporates. The broth cooks for 6 hours at a barely perceptible boil, then at a hard boil for the final 10 minutes. The broth is strained through a fine cotton cloth. Artusi claims the broth will be of fine color and highly nutritious, but he fails to mention if the broth cured his sick friend!

In the back of Artusi's book, there is a section titled "Cucina per Gli Stomachi Deboli," literally, "cuisine for weak stomachs," but meaning in a larger sense the preparation of foods for those with poor digestions, to which he applies his turn-of-the-last-century scientific principles. It includes selected recipes from his book that he feels are appropriate for those who are older, ill, debauched(!), or weak by nature.

Some of the recipes he selects are variations on a simple *dieta in bianco*, but follow similar principles. A few of his most appealing suggestions include broth-based soups thickened with bread crumbs or slices of bread; soups made with small dumplings of semolina, and *zuppa regina*, a soup made of pounded chicken breast and almonds, topped with small bread cubes crisped in butter.

Among frittatas, he especially recommends asparagus frittata and warns against serving either raw or overcooked eggs.

As for vegetables, he suggests preparing *sformati*—mild savory vegetable puddings. They can be made with finely textured purees, produced with a food mill, of spinach, cardoons, artichoke hearts, or fennel, and bound with bechamel and eggs. The *sformato* is baked in the oven and served unmolded.

For salads, he cautions against raw vegetables as being hard to digest, and instead recommends cooked salads, such as a combination of cooked radicchio and beets, or simply cooked asparagus or green beans. I would add that the vegetables should be cooked until completely tender and simply dressed with olive oil and possibly a few drops of lemon. Boiled beef and chicken also meet with his seal of approval, again, simply dressed with a little olive oil, a few drops of vinegar, and salt.

Finally, it seems that most raw fruits are acceptable fare for *stomachi deboli*, as long as they are in season and thoroughly ripe. But he also highly recommends cooked apples or pears, or a compote of cooked pears and apricots. Unfortunately, he banishes all rich pastries, declaring them totally indigestible!

In Italy, my mother and her grandmother always brought rum babas from the local *pasticceria* whenever visiting a sick friend or relative. This *dolce*, a big favorite of mine, is made with a special spongelike brioche soaked in rum syrup (that's where the spongelike quality of the brioche comes in) and filled with pastry cream. According to her grandmother, the rum syrup was good for the sick because it revived them. And if you think of it, the brioche for rum babas is a light, spongy egg bread and the pastry cream is made from egg and milk, so a rum baba does provide nutrition as well as lifting one's sagging spirits.

But Artusi suggests avoiding liquor altogether, since he feels overdoing it could prove fatal to a weak digestion! But he makes an exception for brandy, if served in moderation.

Strict eating *in bianco* Italian style reflects the simplicity of Italian cooking. A *dieta in bianco* requires, above all, restraint in the kitchen and the use of high-quality ingredients. The dishes instantly lose their healing powers when complicated by too many additions. The idea is to rest your system rather than stimulate it, to give enough sustenance to maintain or build strength, but not so much as to tax the body.

I can personally attest to the comfort quotient of these dishes. I always turn to them when I'm not feeling well, and always feel better for having eaten a dish *in bianco*.

The following recipes in this book adhere to the principles of eating *in bianco*. Serve them to anyone not feeling well, including yourself.

MENUS

HERE IS A GROUPING OF INFORMAL MENUS FOR A WEEK, WITH A SPECIAL MENU FOR SUNDAY LUNCH. YOU'LL ALSO FIND A FEW IMPROMPTU MEALS THAT WERE memorable—picnics by the sea or in the countryside—tucked in among the more proto-typical menus.

The one menu item I didn't mention, since it is ever present, is good, rustic bread. It must be on the table or Italians simply cannot eat. With all the following menus, serve an abundance of the best bread you can find.

Also note that recipes appear and reappear, just as they would in a typical Italian house-hold, reflecting both what is in season and the comfort Italians derive from the repetition of favorite dishes.

The menus that follow are based on meals I've eaten during my summers in the Salento.

Lunedì

MONDAY

PRIMA COLAZIONE

Caffè latte (page 24) and Breakfast Biscotti (page 26)

MORNING SPUNTINO

Cappuccino and Pasticcioni (page 31)

PRANZO

Homemade light red wine

Mineral water

Pasta and Tomato Veal Sauce

*Signora Pantella's Basic Zucchini (page 110),
at room temperature, topped with a generous
drizzling of extra-virgin olive oil*

*Fried Zucchini Flowers
with Hot Red Pepper Bread Stuffing (page 114)*

Cantaloupe and cucumbers

Espresso

AFTERNOON SPUNTINO

Gelato di Zuppa Inglese (page 202)

CENA

Homemade light red wine

Mineral water

Signora Pantella's Red Peppers al Forno (page 162)

Signora Pantella's Chicken Salad (page 69)

*Simona's Alkermes cake (sponge cake with pastry
cream, layers drenched in Alkermes), a surprise
treat from Signora Pantella's daughter*

Apricots

Espresso

Martedì

TUESDAY

PRIMA COLAZIONE

Espresso and Breakfast Biscotti (page 26)

MORNING SPUNTINO

Gelato di Melone (page 204)

PRANZO

PICNIC ON THE SCOGLIERA:

Mineral water

Raw sea urchins with lemon and semolina bread

Strips of peeled round local cucumbers

Very fresh and mild pecorino cheese

Bread and chocolate

Cantaloupe

AFTERNOON SPUNTINO

Fresh figs—big green ones with violet flesh

CENA

Local white wine

Mineral water

Linguine with Tomato and Mussel Sauce (page 133)

Thin Swordfish Steaks the Italian Way (page 153)

Salad of green beans and Signora Pantella's Basic Zucchini (page 110)

A bowl of fruit

Espresso

Mercoledì

PRIMA COLAZIONE

Caffè latte, biscotti, a bowl of cherries

MORNING SPUNTINO

A small container of yogurt flavored with kiwi and gooseberries

PRANZO

A PICNIC IN THE COUNTRYSIDE:

*Salad of potatoes, cucumbers, sea fennel, dried wild oregano,
and small tomatoes, drizzled with extra-virgin olive oil*

Aged local pecorino in very thin crumbly slices

Green melon slices

*Fresh ricotta picked up at a masseria, farm, along the way,
and just before eating, sprinkled with a little sugar and ground coffee*

AFTERNOON SPUNTINO

Granita di Caffè (page 35)

CENA

LATE SUMMER NIGHT:

*Spaghetti with tomato and hot red pepper sauce,
sprinkled with a little chopped Italian parsley*

Salad of tuna, wild arugula, cucumbers, little green tomatoes

Fruit feast of watermelon, plums, and figs

Giovedì
THURSDAY

PRIMA COLAZIONE

Caffè latte and Pane, Burro, e Marmellata (page 25)

MORNING SPUNTINO

Stuffed Focaccia with Ricotta Filling (page 53)

PRANZO

Homemade light red wine

Mineral water

*Very thin pasta with Signora Pantella's home-canned
sauce, with a slice of fresh ricotta on the side*

*A stew of wild snails cooked with dried wild
oregano and extra-virgin olive oil*

Watermelon

Espresso

AFTERNOON SPUNTINO

*Iced tea at a bar/caffe with a spoonful of Granita di
Limone (page 34) stirred in, a popular afternoon refresher*

PRANZO

DINING AT A SEASIDE TRATTORIA:

Local white wine

Mineral water

Spaghetti with a Mountain of Tiny Clams (page 132)

"Brown Paper" Seafood Fritto Misto (page 173)

Simple green salad

Fresh fruit and custard tart

Espresso

Venerdì

FRIDAY

PRIMA COLAZIONE

*Caffè latte and Maria's Torta Squisita (page 198),
toasted and spread with peach jam*

MORNING SPUNTINO

Grilled Panino with Ricotta and Winter Savory (page 42)

PRANZO

Homemade light red wine

Mineral water

Zucchini Fritti Impanati (page 111)

Zuppa di Pesce (page 172)

Arugula salad with extra-virgin olive oil and lemon dressing

A bowl of fruit

Espresso

AFTERNOON SPUNTINO

Granita di Limone (page 34)

CENA

Homemade light red wine

Mineral water

Palermo Market Salad (page 60)

Tuna Scaloppine, Lightly Grilled (page 154)

Sopratavola (page 193)

Espresso

Sabato

SATURDAY

PRIMA COLAZIONE

Caffè latte and Breakfast Biscotti (page 26)

MORNING SPUNTINO

Potato "Focaccia" (page 108)

PRANZO

Light red wine

Mineral water

Signora Pantella's Red Peppers al Forno (page 162)

Pasta alla Sangiovanniello (page 163)

Pepate di Cozze (page 164)

Figs and watermelon

Espresso and assorted biscotti from a bakery

CENA

Homemade light red wine

Mineral water

Romano Beans Braised with Garlic in Spring Water (page 95)

Signora Pantella's Basic Zucchini (page 110)

Signora Pantella's Pollo in Umido (page 180)

Sopratavola of cantaloupe and local cucumbers

Espresso

Liquore of choice—select a favorite liqueur

Domenica

SUNDAY

PRIMA COLAZIONE

Granita di Limone con Brioscia (page 34)

MORNING SPUNTINO

Espresso and Pasticcioni (page 31)

PRANZO

Homemade light red wine

Mineral water

A Plate of Prosciutto (page 175) and big green olives

Lasagnette with Sunday Meat Sauce (page 139)

Lamb Spiedini (page 186) on a bed of lettuces

Verdura all'Insalata (page 57)

Maria's Torta Squisita (page 198) with whipped cream and strawberries

Espresso

Liquore—a liqueur of choice

AFTERNOON SPUNTINO

A mix of various flavors of gelato in a coppa
(see "Ordering Gelato Like an Italian," page 205)

PRANZO

DINNER AT A SEASIDE TRATTORIA:

Local white wine

Mineral water

Insalata di Mare (page 68)

Whole Grilled Fish in an Olive Oil and Herb Marinade (page 157)

Boiled green beans all'agro, served at room temperature with olive oil and lemon

A bowl of fruit

Espresso and a piece of pastry tart with crema pasticcera

MIDNIGHT SPUNTINO

WHILE TAKING A PASSEGGIATA BY THE SEA:

Gelato, gelato, and more gelato

La Natura

THE NATURAL WORLD

$\mathcal{S}$pending time in the Salento has brought me closer to a power that is great and all-encompassing. When I'm alone in a forest of ancient olive trees that extends for miles, ending abruptly on either side at the sea—or I climb time-eroded cliffs bleached stark white by the sun to reach a rocky shore of dazzling clarity and enchanting coloration that shifts and changes—or when I walk through a field of red poppies, wild garlic, and thorny thistles with pale purple blossoms, these moments touch me at my core. ✂ Hardly ever is there another soul in sight. Sounds animate this natural world: the sea splashing against limestone rocks or the echo of my voice as I descend into a watery grotto carved in rock by nature's battering forces. A chorus of cicadas screeches in crazy rhythm amid the twisted olive trees, some hundreds of years old. The wind makes its presence known as it whistles through the olive trees, rattling the branches. Birds chatter away or sing the prettiest songs. Then a pesky mosquito dives toward my ear, the buzzing as loud as a jet landing. Add the sudden hiss of a snake, the loud croak of a toad, the whir of a bat passing by my head, the hoot of a straggly owl at dusk, and even, hopefully very far away, the howl of a wolf. ✂ Sometimes in the distance I can hear voices carried on unbroken sound waves, for the Salento is flat with no mountains and very few hills to break their path. At regular intervals the church bells toll the hours, their sound distorted by the distance of its travels. ✂ That flatness spells disaster when the *scirocco* hits, a brutally hot wind that travels from North Africa and carries with it in its mean path the coarse sand that it deposits in every cranny, on cars and houses, plants and terraces, blanketing everything with rusty-pink sand. If you are unfortunate enough to get in its way, the fierce wind scratches your face and burns your skin. If you find yourself by the sea, its raging sound is like a hurricane. ❧ When it is hot—and in the summer that means just about every day—the fragrance of the pines, wild herbs, and grasses is intoxicating. I imagine a priest waving his smoky incense lantern, the penetrating scents filling the air. When the heat turns intolerable, the Salento combusts. It could be small landowners burning excess wood to ward off the danger of fire, or larger fires the *pompieri* struggle valiantly to control, with volunteer firefighters at their side. I've never seen so many flames, so much fire, nor felt such intense heat as in the Salento in summer. Fires large and small produce another incense: the smell of smoldering olive wood and charred herbs. ❧ In the cooler autumn, when the olives are harvested and pressed for their oil, the Salento smells green-gold and fruity. The olive scent turns the air voluptuously unctuous, with a bracing undercurrent, since freshly pressed olive oil is strongly bitter. ❧ Ever present is the smell of the sea. The Salento is an extremely narrow peninsula, and you can drive crosswise from one side of the coast to the other in about an hour and a half, whether you are driving an old *cinquecento* or a supercharged Alfa. Drive in almost any direction in the Salento and, before you know it, you arrive at one of its dazzling coasts. ❧ The salt breeze that crosses the Salento arrives in delicious waves. It holds in its microscopically small droplets the scent of the wild fennel that grows in giant, feathery green wands along the coast and the sea-and-earth smell of the thyme that grows in large clusters on the sandy shore. In this confluence of scents is the fragrance of sea fennel, a small succulent with the licorice-like scent of wild fennel, the hot smell of tar from passing ships, the perfume of driftwood, the briny aroma of seaweed and algae. Piercing these mingled odors is the pungent smell of huge deposits of sea salt from the salt-rich Mediterranean, full of mineral scents, that contributes generously to this elixir of sea air.

The brick-red earth also contributes its scent of iron, as do the limestone rocks that are everywhere—in stone walls that sinuously wind through the countryside, marking the small roads that, like a labyrinth, take me through the heart of the countryside and to the edge of the sea. There are ancient and mysterious architectural constructions of stone: dolmens—enormous slabs of stone held aloft by stacked boulders; menhirs—tall and narrow monoliths, rising from the earth like God pointing up to the sky; and crumbling stone watchtowers at strategic points along the coast like a connect-the-dots drawing. Stone sheds dot the agrarian landscape; boulders are scattered throughout the terrain, as though a meteor exploded and left behind its rocky debris. Bit by bit, stones have been laboriously hoisted up and carried to a spot where they could be of use. But still the Salento remains a landscape of stone.

Tucked away are the religious grottos, shrines, crudely built abandoned churches. I go down steps carved of sheer rock and enter a religious grotto with a small altar, beads of moisture slowly making their way down the damp stone walls. A votive candle in red glass burns in the semi-darkness, effigies of Jesus and Mary stare back at me. A few plastic flowers have been placed in a small vase. Or I come upon a simple shrine, a crucifix, a small religious statue—to comfort me in the midst of all this mystery.

In this land of rock and aridity or winter's occasional diluvial downpours, the people of the Salento have created a miracle: a verdurous, productive land. The color is mostly the silvery green of olive leaves, but there are also the ever-changing hues of the vineyards, fruit trees that burst into pastel bloom in early spring, summer's deep red tomatoes. An amazing variety of shades of green profit from the mineral-red earth; there are the ice-green melons and cucumbers, spring-green fava beans, and the gray-green artichokes that echo the gray-green of the landscape. It's a big, roughly woven basket of abundance. A gift from nature, yes, but earned by hard work.

Sometimes, for example when I'm swimming in the sea and dive down deep, with my mask firmly in place, I'm overwhelmed by the gorgeous otherworldliness of what I see: sea urchins, purple-black pincushions with oversized sharp spines; mineral colors glowing amethyst, rust red, lime green in the glinting blue water; the little fish rushing by on their way to some important appointment; the massive rock formations below the water's surface. I'm awed by how sublimely beautiful it is, yet also a little frightened by it.

Nature makes us feel so many emotions. It can induce fear or exhilaration, be a source of comfort to our souls or discomfort to our bodies. Nature must be God, and God is nature—one and the same. Nature is in us and governs our lives, granting both hardship and happiness. When I'm in the Salento, I feel close to the power that created this wonder and continues to exert its force—as close as I've come to experiencing true religious feeling.

When I look at the list of foods I've gathered and cooked with—wild mint, savory, and thyme; sprigs I've plucked from masses of oregano and rosemary—free for the picking as I wander through the countryside; or when I'm sitting with a friend on a white-as-a-bone rocky cliff overlooking the sea and eating raw sea urchins; or when I'm sitting alone in my kitchen upstairs from Signorina Maria, with a big bunch of wild greens I've gathered spread out on the table, quietly cleaning and trimming them, breathing in their sharply verdant scent, and again, when I sit down to eat the *cicoriella* or whatever green I've gathered, simply boiled and drizzled with a neighbor's gift of olive oil from a personal reserve, I feel a merging of myself with nature. Even though it is notorious for its mean streak—call it God, or nature, or whatever name you choose—this power is generous and kind and loving.

Index

About the Author

VIANA LA PLACE is the author or coauthor of eight previous Italian cookbooks, including the classics *Cucina Fresca*, *Cucina Rustica*, and *Verdura: Vegetables Italian Style*. She has created an influential and enduring body of work that has helped redefine America's perception of Italian cooking. Hailed for her simple, restrained recipes that produce extraordinary results, she is also known for her evocative writing about Italy. She lives in San Francisco and spends her summers in Italy, in a small town by the sea.